Eminent Parliamentarians

Eminent Parliamentarians
THE SPEAKER'S LECTURES

—

Edited by
PHILIP NORTON

Biteback Publishing

First published in Great Britain in 2012 by
Biteback Publishing Ltd
Westminster Tower
3 Albert Embankment
London SE1 7SP

Picture credits: David Lloyd George © Harris & Ewing; Enoch Powell
© Alan Warren; Margaret Thatcher © The Margaret Thatcher Foundation;
Tony Benn © Isujosh; Nancy Astor, Aneurin Bevan, Michael Foot, Iain Macleod
and Roy Jenkins © Press Association.

Every reasonable effort has been made to trace copyright holders of material
reproduced in this book, but if any have been inadvertently overlooked the
publishers would be glad to hear from them.

ISBN 978-1-84954-407-8

10 9 8 7 6 5 4 3 2 1

A CIP catalogue record for this book is available from the British Library.

Set in Baskerville and Bulmer

Printed and bound in Great Britain by
CPI Group (UK) Ltd, Croydon CR0 4Y

Contents

Foreword

When I stood for election as Speaker, I was clear that the House of Commons needed to change to re-engage with the public and enhance the role of backbenchers in holding the government to account. This change continues. I do not, however, believe in change for change's sake, nor think that the past has nothing to teach us. That is why I was keen to provide the opportunity for Members of both Houses to reflect upon, and learn from, some of the illustrious figures who have walked the green carpets of the House of Commons. The first lecture series, 'Eminent Parliamentarians', proved to be very successful. Indeed, there are always more requests for tickets than we are able to accommodate in the State Rooms of Speaker's House. To compensate, the lectures have been made available to a wider audience through their screening on the BBC Parliament Channel and this book will provide a permanent reference for students and all those who share my love of politics.

The lives and careers of the eminent parliamentarians contained within this book have brought something unique to the House of Commons and are rightly garlanded by the Members of both Houses who kindly shared their enthusiasm and knowledge with us. The parliamentarians within this book may make surprising bedfellows – Tony Benn and Margaret Thatcher, for example. These remarkable figures may not share an ideology but they do share the ability to fascinate – and fascinating is just one of the many descriptions associated with this lecture series.

In the pantheon of great liberal figures in British politics, David

Lloyd George will always stand out. If he was renowned for his progressive instincts and contempt for the claims of heredity, he was famed too for his spell-binding oratory which moved to ecstasy or fury all who heard it. Kenneth Morgan recalls Lloyd George's description of the House of Lords as 'Five hundred ordinary men, chosen at random from amongst the unemployed' but, intriguingly, he also quotes Lloyd George damning a speech by Macmillan for containing far too many points. No speaker, Lloyd George suggests, should make more than three points as the challenge is to convey a clear, straightforward message to the immediate listener.

Peter Tapsell, in his meticulously researched lecture, shows us what an exquisite practitioner of repartee F. E. Smith was, not merely in Parliament but in the courts. One concluding exchange with Judge Willis is a delicious example of the genre. Judge Willis: 'You are an extremely offensive, young man'; F. E. Smith: 'As a matter of fact, we both are, but I am trying to be and you can't help it.'

As a strong proponent of the House becoming a closer reflection of the people we serve, I found Shirley Williams's account of Nancy Astor's journey to the green benches particularly intriguing. Lady Astor was no suffragette and, as Shirley interestingly observes, her place in history as the first woman to take her seat 'owed everything to expediency and privilege, not to leadership'. This may come as a disappointment to some, but her place in history cannot be denied, nor can her striking character and piquant turn of phrase. I will leave readers to ponder Astor's assertion that all women marry beneath themselves.

Having his grandson deliver a lecture on Churchill, with his daughter in the front row, was among the most moving moments in the whole lecture series. Nicholas Soames managed to achieve what others could not – a familial, warm and intimate tribute to a towering political figure balanced by an honest analysis of what some might see as Churchill's weaknesses. For a man so revered for his oratory, it is clear that Churchill was not a stump speaker and he would spend hours preparing his speeches and rehearsing tone and inclination. This did not always succeed, however, and Nicholas recounts a number of disastrous speeches. Churchill also spent many years being distrusted and actually disliked by his party, whether it was Liberal or Tory. These insights do not demean or devalue our great war hero, however, but ironically add to our admiration for a man who achieved so much, in spite of those challenges.

The complexity and paradoxes of Bevan were ably chronicled by Gordon Marsden in his lecture. Marsden painted a compelling picture of Bevan and neatly postulated Bevan's likely views on the challenges we face today. Bevan's reaction to the creation of the Independent Parliamentary Standards Authority (IPSA) and the future of the NHS may well be conjecture, but Gordon's lecture provides us with an opportunity to apply historical debate and thought to the preoccupations of current Members of the House. In his book *In Place of Fear*, Bevan wrote in somewhat chilling terms for us today: 'There is one situation fatal for a democratic Parliament – that is helplessness in the face of economic difficulties.'

Opinions on Enoch Powell are, to put it mildly, divided. Philip Norton had the onerous task of giving this lecture on a man whose inclusion on a list of great parliamentarians could, in itself, be seen as controversial. Philip was certainly up to this task and gave a lecture of scrupulous fairness and academic rigour, which provides a multi-dimensional picture of a man often seen as a two-dimensional character. The breadth of Powell's interests may be a surprise to many, but Philip has provided an elegant challenge to this assumption that Powell was a one-trick pony. How does one square Powell's odious, in my view, 1968 Birmingham speech on immigration with his impassioned attack on the killing of Mau Mau detainees by British forces in Kenya? Philip's thoughtful and insightful analysis is required reading for those who want to take their political knowledge beyond simple headlines.

When it comes to the oratory and parliamentary performances

of Michael Foot, I need to declare an interest, for I am a keen admirer. Reading his parliamentary contributions in Hansard, especially in the earlier part of his career, is a must for students of oratory. In a riveting address, Neil Kinnock captured the essence of Michael Foot, the man and the parliamentarian. He conveyed Foot's commitment to the House and what the House could do for good. Neil's description of Foot as 'chromosomal Commons man' says it all.

Douglas Hurd's time as Foreign Secretary provided an invaluable basis upon which he could discuss Macleod's achievements and frustrations as Colonial Secretary dealing with the difficult and risky transformation of Empire into Commonwealth. Interestingly, this lecture also gave us a number of what-ifs. Macleod sadly died a week after becoming Chancellor in 1970 and, with his in-depth knowledge of Ted Heath, Douglas speculates on the likely fortunes of the 1970–74 government had Macleod lived.

Part of the success of the lecture series lays in the differing approaches and styles used by our lecturers. Andrew Adonis's lecture stands as an exemplar of outstanding research and a very Jenkins-like development of his hypothesis on the legacy of his subject. Roy Jenkins is latterly best remembered as one of the gang of four who broke away to form the SDP. What Andrew reminds us of, however, is the huge impact that Jenkins had on day-to-day lives. In just twenty-three months at the Home Office in the 1960s, Jenkins oversaw the legalisation of homosexuality, the introduction of 'no fault' divorce, the prohibition of racial discrimination and the abolition of stage censorship to name but a few. Jenkins's achievements in social freedom to which we have all now become accustomed are many, and Andrew ties these neatly to Jenkins's philosophical approach to politics.

We were privileged to hear from John Whittingdale who worked closely with Margaret Thatcher and who gave us an up-close and personal view of a character we all think we know. What is perhaps less well known is the great importance she

attached to the House and although she enjoyed large majori-
ties, regularly voted in the lobbies. That she prepared fastidiously
for PMQs may not be a surprise to us, but the fact that her leg
trembled at the dispatch box probably is! Margaret Thatcher
remains a potent political figure to this day and my colleague has
done an admirable job in explaining why.

Tristram Hunt had a singularly challenging job when deliver-
ing his lecture as his subject, and his subject's family, was sitting
right in front of him! Tony Benn is an intriguing figure – a
doughty campaigner, a thorn in the side of governments and his
own party and, unusually today, a politician who is a household
name. Tristram brought his skills as a historian to his lecture and
this is reflected in the depth of his analysis of not just Benn the
politician, but also the ideological and historical context of his
beliefs. This lecture provides both student and practitioner of
politics insights into the person and the paradigm, and charts the
journey of the left through the eyes of its best-loved advocate.

I am very grateful to Philip Norton who has edited these
lectures with such skill and sensitivity. I first became aware of
Philip's work when I was myself a student, and he has delivered
an indefatigable stream of thoughtful and rigorous contributions
to the study of public life over four decades. I could think of
no one better to have undertaken the editing of this book, nor
would I have wished for another. My thanks also go to colleagues
in both Houses who shared with us their passion and dedication to their eminent parliamentarian and I am pleased that they
have kindly agreed for their work to be shared with others.

I very much hope that you will gain as much enjoyment and
illumination from this book as I got from sponsoring and attending the lectures.

Rt Hon. John Bercow MP
Speaker

Introduction

Philip Norton

The Parliament Act 1911, as Chris Ballinger has noted, 'is a short act of parliament, which had a profound effect on constitutional and political legislation in the twenti- eth century'.[1] It established the supremacy of the elected House of Commons over the unelected House of Lords. Its passage was politically fraught, achieved only after two general elections and an undertaking by the King, George V, that, if necessary, he would create 500 new peers to ensure that it made it onto the statute book.[2] The Act, as amended by the Parliament Act 1949, continues to govern the relationship between the two Houses of Parliament. It also redesigned the electoral landscape of the nation by reducing the maximum life of a Parliament from seven years to five years.

The centenary of the passage of the Act was marked by several events. Among them was a lecture series initiated by the Speaker of the House of Commons, John Bercow. Rather than simply focusing on the events leading up to the passage of the Act in 1911, he felt it would be appropriate to look at Parliament in the century since the passage of the Act. He commissioned eleven lectures, each devoted to an outstanding MP of the past century. He felt it appropriate that each should be delivered by a present parliamentarian who had a notable interest in history and a particular appreciation of Parliament. Each was delivered in the State Rooms of the Speaker's House and broadcast by BBC Parliament. This volume reproduces the lectures essentially as they were delivered and, as far as possible, comments reflecting the nature of the occasion have been retained.

Each speaker had a particular interest in their subject matter, in some cases a close personal link. Nicholas Soames delivered the lecture on his grandfather, Sir Winston Churchill. In discussion after his lecture, he recounted the occasion when, as a young child, he had wandered into his grandfather's bedroom. 'Are you really the greatest living Englishman?' he enquired. 'Yes,' replied the great man. 'Now bugger off.' Neil Kinnock (Lord Kinnock) delivered the lecture on Michael Foot, his predecessor as leader of the Labour Party. The relationship between the two was affectionate but, as Neil Kinnock recounted, occasionally a little fraught, Foot on one occasion throwing a tray at him in a disagreement over devolution. Andrew Adonis (Lord Adonis) spoke on Roy Jenkins, to whom he had been close in the newly formed Social Democratic Party, and John Whittingdale on Margaret Thatcher, the Prime Minister that he had served as Political Secretary. As he reveals in his lecture, working for Britain's first female Prime Minister could be demanding, but it also had some lighter moments.

Some of the lectures were delivered by historians. Kenneth Morgan (Lord Morgan), an authority on Lloyd George and Welsh politics, was an obvious candidate to deliver the lecture on the distinguished Welshman. Gordon Marsden, a former editor of *History Today*, spoke on Aneurin Bevan, and fellow historian Tristram Hunt delivered the lecture on Tony Benn – the only lecturer whose subject was in the audience when he spoke.

Shirley Williams (Baroness Williams), who when she was first elected as an MP in 1964 was still one of fewer than one hundred women to have been elected to the House of Commons,[3] looked at the life of Nancy Astor, the first woman to take her seat in Parliament. The Father of the House of Commons, Sir Peter Tapsell, spoke on the towering figure of F. E. Smith, whose rooms he once briefly occupied as an undergraduate at Merton College, Oxford. Douglas Hurd (Lord Hurd of Westwell) reflected on the life of another Tory politician, Iain Macleod, whom he had been able to observe prior to Macleod's untimely death. I spoke on one of the most controversial politicians of the latter half of the twentieth century, Enoch Powell, whom I got to know in the later years of his time in the House of Commons.

The utility of having parliamentarians deliver the lectures was a sensitivity to the conditions that their subjects will have faced, not least a critical House, and in seeking to persuade others, not least in their own party, that their declared path was the right one. Parliament can provide a congenial environment but at times a very lonely one.

The lectures covered a distinguished but eclectic array of politicians who made a name for themselves not only in the House of Commons but also in the country.[4] They came from disparate backgrounds, some modest and some privileged, and espoused very different political philosophies. Some closed their political careers by retiring voluntarily, while others were retired by the electorate or by their (or, in Lloyd George's case, another) party. Enoch Powell notably wrote, in his biography of Joseph Chamberlain, that 'all political careers, unless they are cut-off at some happy juncture, end in failure'. Iain Macleod had his career cut off in its prime, dying within days of becoming Chancellor of the Exchequer. Aneurin Bevan died within a year of becoming his party's Deputy Leader.

What, then, unites the eleven figures selected for inclusion in the series? What made them such notable figures in the House of Commons? Though not true of all, some were great orators who could hold the House transfixed while they spoke; others varied in the way they dominated the House. Enoch Powell was a great debater, a parliamentarian who could craft a speech on his feet. Winston Churchill laboured long and hard to produce masterly speeches, but – unlike his father, Randolph Churchill – he was not a natural debater. He was dependent on his script and could not adjust in order to meet the temper of the House. Nicholas Soames recalled the observation of Clement Attlee who, when asked if Churchill had been a great parliamentarian, replied: 'No, he was a great parliamentary figure.'

Some were effective politicians, being able to mobilise supporters to get their way and achieve notable policy outcomes. As I argued in my lecture, Enoch Powell was a great parliamentarian but not a great politician. He held no political office after the age of fifty-one and failed to achieve any of his principal political aims. Margaret Thatcher, by contrast, was a distinguished parliamentarian rather than a great one, but – as Powell recognised – she was a very effective politician. She was able to manipulate the political system in order to get her way. She knew where she wanted to go but, as one of her ministers once put it to me, 'she could recognise a brick wall when she saw one'. All three – Churchill, Powell and Thatcher – could dominate the House, though in Thatcher's case it was only after she became Prime Minister. (Her oratorical skills were not that apparent when she was Leader of the Opposition.[5]) Others, particularly Nancy Astor and Tony Benn, were notable Members of the House, but were never dominant figures. Tony Benn's greatest political achievement came relatively early in his career, when he secured a change in the law (the Peerage Act 1963) to enable peers to renounce their titles. This enabled not only Benn but also the Earl of Home to return to the House of Commons, in the latter case to become Prime Minister. Though a leading MP, Benn's impact was greatest on the party platform and in the television studio.

Michael Foot published a series of essays on politicians in a book entitled *Loyalists and Loners*.[6] Loyalists were devoted to their party whereas loners preferred to act alone in the last resort, as people 'who would always follow their own star or search out their circuitous destiny and who, for whatever reason, would find the association of party loyalty too insulting or irksome to bear'.[7] Some of the eleven were clearly loners. Lloyd George effectively destroyed his party, Churchill had little compunction switching between parties, Jenkins sought to create a new one and Powell – who had voted Labour in 1945 – moved from the ranks of the Conservatives to the

Ulster Unionists. Others were loyalists. Aneurin Bevan, declared
Foot, was, 'for all his splendid individuality and poetic imagination, no loner. He was born and bred a member of the Labour
movement, and could not think of politics except in that context.'[8]

There is, nonetheless, a unifying element: each was driven
by a particular set of beliefs. Popularity and, if necessary, office
came second. There was a belief in the rightness of their goals
and they were prepared to do whatever was necessary in pursuit
of those goals. That encompassed not just impassioned speeches
but, if required, a willingness to resign office or to refuse it.
Churchill spent some years in the political wilderness, espous-
ing causes that did not appeal to most of his friends, let alone
his opponents.[9] Powell only resigned a ministerial office on one
occasion but he declined it on three. Two of the three refusals
were on a point of principle. He and Iain Macleod famously
declined to serve in the Cabinet under Alec Douglas-Home.
Bevan resigned from the government over prescription charges.

Each was prepared to speak and act independently. Bevan
may have been a loyalist, but his loyalty was to the Labour
movement and not to the party whips. He was briefly expelled
from the party in 1939, when he supported Sir Stafford Cripps
in his Popular Front campaign. 'This was the only time in his life
that Bevan was actually expelled from the Labour Party, though
he came close to it on several subsequent occasions.'[10] Michael
Foot was for a period the leading rebel on the Labour benches,
suffering at one point the withdrawal of the party whip (1961–63)
when in opposition and then voting against his own government
sixty-eight times in the 1966–70 parliament.[11] Powell was the
leading dissenter on the Conservative benches during the Heath
premiership, voting against the government on 115 occasions.[12]

Taking the stance they did meant that they did not always
court popularity and indeed at times were out in the political
cold. They favoured their own counsel to that of their party
colleagues. None was an obviously clubbable person. Indeed, as
Nicholas Soames notes of his grandfather and his wartime ally,

General de Gaulle: 'Both of them were … rather lonely men, who preferred to march alone rather than in company.' Some – notably F. E. Smith, Iain Macleod and Roy Jenkins – were not afraid to display their effortless intellectual superiority, albeit not an activity that garnered the warmth or support of their colleagues. The Marquess of Salisbury famously described Iain Macleod as 'too clever by half'. Andrew Adonis's portrayal of Roy Jenkins is affectionate but makes no attempt to hide the fact that Jenkins was well aware of his own ability and had no qualms about demonstrating his love of the finer things in life.

Their single-minded pursuit of their beliefs could instil apprehension or even fear on the part of others. F. E. Smith, like Aneurin Bevan, was a ferocious debater. Peter Tapsell wondered why judges put up with his barbed retorts. In answering questions after his lecture, Douglas Hurd conceded that Enoch Powell was the only politician who scared him. When sat on the government front bench, he was in fear when the Ulster Unionist MP for South Down – with his staring eyes, intense manner and penetrating questions – rose to his feet. Ministers and civil servants often quailed when faced with questioning by Margaret Thatcher. She combined intensity of feeling with a mastery of her brief. John Whittingdale recounts her tendency to grab the telephone and harangue a minister's private secretary when a brief sent to No. 10 was deemed inadequate.

These reflections also convey that a commitment to one's beliefs is a necessary but not sufficient condition for explaining the distinctiveness of the eleven. They were not only committed but also brave in the pursuit of their goals. They exhibited a remarkable strength of character. As Michael Foot noted of one press gallery reporter's coverage of the young Bevan, he 'put his finger on Bevan's most conspicuous quality – his courage'.[13] Lloyd George faced the mobs in his opposition to the Boer war. Nancy Astor took on a somewhat different mob – the ranks of hostile male MPs – and fought for women's rights. Having been associated with appeasement (her home, Cliveden, gave its name to a leading group, the Cliveden set), she was one of the Tory MPs to vote against, and help bring down, the Chamberlain government in 1940. She is the only one of the eleven never to become party leader or a Cabinet minister. Churchill stood alone in the 1930s and was resolute in time of war. Even after accepting the premiership, he had to face a Parliamentary Conservative Party that was wary if not hostile. Benn faced considerable hostility in his attempts to get the peerage law changed as well as during his later spats with others in the Labour Party. He was one of the most divisive figures in the Labour Party in the latter half of the 1970s and early 1980s. Margaret Thatcher showed notable resolve in challenging the incumbent, and former Prime Minister, Edward Heath, for the Tory leadership in 1975 and remarkable courage in her reaction to the attempt to assassinate her at the Conservative Party conference in Brighton in 1984. Powell, another potential terrorist target, insisted on publishing his home address and eschewed bodyguards.

It was also perhaps this particular quality that they recognised in others. Powell and Foot exhibited great respect for one another and, indeed, proved effective allies in 1969 in helping destroy the Parliament (No. 2) Bill to reform the House of Lords. Foot described Powell as 'the soul of honour and loyalty'.[14] Foot was an outstandingly eloquent speaker in the Commons. 'Only Enoch Powell, perhaps, could challenge him, and he and Foot became significantly close friends.'[15] Powell admired Thatcher as a politician and Thatcher, despite Powell's attack on her over the Anglo-Irish Agreement, held him in near reverence. Foot followed in Bevan's footsteps by taking over his seat. Foot may not have revered Nancy Astor in the way his father did[16] (Isaac Foot was her Liberal opponent in Plymouth Sutton in 1919) but he penned a notably sympathetic portrait.

The eleven chosen for the series thus stood out. They were clearly distinctive, meriting the accolade of eminent parliamentarians, though not unique. There were others who merited inclusion – it would be a sad reflection on the House of

Commons if this was not the case. The century saw some brilliant debaters, not all of them remembered today, and some distinguished figures who could hold the House and who were resolute in pursuit of their ideals. One thinks of recent politicians such as Robin Cook, 'one of the great dispatch box orators of the modern generation',[17] who resigned from the Cabinet in opposition to the Iraq war; Denis Healey, 'a very strong politician, the strongest of his time',[18] and 'a brilliant if sometimes brutal parliamentary debater';[19] and Michael Heseltine, a flamboyant performer at the dispatch box, though – like Tony Benn – someone who was possibly even more effective on the party platform than he was on the floor of the House of Commons.

Lesser-known politicians from earlier generations include Ellen Wilkinson on the Labour benches and Nigel Birch on the Conservative. Wilkinson – 'Red Ellen' – was a noted campaigner, with significant organisational skills, who moved from the public platform to the chamber of the House of Commons as MP for Jarrow; rather like Michael Foot, she was at her best on the back benches rather than in ministerial office.[20] Birch, following his election to Parliament in 1945, 'quickly made a formidable reputation ... for his mordantly witty interventions and speeches'.[21] He resigned ministerial office in 1958, along with fellow Treasury ministers Peter Thorneycroft and Enoch Powell, in opposition to the government's failure to approve cuts in public expenditure. He could contribute eruditely to economic debate, often speaking without a note, though is perhaps best remembered for his speech following the Profumo scandal in 1963 when he called on the Prime Minister, Harold Macmillan, to resign, quoting Browning: 'Never glad confident morning again.'[22] 'No leader,' wrote Clive Irving, 'could have been knifed by a more exquisitely honed blade.'[23]

Shall we see their like again? The history of Parliament is littered with Members complaining about the disappearance of the parliamentary greats. Recent decades have also been littered with complaints about the demise of the independent-minded party MP, willing to stand up to party leaders. These, though, are myths, albeit myths that are taking a long time to disappear. The high point of party loyalty was actually the 1950s with two parliamentary sessions in which not a single Conservative MP voted against the whips.[24] MPs loyally obeyed the whips, a situation that changed in later years, and especially so in the 1970s with an upsurge in intra-party dissent in Conservative ranks.[25] More recent years have seen unprecedented levels of backbench dissent[26] and the first session of the Parliament elected in 2010 set new records.[27] Some Members have exhibited courage, independence of mind and a commitment to the institution of Parliament, as well as a capacity to argue their case in a compelling manner. Were a future Speaker to commission a series of lectures on outstanding parliamentarians of the twenty-first century, it would likely include some already occupying the green benches of the House of Commons.

1   Chris Ballinger, 'Hedgers and Ditchers: The Parliament Act 1911', in Philip Norton (ed.), *A Century of Constitutional Reform* (Chichester: Wiley-Blackwell, 2011), p.19.
2   See, for example, Roy Jenkins, *Mr Balfour's Poodle* (London: Heinemann, 1954), Harold Nicolson, *King George The Fifth: His Life and Reign* (London: Constable, 1952), pp.125–55, and Philip Norton, 'Resisting the Inevitable? The Parliament Act 1911', The History of Parliament Annual Lecture, *Parliamentary History*, Vol. 31 (3), 2012, pp.472–88.
3   See Melville Currell, *Political Woman* (London: Croom Helm, 1974), pp.53–73.
4   This draws on the author's article, 'Centurions of the chamber', *The House Magazine*, No. 1404, Vol. 36, 12 January 2012, p.56.
5   See Philip Norton, 'Margaret Thatcher, 1975–9', in Timothy Heppell (ed.), *Leaders of the Opposition from Churchill to Cameron* (Basingstoke: Palgrave Macmillan, 2012), pp.97–108.
6   Michael Foot, *Loyalists and Loners* (London: Collins, 1986).
7   Foot, *Loyalists and Loners*, p.186.
8   Foot, *Loyalists and Loners*, p.14.
9   See, e.g., Martin Gilbert, *Winston Churchill: The Wilderness Years* (London: Macmillan, 1981).
10 John Campbell, *Nye Bevan: A Biography* (London: Hodder & Stoughton, 1994), p.83.
11 Philip Norton, *Dissension in the House of Commons 1945–74* (London: Macmillan, 1975), p.613, n.8.

12 Philip Norton, *Conservative Dissidents* (London: Temple Smith, 1978), p.253.

13 Michael Foot, *Aneurin Bevan*, Vol. 1: *1897–1945* (London: Paladin edn, 1975), p.119.

14 Foot, *Loyalists and Loners*, p.186.

15 Kenneth O. Morgan, *Michael Foot: A Life* (London: HarperPress, 2007), p.484.

16 See Foot, *Loyalists and Loners*, p.231.

17 John Kampfner, *Robin Cook* (London: Victor Gollancz, 1998), p.10.

18 Kenneth O. Morgan, *Labour People* (Oxford: Oxford University Press, 1992), p.325.

19 Stephen Howe, 'Denis (Winston) Healey', in Keith Robbins (ed.), *The Blackwell Biographical Dictionary of British Political Life in the Twentieth Century* (Oxford: Blackwell, 1990), p.194.

20 On Wilkinson, see Betty D. Vernon, *Ellen Wilkinson* (London: Croom Helm, 1982).

21 Enoch Powell, '(Evelyn) Nigel (Chetwode) Birch', in Hugo Young (ed.), *Political Lives* (Oxford: Oxford University Press, 2001), p.115.

22 See, e.g., Anthony Sampson, *Macmillan: A Study in Ambiguity* (Harmondsworth: Penguin Books, 1967), p.239.

23 Clive Irving, with Ron Hall and Jeremy Wallington, *Scandal '63* (London: Heinemann, 1963), p.170.

24 Philip Norton, *Dissension in the House of Commons 1974–1979* (London: Macmillan, 1975), p.426.

25 Norton, *Dissension in the House of Commons 1945–74*, Norton, *Conservative Dissidents*, Norton, *Dissension in the House of Commons 1974–1979*.

26 See especially Philip Cowley, *Revolts and Rebellions* (London: Politico's, 2002), Philip Cowley, *The Rebels* (London: Politico's, 2005), and Philip Cowley and Mark Stuart, 'A Rebellious Decade: Backbench Rebellions under Tony Blair, 1997–2007', in Matt Beech and Simon Lee (eds), *Ten Years of New Labour* (Basingstoke: Palgrave Macmillan, 2008), pp.103–19.

27 Philip Norton, 'Coalition Cohesion', in Timothy Heppell and David Seawright (eds), *Cameron and the Conservatives* (Basingstoke: Palgrave Macmillan, 2012), pp.181–93, Philip Cowley and Mark Stuart, 'A Coalition with Two Wobbly Wings: Backbench Dissent in the House of Commons', *Political Insight*, Vol. 3 (1), 2012, pp.8–11.

David Lloyd George

Kenneth O. Morgan
Delivered on 11 January 2011

Biographical note

David Lloyd George

Born 1863, son of William George, former master of Hope Street Unitarian School, Liverpool, and Elizabeth, daughter of David Lloyd, Baptist minister. Married first in 1888 Margaret Owen (died 1941), second in 1943, Frances Louise Stevenson. Educated at Llanystumdwy Church School and privately. Solicitor. Liberal MP for Caernarfon Boroughs April 1890 to January 1945. President of the Board of Trade 1905–08; Chancellor of the Exchequer 1908–15; Minister of Munitions 1915–16; Secretary of State for War 1916; Prime Minister 1916–22. Leader of the Liberal Party 1926–31 and Independent Liberal Group 1931–35.

Privy Counsellor 1905; Constable of Caernarfon Castle 1908; Lord Rector of Edinburgh University 1920–23. Awarded Order of Merit 1919. Father of the House of Commons 1929–45. Created Earl Lloyd-George of Dwyfor 1945. Died 26 March 1945, shortly after accepting the peerage.

A fiery and ambitious politician, his 1909 Budget precipitated the constitutional crisis leading to the Parliament Act 1911. He engineered Asquith out of the premiership in 1916, succeeding him as Prime Minister and irrevocably splitting the Liberal Party. He was an outstanding wartime Prime Minister. Dependent on Conservative support, his peacetime leadership proved contentious and in 1922 Conservative MPs voted to withdraw from the coalition.

I t is a great honour to be invited by Mr Speaker to give the first of these lectures. It is fitting that Lloyd George should launch the series. I believe that it is intended not simply to recall the momentous passage of the Parliament Act a hundred years ago, but also to celebrate the influence and authority of Parliament over our national life. No one in the twentieth century illustrates that more emphatically than 'the little Welsh attorney', whose epoch-making People's Budget brought the Parliament Act into being in the first place.

The seventeen-year-old trainee solicitor first set eyes on Parliament in November 1880 on his first visit to London. He gave it a somewhat mixed review. 'Grand buildings outside but they are crabbed, small and suffocating', especially the House of Commons. But, significantly, he went on, 'I will not say but that I eyed the assembly in a spirit similar to that in which William the Conqueror eyed England on his visit to Edward the Confessor, the region of his future domain.'[1] The young man was already thinking in terms of conquest of that great institution, 'the great assize of the people', and over the next half century that is manifestly what he achieved.

He was, of course, a uniquely controversial parliamentarian, both in his public career and his private life, and it was a long while before Parliament gave him his due. Back in the 1930s, the French put up a statue of Lloyd George's wartime ally, Georges Clemenceau, in the Champs-Élysées. He stands tall there with his cape, his cane and his black leather boots, and was universally hailed as 'Père la Victoire'.[2] It was not until November 2007 that Lloyd George's appropriately dynamic statue was unveiled in Parliament Square by Prince Charles. He was the first radical to feature there, alongside five Conservative Prime Ministers and a conservative king. I note that Winston Churchill's statue was decorated by anti-capitalist demonstrators and latterly some protesting student militants. It is agreeable to think that Lloyd George's statue may sometime be adorned by the pheasant-shooting wing of the Countryside Alliance.

He was a parliamentarian almost from birth. At the age of five, he was carried on the shoulders of Uncle Lloyd to hail the great Liberal victory in Caernarfonshire in the general election of 1868. He was an intensely political young schoolboy at Llanystumdwy national school, where he led a strike of his schoolfellows to prevent them reciting the Anglican creed before the headmaster. He began professional life as a country solicitor in Portmadoc, an ideal platform for engaging in an assault on the Anglican 'Unholy Trinity' of the Bishop, the Brewer and the Squire who dominated the rural scene in Nonconformist Wales. His boyhood hero was the recently assassinated Abraham Lincoln – indeed the image of another country lawyer who went from log cabin to become President of the United States was made much of by his admirers. *From Village Green to Downing Street* was the evocative title of one early biography.[3] He was thought of as a possible Liberal candidate for Merioneth in the 1885 election when he was a mere twenty-two. He entered the Commons in 1890 when he was twenty-seven. His victory in Caernarfon Boroughs was actually a Liberal gain. Down to 1906 he conducted a bold and brilliant start to his parliamentary career in a highly marginal constituency. The Anglican influence in the cathedral city of Bangor was always a looming threat.

From the start of his time in the Commons, he emerged as a speaker of extraordinary power and charisma. His maiden speech on 13 June 1890, on the congenial topic of temperance and the prospect of compensation for publicans, included bold satire of two parliamentary giants, Joseph Chamberlain and Randolph Churchill (something of a hero for the young Lloyd

George) whom he compared to two contortionists who set their heads in one direction and their feet in the opposite. He told his young wife back in Caernarfonshire, 'There is no doubt I scored a success and a great one' – no false modesty about Lloyd George. He also told his wife that he would take time in making a second speech to give it the more impact.[4] Soon he was established as one of the most admired and feared Members of the House.

It is worth examining why his speeches were so effective. Clearly there was the influence of the Nonconformist pulpit – the lyrical language (in Welsh quite as much as in English), the compelling rhythm, the Biblical imagery and the use of homely metaphor (such as, famously, his reference to picking up fire-wood in greater abundance after stormy weather). But he was also moved by another late-Victorian institution – the music hall. He also made much use of humour, not commonly a feature of Nonconformist chapel sermons, especially in Wales. The Prime Minister of Great Britain reflected something of the style of George Robey, the Prime Minister of Mirth. Lloyd George was always infinitely adaptable as an orator. He could move easily, effortlessly, from the slapstick to the sublime, from partisan knockabout to supra-party moral consensus.

There were great figures in the Commons when he entered it in 1890. He was most impressed by the titanic personality of Gladstone – 'Head and shoulders above anyone else I have ever seen in the House of Commons.'[5] Lloyd George marvelled at his power of gesture, language, fire and, latterly, 'wit', also the transfixing power of the Grand Old Man's 'terrible eye'.[6] His one criticism was that at times Gladstone would go on too long, seldom something for which Lloyd George himself could be criticised.

Lloyd George's speaking style, in the Commons and else-where, depended heavily on communion with his audience. He was always subtly responsive to his listeners, in parliamentary debate and in meeting deputations as a minister. He was also outstanding at listening to others. In the famous phrase, he 'could charm a bird off a bough'. He loved heckling and, like his countryman, Aneurin Bevan, fed off it richly. He could be exceptionally devastating and ruthless in personal attack. On the platform he would describe Herbert, Viscount Gladstone, as 'the finest living embodiment of the Liberal principle that talent was not hereditary'.[7] Hereditary peers were elevated on the 'principle of the first of the litter – you would not choose a spaniel on those principles'. The House of Lords was dismissed as 'five hundred ordinary men, chosen at random from amongst the unemployed'.[8] He could also be hugely effective in turning defence into attack, notably in the Maurice debate of May 1918 when he destroyed the motion of censure timidly moved by Asquith. He could also be uniquely sensitive in winning over the House. During the debate on the Marconi case in 1912, when he was accused of corruption by making money through investing in a company contracted to the British government, he delivered an extraordinarily passionate plea of his innocence and honesty. Mrs Lucy Masterman, the wife of his colleague Charles Masterman, wrote in her diary of this debate, 'The whole House was soon crying. Winston had two large tears rolling down his face. Rufus [Isaacs] was sitting with his head bent so that no one could see his face. Charlie [Masterman] was crying. The PM [Asquith] was crying.' A Liberal backbencher 'boo-hooed in a very vocal manner'.[9]

Another important parliamentary quality of his on occasion was generosity. Thus when he was fiercely attacked by the young Nye Bevan over the Coal Mines Bill in 1930 – 'better dearer coal than cheaper colliers' – Lloyd George responded with much grace, perhaps mindful of his own onslaughts on the great Joe Chamberlain. An observer wrote that he was 'confronted with the ghost of his own angry youth'.[10]

Compared with Winston Churchill, Lloyd George was far more spontaneous a speaker. Churchill prepared his speeches with intense care and largely read from them (he broke down in

1904 as a young MP when he departed from them). Lloyd George spoke to his listeners; Churchill spoke to, and for, history. Lloyd George's major speeches usually had two kinds of material. He carefully had typed out the main themes, including key phrases (e.g. 'cowardly surrender').[11] Then he would use pencil notes as well, which gave him the maximum of flexibility in debate. His People's Budget speech in April 1909 was backed up by a jumble of scarcely coherent or legible pencilled statistics to illustrate the details of land taxation and valuation.[12] His spontaneity could be immensely effective (as in the 1940 Norway debate speech which helped to bring down Neville Chamberlain) but it could also be dangerous (as with Michael Foot) if he departed from his text without due care. One such instance was his speech at Bristol in the 'coupon' general election in December 1918, when he responded to the encouragement of his audience with references to Germany 'paying to the very last penny' and rashly mentioned a specific sum of damages (£24m).[13] If Lloyd George's spontaneity could give hostages to fortune, the care which Churchill took in his speeches could be immensely powerful and indeed moving. Thus in late March 1945, when Churchill was almost overwhelmed with critical political issues after the Yalta conference as the war came to its end, he took a remarkable amount of time in composing a personal tribute to his old comrade in arms over forty years: 'the greatest Welshman produced by that unconquerable race since the days of the Tudors'.[14]

Another Prime Minister has given us the greatest insight into the impact of Lloyd George's speeches on the House. Harold Macmillan was a huge admirer:

> The wonderful head, the great mane of white hair … the expressive features, changing rapidly from fierce anger to that enchanting smile, not confined to the mouth but spreading to his cheeks and eyes: above all, the beautiful hands, an actor's or an artist's hands, by the smallest movement of which he would make you see the picture he was trying to paint.

He gave Macmillan, as a young backbencher, advice in his private office on how to speak in the House, how to vary his pace and his pitch. He taught him to 'use his arms, not wrists, not hands, not ineffective posturing but the whole of the arms and shoulders, even the back, in a total integration of body into words'. Macmillan once sat next to me at lunch in Oxford and told me that Lloyd George advised him always to let the gesture follow the words, as in 'there is a man who has betrayed his country' – pointing at the victim immediately after, not during, these comments. He once criticised one of Macmillan's early speeches. It was not, said Lloyd George, a speech at all, but a contribution to an economic journal.

> You made twenty-five points all leading on to one another. That's not the way to speak. You want to make one, if you are a backbencher, two if you are a Minister, possibly three, but better still two... The art of speaking is to leave on the audience a clear picture of what it is you want.[15]

Lloyd George was almost always true to his word.

The supreme communicator in the politics of his day, only one form of communication defeated him, and that in old age. He was never at home with radio broadcasting. With no human audience visible in front of him, he could not blossom. His daughter, Megan, tried to get him to be at ease in BBC studios – but 'there was nothing'. The giant of platform, pulpit and Parliament was suddenly anonymous, almost tongue-tied.

At every stage of his fifty-four years in the Commons, he was a powerful influence in the House. As a backbencher between 1890 and 1905, he often focused on the local affairs of Wales, frequently in speeches that were satirical and somewhat lightweight. He made a national impact for the first time with his passionate attacks on his old hero, Joseph Chamberlain, during the South Africa War – 'this electro-plated Rome and its tin Caesar'. He accused Chamberlain, with powerful effect, of profiteering personally from war contracts with the army.[16] But he could also strike a higher note, as when he passed on to his leader, Campbell-Bannerman, Emily Hobhouse's first-hand verdict on the atrocities inflicted on Boer women and children in the British concentration camps on the Veldt – 'methods of barbarism', three words that changed the culture of Edwardian politics. During the debates after the 1902 Education Act, he could move on from Nonconformist 'revolt' against an Act which aided Anglican schools to an appeal to transcend religious sectarianism where education was concerned.[17]

As a government minister between 1905 and 1916, he would be brilliantly effective in presenting highly complex proposals. As it happened, perhaps his most important statement was just about his worst. His People's Budget speech on 29 April 1909 saw him almost break down through sheer strain and fatigue. The House took a break to let him recover his stamina. But he did recover, and ended with a powerful peroration about the government's plans to make poverty in Britain as remote as the wolves which once infested its forests. That summer, he handled the difficult committee stage with courtesy, charm and humour. He was also excellent in conducting the committee stage of the National Insurance Bill in 1911. Some jaundiced critics wondered whether he had really understood the arcane minutiae of his own bill. In debate in the House, Lloyd George showed emphatically that he had.

A quite different kind of speech was an astonishing polemic in the second reading debate on the Welsh Disestablishment Bill in May 1912. The Duke of Devonshire had claimed that the disendowment of the Welsh Church was the robbery of God. Lloyd George (perhaps helped in his researches by a strong Liberal, A. F. Pollard, a distinguished historian of the Tudors, and grandfather of the celebrated psephologist David Butler) responded that the fortunes of the duke, like those of many other landowners such as the Cecils, were 'laid deep in sacrilege' during the era of the Reformation, which saw the dissolution of the monasteries.

They robbed the Church. They robbed the monasteries. They robbed the altars. They robbed the alms-houses. They robbed the poor. They robbed the dead. Then they come here when we are trying … to recover some of this pillaged property for the poor to whom it was originally given, with hands dripping with the fat of sacrilege, to accuse us of robbery of God.[18]

He was strongly backed by G. K. Chesterton, who countered F. E. Smith's claim that the bill would offend the souls of Christian people everywhere with the satirical poem 'Anti-Christ', with its memorable finale: 'Chuck it, Smith!'

As Prime Minister between 1916 and 1922 his survival in the House depended on his rhetorical skills. He was a Prime Minister without a party and, unlike Churchill in 1940–45, had no assured majority in the House. In the peacetime coalition of 1918–22 he depended solely on the goodwill of the dominant Conservative (or Unionist) Party. Much depended on the Prime Minister's oratorical command, his ability to play on the emotions and at times to strike a tone of high patriotic idealism. Thus, in the Maurice debate, he destroyed Asquith's feeble case and the undercover manoeuvring of the military high command with a devastating performance.[19] General Maurice had claimed that the government had not been telling the truth about the comparative number of British troops at the front in 1917 and 1918, and the reasons for the extension of the British line on the western front. Lloyd George showed that in fact his figures came from Maurice's department, the Department of Military Operations (DMO), at the War Office, and that he had never challenged them there or at Cabinet meetings. He also underlined the inconsistency of Maurice acting with such disloyalty and insubordination while claiming to try to be reassuring morale in the armed forces. He ended on a high patriotic note. He appealed 'on behalf of our common country' that 'there should be an end of this sniping'.[20] While historians have debated the statistical evidence on these matters at length subsequently, at the time Lloyd George enjoyed a complete triumph. His enemies, political and military, were annihilated.

Lloyd George exerted his unique personal authority again in April 1919, when he confronted newspaper and other critics that he was being too soft on the defeated Germans in the Paris peace conference. He delivered a slashing attack on Lord Northcliffe, owner of *The Times*.[21] He referred to his 'disease of vanity', tapping his head significantly as he did so. Northcliffe was sowing dissension among the Allies at Paris. 'Not even that kind of disease is a justification for so black a crime against humanity.' Northcliffe was derided and ridiculed. Later on in 1922, when Northcliffe was dead from a mysterious blood infection, Lloyd George meditated a kind of posthumous revenge by becoming owner or even editor of *The Times* himself.[22]

Finally, as elder statesman, from his downfall as Prime Minister in October 1922, he remained a powerful force in debate. He was very much a front-line player whose return to government was widely canvassed, down to the general election of 1935, when he was seventy-two. In the 1920s he spoke a good deal on economic policy and measures to combat economic depression and mass unemployment. In the 1930s, he lent his matchless prestige to debates on international affairs. He often struck an ambiguous note, perhaps a dangerous one, notably with his remarkable enthusiasm for Hitler after his visit to Berchtesgaden in August 1936. This was by far the most appalling misjudgement of his career.

Conversely, his abiding power as a senior politician was shown in the remarkable impact of his speech of 18 June 1936, attacking the government for its failure to impose sanctions on Italy after the invasion of Abyssinia. He launched a ferocious assault on the government, in what Stanley Baldwin called 'an extraordinarily brilliant speech'. He made merciless use of quotations from government ministers. Baldwin had spoken of Britain 'standing like a rock in the waves'. Lloyd George observed that 'the rock has turned out to be driftwood'. The government he compared to an aeroplane popularly known as 'the flying flea'. Neville Chamberlain had spoken of avoiding 'a cowardly surrender'. 'Tonight,' declared Lloyd George, 'we have had the cowardly surrender and there [pointing at the government front bench] are the cowards.'[23]

Frances Stevenson, his private secretary, wrote that the government front bench 'was literally cowed before his onslaught'. A young Tory MP told Churchill that he had never heard anything like it in the House. 'Young man,' replied Churchill with rare generosity of spirit, 'you have been listening to one of the greatest parliamentary performances of all time.'[24]

There was an even later oratorical triumph in the Norway debate on 8 May 1940, Lloyd George's last great speech in the House. This was very different, almost unplanned. He had not thought of speaking but was persuaded to do so by Clement Davies, Robert Boothby and others. He spoke largely off the cuff from rough notes only, which added to the powerful effect on his Commons audience. He ended with a tremendous finale. The Prime Minister had asked for sacrifice. He should set an example himself, because he could make no greater contribution to victory in the war than to sacrifice the seals of office.[25] Chamberlain resigned following a major Conservative backbench revolt. Thus the colossus of the First World War helped pave the way for the elevation of the colossus of the Second.

Beyond Lloyd George's personal career, his wider impact on his country and his world was immense, probably greater than that of anyone else in this series of lectures. Churchill, after all, was identified with a dying world, that of the later Victorian empire, and a fading class system. Lloyd George more emphatically looked to the future.

As regards the constitution, Lloyd George and Asquith, that great partnership, between them transformed relations between the Commons and the Lords for ever. The 1911 Parliament Act tilted power decisively to the elected House. If the statesman's craft of getting the Act through came from Asquith, it was Lloyd George's 1909 Budget that brought matters to the proof. It was the powers of the Lords that always concerned Lloyd George, not its composition. He demonstrated this as Prime Minister with his mass creation of so many peers, many of them capitalists of dubious origin. He told J. C. C. Davidson that it was better to sell titles than to sell policies, as happened in politics in America: 'It keeps politics far cleaner than any other method of raising funds.'[26]

Constitutionally, his premiership of 1916–22 was a massive landmark. It was the first clear instance of a move towards a presidential type of premiership. Richard Crossman and John Mackintosh were later to see his regime as the first indication of prime ministerial government replacing classical Cabinet government. He set up the Cabinet Office to enable the Prime Minister to control government business and ensure, through his powerful secretaries, Maurice Hankey and Thomas Jones, that decisions were taken and followed up. He also had his own cadre of unelected special advisers, notably the 'Garden Suburb', his own personal secretariat headed by Philip Kerr who worked in huts set up in the garden of 10 Downing Street. He absented himself from Parliament for long periods at a time and was satirised for it by Bernard Partridge in *Punch* cartoons. The Cabinet met erratically and was often by-passed by carefully chosen 'conferences of ministers'. On one occasion in 1921, the British Cabinet met, not in London, not even in England, but in Inverness town hall, to accommodate the Prime Minister who was having a holiday in the Highlands.[27] His maverick style was strictly personal, heterodox, unpredictable. He negotiated industrial relations with trade unionists like Jimmy Thomas over a Welsh Nonconformist's equivalent of beer and sandwiches at No. 10. He held private conclave with wealthy capitalists about party political funding. He gave confidential briefings to press editors and journalists from home and overseas, and was freely on view for paparazzi: with his Inverness cloak, his long mane and his delicate feet, he was the most media-conscious politician of his day. He largely conducted foreign policy himself via summit diplomacy: he barely concealed his contempt for the official Foreign Secretary, Lord Curzon. Lloyd George, in short, was the first exponent of sofa government, Tony Blair *avant la lettre.*

Two other constitutional changes stand out. Lloyd George's government transformed the political status of women. In his 1918 Reform Act, women of thirty and over got the vote. In 1919, Lady Astor became the first female MP to take her seat. This was appropriate. Lloyd George, unlike Asquith and Churchill, was always a supporter of women's suffrage, even if his pre-war efforts, like those of most men, proved disappointing to the suffragettes.

Secondly, Lloyd George ensured that Ireland was removed from centre stage in British politics after the Free State Act of January 1922. After a terribly dark period of bloody retaliation in the era of 'Black and Tans', Lloyd George made the great diplomatic breakthrough with Sinn Féin leaders with the creation of a self-governed, if partitioned, Ireland. It owed everything to the Prime Minister's Celtic guile. He pointed out to Éamon de Valera that neither the Welsh nor the Irish languages had a word for 'republic', which he felt to be significant.[28] He created a settlement that endures, for good or ill, to the present day. No longer would there be an Irish Nationalist party which might control the balance of power in the House. He had succeeded where Pitt, Peel and Gladstone all failed in finding a solution to the Irish impasse that, if highly controversial, nevertheless stood the test of time. A different, more pluralist, vision of the union of the United Kingdom would henceforth emerge. This was appropriate since Lloyd George in his *Cymru Fydd* (Young Wales) days in the 1890s had been an early proponent of devolution. What took place in 1999 in Scotland and Wales was partly his legacy.

He also had a massive impact on the party system. Here was a highly paradoxical figure – a vehement partisan who aroused strong emotions among friends and foes, yet was also the great

champion of coalitions. Through his career, he showed a
disposition to work with political opponents in search of higher
objectives – as he did back in Wales as early as 1895 over possible Welsh home rule. In 1910, he astonished the political world
at a time of high political emotions over the Budget and the
Parliament Bill by proposing to Balfour and some Conservative
leaders that there should be a coalition to by-pass what he called
'uncontroversial' issues like free trade and Welsh disestablishment in pursuit of the higher objectives of national defence and
social reform. [29]

As a Prime Minister, of course, he headed a coalition
himself. After the successful outcome of his alliance with the
Conservatives during the war, he put forward in 1919–20 the idea
of a kind of government of national unity on the lines of the
'unity of command' achieved during the war. His heroes were
men who broke with their own parties – Joseph Chamberlain
over Irish home rule and Theodore Roosevelt who formed his
breakaway Progressive Party under the banner of the New
Nationalism in 1912.[30]

In fact, the outcome of his coalitions with the Conservatives
in wartime and in peace was a very mixed one. His coalition of
1918 (based on the notorious 'coupon' of electoral co-operation)
destroyed the Liberals as a party of government when they
split into two. If anything, it also created the Labour Party as
the clear voice of progressive opinion: in 1918 the party wisely
followed Bernard Shaw's advice – 'Go back to Lloyd George
and say nothing doing.' Arguably, he had laid the basis for the
Labour Party becoming some day a party of government with
his Treasury Agreement with the trade unions in 1915, as earlier
with his use of unions as agencies for national health insurance
in 1911. The essentially Lib-Con coalition of 1931 (which Lloyd
George vehemently opposed) destroyed the Liberals not just
as a party of government, but as a party of opposition as well
when they split into three, the National Liberals under Sir John
Simon in effect becoming indistinguishable from the Tories.

What rewards or calamities the coalition of 2010 will visit upon the heirs of the old Liberal Party remain to be seen. After the university fees imbroglio, and the failure of the AV referendum and Lords reform, the omens do not look too promising.

For domestic British politics, Lloyd George's impact was truly remarkable. He was indeed the 'dynamic force' of which Baldwin spoke apprehensively at the Carlton Club meeting of 1922. He was always concerned with ideas and long-term policy objectives. His associates were not just shady people who traded titles or armaments, but distinguished intellectuals like Charles Masterman, Seebohm Rowntree, William Beveridge, the great historian H. A. L. Fisher, the economists of the Liberal Summer School in the 1920s and, of course, Maynard Keynes, who famously declared, 'I oppose Mr Lloyd George when he is wrong, and support him when he is right.'[31] Much of the time, the road that Lloyd George took was the high road. Lloyd George was thus a foremost architect of the welfare state. His National Insurance Act of 1911, following on his Old Age Pensions Act of 1908, created the base for future social policy down to the Beveridge report and the National Health Service. It created a new vision of the enabling state and of social citizenship. It is surely Britain's great progressive contribution to modern civilisation, and Lloyd George was its founding father.

His Budget of 1909 and (lesser regarded) that of 1914 laid down new principles of progressive, redistributive, graduated taxation which shaped the policy of all political parties down to the 1980s. With higher estate duties, a new supertax and social novelties such as child allowances, it provided a powerful free-trade solution to financing social welfare. The tariff reformers had argued that 'the foreigner will pay'; Lloyd George's riposte was 'the rich will pay'. Ironically, the least successful part of his taxes were the controversial land duties which yielded almost nothing and were repealed, embarrassingly, in 1920 when Lloyd George was Prime Minister.

The post-war coalition of 1918–22 was also far from negligible in social policy. It began publicly subsidised housing policies in the Addison Act, it set up a national framework for free state education in the Fisher Act, it revised and extended the system of unemployment insurance, fortunately in view of the mass unemployment to follow, and it created a Ministry of Health. Until extinguished by economic depression in the latter part of 1920, it was perhaps the last hurrah of the pre-war New Liberalism.

In opposition in the 1920s he promoted far-sighted new policies for economic revival and pump-priming policies to combat unemployment. In *The Yellow Book* and *The Orange Book*, he was a Keynesian before Keynes: after all *The General Theory of Employment, Interest and Money* was not published until 1936, whereas Lloyd George's creative mind was at work on these issues a decade earlier. The spectre of the National Debt never terrified him and he condemned the dismal deflation of the National government. Today, many economists like Lord Skidelsky seem to believe that, following the credit crunch, the programmes of public investment to sustain employment pioneered by Lloyd George eighty years ago still provide the key to long-term, sustainable economic recovery.

Finally, there is his legacy in international politics. He was very much a maker of our world. He had great responsibility for the peace settlement of 1919–22. There has been massive criticism of how the Versailles Treaty came about, most famously by Keynes: Margaret Macmillan's *Peacemakers* (2001) has cogently argued the opposite case and sees the view that Versailles led inexorably to another war as simplistic. Of course, there were immense problems resulting from the settlement in the Middle East, the mandate system and the colonial restructuring that followed the end of the old Ottoman Empire. But the post-imperial Europe of Versailles and the later treaties, based on the broad principle of nationality, is still our inheritance. It has, it is true, seen the break-up into lesser states of both Yugoslavia and Czechoslovakia, but in fact Lloyd George had grave doubts about both of them as artificial hybrid creations. Edvard Beneš of

Czechoslovakia was a particular *bête noire*. In any case, alone of the post-war peacemakers, he sought to revise the peace treaties in 1920–22, both with regard to territories and reparations payments, and in time Keynes, his bitterest critic, came to endorse his views.

Our world, therefore, bears Lloyd George's imprint. Every day the newspapers and television bulletins remind us of his legacy. *Si monumentum requires, circumspice.* Much of it is benign. But far from all. Since the 1960s, British governments have been plagued by three great problem territories – Northern Ireland, Palestine, Iraq. They have one thing in common. Like all things wise and wonderful, Lloyd George made them all.

1   Diary entry of 12 November 1880, quoted W. R. P. George, *The Making of Lloyd George* (London: Faber and Faber, 1976), p.101.

2   See Kenneth O. Morgan, 'The Goat and the Tiger', *Ages of Reform* (London: I. B. Tauris, 2010), pp.93ff.

3   J. Hugh Edwards and Spencer Leigh Hughes, *From Village Green to Downing Street: Life of the Rt. Hon. D. Lloyd George MP* (London: Newnes, 1908).

4   David Lloyd George to Margaret Lloyd George, 14, 19 June 1890, in Kenneth O. Morgan (ed.), *Lloyd George, Family Letters* (Oxford: Oxford University Press, 1973), pp.29–30. These papers are in the National Library of Wales, Aberystwyth.

5   *Lord Riddell's War Diary* (London: Nicholson and Watson, 1933), p.67 (7 March 1915); *Lord Riddell's Intimate Diary of the Peace Conference and After, 1918–1923* (London: Gollancz, 1933), p.158 (1 January 1920).

6   For Gladstone's 'terrible eye', see A. J. P. Taylor (ed.), *Lloyd George: A Diary by Frances Stevenson* (London: Hutchinson, 1971), p.306 (17 April 1935).

7   Speech at Manchester. *The Times*, 15 October 1922.

8   Speech at Newcastle. *The Times*, 10 October 1909.

9   Richard Toye, *Lloyd George and Churchill* (London: Macmillan, 2007), p.97, quoting Lucy Masterman's diary.

10 Michael Foot, *Aneurin Bevan*, Vol. I (London: McGibbon and Kee, 1962), p.117.

11 Notes of speeches in Lloyd George papers (Parliamentary Archives, House of Lords), e.g. notes on Abyssinia speech, 18 June 1936 (G 186/5).

12 Lloyd George papers (C/26/folder 1).

13 *The Times*, 12 December 1918.

14 House of Commons: Official Report (Hansard): 28 March 1945, Vol. 409, col. 1380

15 Alastair Horne, *Macmillan*, Vol. I (London: Macmillan, 1988), pp.77–8. Conversation of the present writer with the Earl of Stockton, *c*. 1970.

16 House of Commons: Official Report (Hansard): 8 August 1900, Vol. 87, cols 1008–13..

17 Kenneth O. Morgan, *Wales in British Politics 1868–1922* (Cardiff: University of Wales Press, 1963), pp.188ff.

18 House of Commons: Official Report (Hansard): 16 May 1912, Vol. 38, col. 1326.

19 House of Commons, 9 May 1918. Notes of speech in Lloyd George papers, F/235.

20 Notes of speech in Lloyd George papers, F/235.

21 House of Commons: Official Report (Hansard): 16 April 1919, Vol. 114, cols 2936–56.

22 *History of the Times*, Part II, 1921–48 (London: The Times Publishing House, 1952), pp.685ff.

23 House of Commons, 18 June 1936: notes of speech, Lloyd George papers, G/186/5.

24 *A Diary by Frances Stevenson*, p.324 (20 June 1936).

25 House of Commons: Official Report (Hansard): 8 May 1940, Vol. 360, col. 1283.

26 Memorandum by J. C. C. Davidson, 1927, printed in Robert Rhodes James, *Memoirs of a Conservative* (London: Weidenfeld and Nicolson, 1969), p.279.

27 On 7 September 1921, to consider de Valera's latest proposals for Ireland.

28 Keith Middlemas (ed.), *Thomas Jones: Whitehall Diary, III, Ireland 1918–1925* (Oxford: Oxford University Press, 1971), p.89. In Welsh the words 'Democrat' and 'Republican' are identical – *Gweriniaethwr*.

29 See the memorandum on the proposed coalition in 1910 printed in Kenneth O. Morgan, *The Age of Lloyd George* (London: Allen and Unwin, 1971), pp.150–56.

30 For Lloyd George's views on Theodore Roosevelt, see his *The Truth about the Peace Treaties*, Vol. I (London: Gollancz, 1938), pp.231–2. Lloyd George thought Roosevelt was far superior to his great rival, Woodrow Wilson, in every way.

31 Robert Skidelsky, *John Maynard Keynes*, Vol. 2 (London: Macmillan, 1992), p.249.

F. E. Smith

Peter Tapsell
Delivered on 1 February 2011

Biographical note

F. E. Smith

Frederick Edwin Smith, born 12 July 1872, Birkenhead, son of Frederick Smith, barrister. Educated at Birkenhead School, Wadham College, Oxford (First, Jurisprudence). Married 1901 Margaret Eleanor, daughter of the Rev. H. Furneaux. Barrister (KC 1908). Fellow and Lecturer, Merton College, Oxford, 1896–99; Lecturer, Oriel College, Oxford, 1897. Unionist MP for Liverpool Walton, 1906–18, and for Liverpool West Derby, 1918–19. Special duty with expeditionary force, 1914. Solicitor-General 1915; Attorney-General 1915–19; Lord Chancellor 1919–22; Secretary of State for India 1924–28. Director of ICI Ltd and Tate & Lyle Ltd 1928–30.

Knighted 1915, Bt. 1918. Created Baron Birkenhead 1919, Viscount 1921, Earl 1922. High Steward of Oxford University 1922–30. Rector of Glasgow University 1922–25 and Aberdeen University 1927–30. Died 30 September 1930.

Always known as 'F. E.', Smith was one of the most outstanding barristers of his generation – renowned for his clashes with judges – and was appointed Lord Chancellor at the age of forty-seven. He was known for his debating skills, sharp mind and his liking for a lavish lifestyle, something he found difficult to maintain on a ministerial salary.

Smith's first two names being Frederick Edwin, he was unaccountably but universally known from an early age and ever since as F. E. He was born in 1872 in Birkenhead, from which he later took his title, Earl of Birkenhead. F. E. always expected to die young, which may partly explain the frenetic energy with which he led every aspect of his packed life.

At the age of ten, on his first day at a new school, F. E. informed his classmates that he intended to be either Lord Chancellor or Prime Minister. Fortunately, his father had taught him to box, so he survived to tell the tale. Indeed, his grandfather was a famous bare-knuckle fighter in the north and F. E. inherited many of those fighting qualities in his own personality. Educated at local schools in and around Birkenhead, he was an outstanding boy athlete, with the reputation for being rough and tough on the rugger field and elsewhere. In 1891, he won a scholarship to Wadham College, Oxford. He arrived at Wadham aged twenty-one, determined to get a First, and become president of the Union as he made clear to everyone.

Wadham enjoyed a golden age in the 1890s. F. E.'s contemporaries included, among a galaxy of talent, the legendary all-round athlete C. B. Fry, and the future Foreign Secretary and Lord Chancellor, John Simon. C. B. Fry was probably the most famous athlete England has ever produced – W. G. Grace was in the shadows by comparison. It was said that when Fry was an undergraduate at Oxford and walked down one of the pavements on the high street, heads of houses on the other side of the road used to raise their hats to him. Despite that competition and despite his northern background, which was thought to be a disadvantage to him, F. E. outshone them all, endowing his bare initials with a glamour that lasted all his life. Advised to get rid of his northern accent if he was to do well at the Bar later, he did so within six weeks, putting Eliza Doolittle to shame. It is a mystery how that was achieved; whether he met either Professor Higgins or the man who cured the King's stammer is unclear, but he certainly did it – although one of my colleagues has just reminded me that apparently the BBC has no recording of him speaking even though he lived until 1930. He spoke for the rest of his life with a universally admired rasp to his voice and with a wit that gained the approval of the social and political hostesses who were soon to lionise him at their sparkling receptions in London and in their grand country houses.

To an unusual extent, Smith made his name at Oxford – tall, darkly handsome, unashamedly ambitious, endowed with a scathing wit and an inexhaustible appetite for life and pleasure, he soon made himself the epitome of an Oxford Union star. Smith's verbal duels with Hilaire Belloc remain the stuff of Oxford legend. He switched from classics to law after he only achieved a second in Mods, and became president of the Union in his third year, but still managed with a heroic last six months of intense hard work to get his coveted First – always a rare double at Oxford. Those were the days when Firsts were Firsts. Even Curzon got a Second and Alec Douglas-Home got a Third.

Much of Smith's time at Oxford was spent on the playing fields or riding horses or attending Bullingdon-type parties. Two lasting characteristics were established. First was his love of fun and equally his capacity, when absolutely necessary, for sustained hard work. His nickname at Oxford was 'Don't Care Smith'. In later years, one of his hunting friends from Oxford described him as 'the bravest man I ever saw riding to hounds'.

Smith plunged heavily into student debt, on a scale that a

modern Lib Dem would find distressing. Six months before his finals, he assembled all the tradesmen – wine merchants, livery stablemen etc. – whose bills he could not pay and told them that if they would be patient he would get a First in law and go on to have a dazzling and highly lucrative career at the Bar. Improbably, his oratory and personality won their agreement. Thereafter, for at least six months before his finals, he worked at his law books for fourteen hours a day. He gave up his social life completely, but not the Oxford Union, at which he took part in two debates, one on drink and one on women. He duly got his First. He went on to win the coveted Vinerian law scholarship and was elected a Fellow of Merton College – my old college; I am wearing the Merton tie in his honour – founded in the thirteenth century, and in the hall of which his portrait, in the splendid robes of a Lord High Chancellor, proudly hangs. I used to stare at it during college meals during my very happy years at Merton.

Smith was a Fellow at Merton for three years, from 1896 to 1899, and studied law intensely during that period. By an extraordinary coincidence, during vacations – because my parents were in East Africa – I was allowed to stay in what I subsequently learned were his rooms, free of charge, the college being very generous to me. It is generally believed that when Smith was at Merton, he gained an extent of legal learning that later surprised his critics at the Bar and in the wider public, who often sought to write him off as merely a flashy politician. F. E. was very happy at Merton. It is said that he even considered remaining as a don for the rest of his life, but I find that unbelievable. Certainly, however, it was the only placid phase of his life, and he looked back on those years with nostalgia.

The college next to Merton is Corpus Christi. Smith fell in love with the daughter of a formidable classics don at Corpus, Margaret Eleanor Furneaux, and married her. They first met playing in a mixed hockey match. Any man who has ever played mixed hockey will know how rough and dangerous a game it is.

Told in advance that a don would be playing, his soon-to-be wife is reputed to have said, 'Oh, not a fusty old don, for heaven's sake', but when she had taken one glance at him she instantly changed her mind. She made him an excellent, spirited and deeply loyal wife throughout his turbulent career. She must have been a remarkable woman to put up with a husband always so active, always in the glare of controversy and burning every sort of candle at both ends right up to his early death at the age of fifty-eight.

Later, F. E. often claimed that he only left Merton because he could not support a wife on the £300 stipend of a don. When he finally left Oxford in 1899, at the start of the Boer war, with Queen Victoria still on the throne and the great Lord Salisbury, uncle of Balfour, nearing the end of his immensely long premiership, and having eaten his dinners at Gray's Inn and passed his Bar finals top equal of the list that summer, he returned to Liverpool to set up in practice on the Northern Circuit.

One of F. E.'s many attractive characteristics was his deep loyalty to his friends and institutions. Throughout his career, he always gave favoured treatment to anyone from Wadham or the Northern Circuit. When, as Lord Chancellor, he promoted a county court judge to the High Court – the first time it had ever been done – amid much disapproval from senior judges, no one was surprised to find that the newly promoted judge was a product both of Wadham and of the Northern Circuit.

Returning to his northern roots, but without his northern accent, which must have bemused and amused his old friends there, even F. E. had to wait a few months before briefs started coming his way. In the first six months of his return to the north he earned eighteen guineas, but he filled in the time by plunging into northern politics, speaking widely in favour of tariff reform, as protection was then known. At one great dinner he was invited to move a vote of thanks to the visiting guest of honour. The reason why he was invited to do so was that by then he had become a parliamentary candidate for a marginal seat of a kind, which I remind Mr Speaker I also captured – the first time a Conservative had ever won it – before losing it five years later.

Smith was a candidate and the other seven people at the top table were already MPs, so Alderman Salvidge, who dominated politics in the north west in the days when lord mayors really ran the show – later Alderman Salvidge refused a seat in Lloyd George's Cabinet, saying, 'I'm not going to give up being Lord Mayor of Liverpool for a mere job in the Cabinet' – and who needed a speaker to move the vote of thanks, asked F. E. to do it because if he asked any of the other seven – the MPs – there would have been jealousy among them, MPs being particularly prone to jealousy of each other.[1]

I mention that incident at some length because it subsequently proved of enormous significance in his later career. Joe Chamberlain, the father of Austen and Neville Chamberlain, had long been a dominant figure in the House of Commons. He achieved a double: he destroyed the Liberal Party by supporting the Tories over the issue of home rule for Ireland twenty-five years earlier, and went on to destroy the Tory Party by dividing it over protection versus free trade. He was famously known as the man who made the political weather; his barometer always pointed towards stormy.

Chamberlain made his customary great speech. F. E. was then called and stood up and moved the vote of thanks in a speech of such brilliance and wit that no one present ever forgot it. While F. E. was speaking, Joe Chamberlain twice asked the chairman, Alderman Salvidge, 'Who is he?' After F. E. sat down, Chamberlain went over to him and said, 'I have told Salvidge that he must get you a safe seat. You will be returned to Parliament, come up to me in the lobby of the House of Commons and recall yourself to my recollection.'[2] As I say, the encounter had a hugely important consequence for F. E.

While F. E. was in the north, he struggled on as young barristers have to do – at least before legal aid – and earned very little, but he gradually gathered momentum and his big break came when there was a tremendous clash between two titans: William Lever, later Lord Leverhulme, who owned most of the soap business, and Lord Northcliffe, who owned most of the newspapers – he was an earlier version of Rupert Murdoch, and a rather greater man. I do not say that contemptuously; Lord Northcliffe was a very great man – there is no question about that. Northcliffe's newspapers had accused Lever of establishing a monopoly in soap. That was very damaging to Lever and he wanted to sue the Northcliffe press, which at the time was as heinous as suing the News International group. Lever instructed two senior counsel in succession to look at all the papers and they both advised him that it would be very unwise to sue Northcliffe; his case was not strong enough and he would probably lose, which would have destroyed him and his company. For reasons that I have never seen explained, Lever sent for the very young F. E. Smith and asked him to look at the papers. For reasons that, again, I do not understand, there was a deadline: F. E. had to produce the results of consultation of the papers by 11 am the following morning. He worked on the papers for fourteen hours non-stop and at the end he wrote an opinion in two sentences, which I quote from memory: 'You have an unanswerable case. The damages will be enormous.' On that basis, Lever went ahead and sued. He briefed the young F. E. to represent him. It was a sensational case involving two of the most famous men in Britain.[3] F. E. was brilliant. He won the case and, taking the appeal into account, it cost Lord Northcliffe £220,000 – a fabulous amount in those days.

Instead of regarding F. E. as a dangerous young man who had to be pilloried in the press thereafter, Lord Northcliffe took exactly the opposite view – as I said, he was a great man – and told F. E., 'I want you to represent my newspapers in any legal action in the future.' That is exactly what F. E. did, with staggeringly highly paid briefs. When everybody knew that he was acting for Lord Northcliffe, they all wanted to brief him too. That was how he made his original breakthrough.

We have a marvellous Commons Library staff and Miss Jude's

research has been a great help to me in this lecture. She tells me, among much else, that £10,000 in 1910 would be the equivalent of £880,000 today. Between 1911 and 1912, F. E.'s fees totalled nearly £10,000. In 1912–13, they were £10,810 and in 1913, they were £14,195, well over £1m in today's money. Characteristically, in after years F. E. said that those figures were a great under-estimate of what he actually earned; he talked about receiving £30,000 to £40,000 a year. That was at a time when Cabinet ministers received £5,000 a year and fairly well-to-do middle-class businessmen were happy to scrape along on a few hundred pounds a year. Mesmerised by his earnings, it was easier for contemporaries to overlook the prolonged intensity of hard work by F. E. that produced them.

At the time, F. E. was also playing a leading role in politics and he had a very active social life. His persuasiveness as an advo-cate, whether acting for great companies in complicated cases of commercial law or headline-commanding criminal cases, such as his successful defence of Dr Crippen's mistress on a charge of murder, were universally admired by the Bar, judges, the Northcliffe press and public alike. He became as famous as Beckham. In the golden era of advocacy – Edward Carson, Marshall Hall, Rufus Isaacs and Norman Birkett – F. E. was pre-eminent.

His near irresistible advocacy in court was based on his extraor-dinary combination of arrogance, fearlessness, legal scholarship, intellectual certainty and brutal biting wit. The choicest examples, which have echoed over the generations, were aimed at judges whom he affected to regard as nincompoops. Why they allowed him to insult them with impunity is a mystery. Today I suspect he would have been ordered out of court, shunned by solicitors and perhaps disbarred, but each of his numerous insulting sallies seemed to increase his standing at the Bar, his fame in the country and the amount of his future fees. His most famous exchanges are well known, but they bear recounting because they always seem as fresh as when they first impacted on us, like a cherished extract from a famous book, play or film. They stand comparison in their fame with my favourite line of dialogue in the history of cinema, Humphrey Bogart's 'Play it again, Sam', in *Casablanca*, so I shall play some of them again.

Judge: Are you trying to show contempt for this court, Mr Smith?
Smith: No, my lord, I am attempting to conceal it.

Smith to witness: So, you were as drunk as a judge?
Judge, interjecting: You mean as drunk as a lord.
Smith: Yes, my lord.

Master of the Rolls: Really, Mr Smith, do give this court credit for some little intelligence.
Smith: That is the mistake I made in the court below, my lord.

Most famous of all are Smith's exchanges with Judge Willis in the Southwark county court, described by Winston Churchill in his wonderful book *Great Contemporaries*.[4] A boy who had been run over was suing the tramway company for damages. F. E. appeared for the company. The case for the lad was that the accident had led to blindness. The judge, a kindly if somewhat garrulous soul, allowed sympathy to outrun discretion. 'Poor boy, poor boy,' he exclaimed, 'Blind. Put him on a chair so that the jury can see him.' This was weighing the scale of justice and F. E. was moved to protest: 'Perhaps your honour would like to have the boy passed around the jury box,' he suggested. 'That is a most improper remark,' exclaimed the judge. 'It was provoked by a most improper suggestion,' F. E. replied. Judge Willis tried to think of a decisive retort. At last it arrived: 'Mr Smith, have you heard of a saying by Bacon – the great Bacon – that youth and discretion are ill-wedded companions?' 'Yes I have,' came the instant riposte, 'and have you ever heard the saying of Bacon – the great Bacon – that a much-talking judge is like an ill-tuned cymbal?' 'You are extremely offensive, young man,' exclaimed the judge. 'As a matter of fact,' said Smith, 'we both are, but I am trying to be and you can't help it.'

As Churchill adds: 'Such a dialogue would be held brilliant in a carefully written play, but that these successive rejoinders, each one more smashing than the former, should have leapt into being upon the spur of the moment is astounding.' Scarcely less striking is the fact that Judge Willis went on giving openings for F. E.'s merciless wit: 'What do you suppose I am on the bench for, Mr Smith?' 'It is not for me, your honour, to attempt to fathom the inscrutable workings of providence.'

The same lightning flashed from Smith on the public platform and in conversation. His *obiter dicta* outside the courtroom are legendary. This is one of my favourites, which has a contemporary sting. F. E., having lunched well in the Strand, often at the Savoy after a morning in court, usually walked to the House of Commons. His walk took him past the National Liberal Club – a great political force in the world in those days. Having lunched and drunk well, he would stop at the club to relieve himself. One day, the head doorman said to him, 'Sir Frederick' – he was by then Solicitor-General and had received the customary knighthood – 'the chairman of the club has asked me to remind you that this is not a public lavatory.' 'Oh,' said F. E., 'I always thought it was.'

In society, his conversational shafts were often both witty and brutal. At a smart party, a lady came up to him and said rather pompously, 'My name is Porter-Porter, with a hyphen.' F. E. answered, 'Mine is Whisky Whisky, with a siphon.' It is a joke that would delight a ten-year-old. That was part of his genius; his humour was as simple as it was brilliant. It appeals to all ages and to all classes across the generations.

F. E.'s fame rests above all on the undisputed fact that his maiden speech in the House of Commons was the most sensationally successful ever delivered in 600 years of parliamentary history. It was not just the speech but the occasion, which I shall briefly describe for those of you who did not read history at Oxford.

For reasons that I will not go into now, the Conservatives had lost the January 1906 general election – to their vast surprise, because there were no polls in those days – by a massive majority. It was the biggest defeat ever suffered by the Conservatives in the twentieth century, much bigger than 1945 or 1997. They came back with only 156 seats out of 670. F. E. had scraped in for the Walton division of Liverpool.[5] The Conservatives in the new House were deeply depressed, with the Liberals occupying four-fifths of the chamber in an absolutely triumphant and bumptious mood – and we all know what Liberals are like when they are in that sort of mood.

F. E. decided to stake everything on a spectacular maiden speech. Only those who have made maiden speeches in crowded debates on a controversial topic can fully comprehend the courage and recklessness that are required at the moment when they are called to stand and address the House of Commons for the first time. Benjamin Disraeli had attempted it and it was an absolute disaster. He was shouted down and after about ten minutes he said, 'I will sit down now, but the time will come when you will listen to me.' F. E. knew all about that, but he determined to go for a repeat performance. He waited impatiently from January until March, and then he spotted an opportunity. There was to be a one-day debate on free trade. This is how F. E. describes the occasion in his memoirs:

> The House was crowded almost beyond human memory for the whole of the day, and almost everybody desired to speak. It was extremely difficult to obtain an opportunity to take part in the debate. I asked Mr Joseph Chamberlain [this is where the famous meeting in Liverpool paid off] with whom I had established some intimacy whether he would use his influence with Mr Speaker in order that I might be called.[6]

I am sure Mr Speaker never allows anybody to use their influence on him, but that Speaker did. F. E. tells us:

He [Chamberlain] most generously accepted the task and returned with the message that I should be called at the best hour in all the debate, ten o'clock at night, and he added the words, 'This is the chance of your life, my friend. See that you use it.' ... When I rose to speak the House was densely crowded. Not one in twenty had the slightest idea who I was. [That was uncharacteristic modesty.] I had made up my mind that I would try a dazzling gamble. It seemed to me that my party was almost in despair. Never in its history had it sustained such a disaster in the polls. The swollen insolence and bad parliamentary manners of the mammoth majority, which overflowed over four-fifths of the available sitting space, seemed to me to have a depressing – almost a cowing – effect upon the tiny Conservative minority... I asked for no indulgence because I was making a maiden speech... I spoke for sixty-five minutes, which I believe to be a record for a maiden speech; and I spoke with a degree of calculated inso-lence and sustained invective which I am quite sure has never been attempted before or since by one who addressed the House of Commons for the first time. As I drove down to the House of Commons with my wife, I said, 'I shall either make a brilliant success or a greater failure than that of Disraeli.' Before I sat down, it was obvious that it was a *tour de force*; the speech had at least, whatever its real merits, been a great success. How great a success I did not realise until I read the papers the next day...[7]

The speech[8] was indeed a sensational success. Asquith, Lloyd George, Chamberlain, Bonar Law and Churchill are all recorded as roaring with laughter at Smith's sallies. It was an epic occasion in the history of Parliament, never to be forgotten. When he sat down, Lloyd George rose to reply for the government and referred to it as 'a very brilliant speech'. Yet there are certain mysteries about it. No one seems to have read it and, when I did so for the first time, to give this lecture, I found it fairly heavy going. It lacks any of the single-sentence knockout words he so often used in court and on the public platform.

Secondly, there is no agreed text of what F. E. actually said. He spoke from few notes. There was continuous noise from his audience and no amplification from loudspeakers. The Hansard reporters had none of their modern equipment and they always complained of him – they do not of me – that he spoke with a speed that exceeded their command of shorthand.

Thirdly, why did the vast Liberal majority listen to him for so long, so attentively and with so much admiration when he was pouring scorn on them by the bucketful, with long, intricately worded, convoluted sentences? Today, some idiot would have tried to wreck the speech by rising on a bogus point of order. No one did. One can only guess that the Liberals were so self-confident at that moment in their history, with their vast majority, that they felt they could humour this David with his tiny sling and enjoy his oratory. They never made the same mistake again. In fact, when, a few years later, on the next really big occasion when he spoke, during the Third Reading of the Parliament Bill, they barracked him so hard he had to sit down with his speech unfinished.

I suggest that the answer to the questions I have posed is star quality. Smith spoke with one hand in his pocket much of the time, seldom glanced at notes and, apparently completely at ease, poured out often violently worded abuse laced with wit, so that people were transfixed by his appearance, his voice, his fluency and no doubt – one hopes – the sense that they were present at a unique parliamentary occasion.

F. E. always maintained that no one was born a great orator, and that it required intense hard work and much practice. He said that there were five types of public speaking and that proficiency in one or even two of them was no guarantee of success in the others. There was the platform speech, the court of law speech, the after-dinner speech, the House of Commons speech and the House of Lords speech. Each required a different technique and a different content. With a characteristic absence of mock modesty, he said that he was rare in having mastered all of them.

No one could doubt it, as he continued to demonstrate for many years. He could have added a sixth – conversation speech – which would no doubt have made him a star performer on modern television. Only Lloyd George exceeded him in exotic charm in private conversation.

Shortly after F. E. entered the House in 1906, and shortly after he made his famous maiden speech, he struck up a close friendship with Winston Churchill, who was not very popular in the Conservative Party at the time because he had just crossed the Floor and joined the Liberals and been promoted to ministerial office as a reward. The Tories were not very keen on him, but F. E. and Churchill got on famously from the word go and remained tremendously close friends.[9] Churchill always said that F. E. was the best friend he had in his life and I think the feeling was reciprocated. Their friendship had impacts. Churchill was the grandson of a duke and was born in Blenheim Palace. His mother, Lady Randolph Churchill, was a famous political and social hostess, and allegedly one of King Edward VII's mistresses when he was Prince of Wales. Winston Churchill obviously moved in the highest social circles, whereas F. E., a young barrister just down from Liverpool, was certainly not used to doing so.

The wives of both men disapproved of the friendship from the beginning. Churchill's wife thought that F. E. led Winston into extravagance and gambling for sums far above his means. F. E.'s wife, rather strangely, thought that Winston would lead F. E. into drinking more than he should, although I would have thought that was impossible.

However, both wives were absolutely right, as a wife usually is when sitting in judgement on the faults of her husband, though neither man needed encouragement from the other. There is no doubt that Churchill was led by F. E. into gambling. An early example shows why F. E. was able to gamble so wildly. He was earning huge money from the Bar and was staying at Blenheim Palace where, from the terrace, he addressed huge audiences from all over Oxfordshire. On one occasion when they were gambling, the Duke of Marlborough said to F. E., 'How high would you like the stakes to be?' to which F. E. replied, 'As high as you wish – for your damned palace if you like.' That shows a degree of confidence and arrogance, but nobody ever seemed to take offence.

Shortly after Churchill and Smith became friends, they set up a dining club – the Other Club.[10] I shall not go into detail now, because Nicholas Soames is still secretary of the club. It was a famous club, and unique for the fact that Smith and Churchill persuaded the leaders of both parties to join. Asquith and Balfour both joined, as did many other leaders from both parties. They met regularly to dine and the conversation was friendly. One of the rules of the club was that nothing should prevent the most violent altercations, but it is difficult to imagine Mr Miliband and Mr Cameron wanting to join the same dining club in order to have friendly dinners once a month.

All the leading politicians from both sides used to address each other in the House of Commons with a degree of violence that would shock a modern Speaker. In a way, the club was the most permanent achievement of F. E., who I think was the leading light in suggesting it, and he helped to draft the rules, which are fascinating. The fact that the club has survived so long that Winston Churchill's grandson is now its secretary is a fascinating aspect of our affairs.

As I have been told to talk about F. E.'s personality, I do not want to give a history lesson about what happened between 1906 and 1928 – the years that span his parliamentary and ministerial career – but I shall touch on a few aspects to give some verbal snapshots. His way of life was fascinating. At Oxford, he hunted a lot; hunting was his chief hobby before the war, as was sailing in his splendid yacht, the *Mallory*, after the war. He bought what he called a cottage at Charlton on the borders of Oxfordshire and Northamptonshire shortly after he and his wife went to London. Every time he got a large brief, he would add to the cottage and eventually people said it looked like Wadham College. What he did there was amazing. He put in stabling for twelve horses. He had innumerable cars, including a Rolls-Royce. He hardly ever used them himself; he almost always rode everywhere on horseback when he was in the country, using the cars to collect people from the local railway station. He treated his cars as though they were horses. He thought they should not be tired, so if the car was used for half a day it had to have a rest, which is why he had so many of them.

Smith was passionately keen on dogs and had an enormous number. As you might expect, he had only very small Cairn terriers or very huge Irish wolfhounds. He adored his dogs and took them everywhere. When he went by train there would be a dog sitting on his knee. There was always a dog on his bed – I do not know what his wife said about it. He even took them on the yacht. Everywhere he went, he took dogs.

F. E. created a magnificent library. After a time, he bought what was really a palace in central London, in Grosvenor Gardens. It was a vast house and he filled it with the most exquisite furniture and paintings, and there was a fine wine cellar, but the most stunning thing about it was the library. He had a passion for buying first editions of the greatest and rarest books; he had everything from *The Faerie Queen* to *Ulysses*. Arnold Bennett, who saw the library in 1918, said afterwards: 'The library is even equal to his own boasting about it.'

F. E.'s yacht was the supreme affection of his last years. He used to say: 'The earth belongs to every man, but the sea is free.' He did not act the grand *seigneur* when he was in the country or at any other time. He encouraged his children to play with the local children and he frequently dropped in at the local pub. He very much loved his wife and his three children – two daughters and a son. He loved to entertain and was happiest when surrounded by energetic young people. He took tremendous pride in his own athleticism even when he was in his early fifties. After a tremendous dinner at Christ Church – he always drank vast quantities of brandy – he bet a famous runner called Milligan that he could

run six times round Tom Quad quicker than Milligan could run
eight times round. I do not know whether any of you who are
over fifty would think of running around Tom Quad even once
after a heavy dinner, but the Lord Chancellor, as he then was, in
full evening dress and pumps, set off. Sure enough, long before
Milligan had finished his eight circuits, the Lord Chancellor had
done six and won the bet. That was typical of him.

From 1906 until the outbreak of the Great War in 1914, F. E.
was active in the turbulent party politics of those years, as well
as earning stupendous sums of money at the Bar. The House
of Commons always filled when he rose to address it. I shall not
burden you in detail with his contributions to debates of the Lloyd
George Budget and the Parliament Act of 1911 or on the suffragette movement, the Ulster crisis or the 'Balfour Must Go'
campaign, to name only some of the issues on which he spoke
and conspired. I shall confine myself to a few snapshots.

When one looks back, it is interesting to see how little anything
changes. Lords reform is fascinating. Nobody would have thought
that Lord Prescott and Lord Foulkes would be using almost
exactly the same words to defend the privileges of the House
of Lords as were used by Lord Lansdowne and Lord Curzon a
hundred years ago. No doubt the accents were slightly different
and the grammar, particularly in the case of the former Deputy
Prime Minister, might not have been quite as eloquent as that of
the Marquess of Lansdowne, but the arguments were the same.
The argument was that the Lords were the ultimate safeguard
of the liberty of the people, because a majority in the House of
Commons, without the check of a second chamber, was a real
threat to liberty – a view that F. E. held very strongly indeed. He
thought that unicameral government was absolutely the road to
tyranny, as do I; in fact, I told the Chief Whip so last night, in an
ill-considered moment.

As F. E. pointed out, in the House of Commons the whips
can organise ambitious young Members who want to become
Parliamentary Private Secretaries to support policies that they

often do not really approve of. A dominant Prime Minister is virtually a dictator. After F. E. had served in the House for five years, he came to the view that the idea that backbenchers have any brake or control on the executive is nonsense. Except on certain occasions when the Prime Minister has lost the confidence of his party, the Prime Minister and a small coterie of his friends run the country; even most of the Cabinet is not taken into account. The latest information we have about the run-up to the Iraq war suggests that nothing has changed.

F. E. was passionately against anything that looked like unicameral government. It was not that he had high regard for the peers as such, although he was perfectly prepared to accept their hospitality in great houses in London and elsewhere, and he was delighted at each step he took in the social world. In rapid succession he was given a knighthood, a baronetcy, a viscountcy and then an earldom, and he was delighted with each, but he never had a high opinion of Lords as such.

He took the view at the time of the conflict over the 1911 Parliament Bill that much wiser than tremendous confrontation would be a coalition of the two great parties.[11] He, Lloyd George and Churchill got together and drew up a plan whereby there would be a coalition government that would push out the Labour Party and the Irish, who by then held the balance of power and were causing a lot of political crises. Curiously enough, Austen Chamberlain and Balfour, the leaders of the Conservative Party, were not particularly opposed to the scheme and F. E. wrote a letter to *The Times* in 1910, headed 'Compromise', which set out the proposals in some detail.[12] They planned to co-operate over a wide range of things, because there were so many problems damaging the country.

The problems have not changed. There was unrest between the Muslims and the Hindus in India. There was serious unrest in Egypt. Indeed, sixty-one years ago, as a boy officer, I was in the back streets of Suez trying to persuade Egyptians not to riot against the Wafd Party and King Farouk. Things do not change very much; the problems that F. E. dealt with are still with us. He always regarded the 1911 Parliament Bill as unfinished business. Only the whips, of whom he had a poor opinion, prevented the coalition from starting at the time.

One of the interesting things about F. E.'s career was that although he was ferociously outspoken in public attacks on his political opponents, in private he always advocated a moderate line of approach, which was something some of his critics fastened on as a sign that he was two-faced. In fact, his whole ministerial career, apart from the last two to three years, was in coalition governments, under Asquith and Lloyd George.

Having failed to get a coalition government, F. E. played a role in other events. The suffragette movement was important at the time. He was strongly opposed to women having the vote. One of his speeches on the subject contains as offensive a sentence as was ever aimed at womankind: 'I venture to say that the sum total of human happiness, knowledge and achievement would have been almost unaffected if Sappho had never sung, if Joan of Arc had never fought, if Siddons had never played and if George Eliot had never written.' He graciously went on to say that nevertheless women were quite useful because without them we could not perpetuate the species. You might think that would cause some offence, and no doubt it did to some of the leading suffragettes, but F. E. was immensely popular with women of all classes and ages. Many young working-class women used to keep his photo under their pillow.

Funnily enough, F. E. supported and helped to draft the Bill in 1918 that gave votes to women. By then he thought they had earned their voting rights by working in factories in the war. He was quite right about that.

On another contemporary problem, F. E. was an early supporter of salaries for MPs. His view on that, which was not held by most of his colleagues, was that he wanted to free them from the domination of the trade unions; if they had no salary, it was paid by a trade union. The 1910 election was the first when a sizeable number of Labour MPs were elected and he wanted to give them freedom from the dominance of the trade unions. That, too, is unfinished business because, as we all know, the new leader of the Labour Party was put in by the trade unions, against the wishes of Labour backbenchers. There was no talk of expenses in those days; he did not go as far as that.

The outbreak of war in 1914, when F. E. was forty-two and at the peak of his reputation, wealth and domestic happiness, changed his life for ever, as it did the lives of millions of people all over the world. Like most people, he thought that the war would be over by Christmas; Kitchener was one of the few who did not think that. F. E. always looked back with nostalgia to pre-1914 Britain, as did Harold Macmillan as he told me on two or three occasions. Macmillan used to use the phrase from Talleyrand – *le plaisir de vivre*. The full translation is, 'He who has not lived during the years before 1789 cannot know what is meant by the pleasure of life.' F. E. felt that England was never the same after 1914. When the war came, it effectively ended his career at the Bar and the huge income he had been earning, which led to great problems later. He was asked to establish a press bureau to influence newspaper reports and censor reports from France – a job given to Duff Cooper at the beginning of the Second World War. Neither was any good at it; neither was suited to the role of a Coulson or an Alastair Campbell. F. E. resigned after only seven weeks.

F. E. was put into uniform and served as an intelligence officer with the Indian Corps in France until after the battle of Neuve Chapelle, by which time he had risen to the rank of Lieutenant Colonel. Soon after he left London, a case came on in the law courts in which he was to have appeared. The barrister who took over from him said: 'My friend, who was Mr F. E. Smith and is now Major F. E. Smith, was originally briefed in this case', to which Mr Justice Darling replied, 'I should think he is General F. E. Smith by now.'

With the exception of Field Marshal Sir John French, who first commanded the British forces in France – whom F. E. detested – the generals liked F. E. very much. Lord Kitchener held him in the highest regard. After F. E.'s death, General Willcocks wrote that F. E. was 'an extraordinarily attractive personality. He could say in one pithy sentence what others would take a page to describe. It was perhaps this very gift that secured him enemies. He was a resolute man who if he had started as soldier would have reached the highest rank.' As the generals of the First World War almost unanimously disliked and despised the 'damned politicians' as they called them, that was superlative praise.

In 1915, Asquith, under growing criticism that he was an ineffectual wartime leader, tried to bolster his position by bringing some Conservative ministers into his government, and F. E. became Solicitor-General. He was to continue in ministerial office as a law officer – first as a Solicitor-General, then Attorney-General and Lord High Chancellor – for the next seven years in a succession of coalition governments. What F. E. could never bring himself to understand was that the war had brought his stupendous earnings crashing down. Indeed, in 1914–15 he had to repay a large sum of money in respect of briefs he had been given shortly before the war that had to be transferred to other barristers. Nevertheless, he continued to live in his usual tremendous and wildly extravagant style, both in the country and in London. He had never been a very rich man in the sense of having much capital, because he spent money with the same abundance as he acquired it. His early earnings at the Bar financed his ministerial career throughout the war years, but his continued extravagance held dangers for the future of his family and his servants. He was of course always confident that he could quickly salvage the situation by returning to the Bar where he was fond of saying, probably truthfully, that he could immediately earn £40,000 a year, as indeed John Simon was doing, but the opportunity never occurred; his political ambitions were too strong.

F. E. was a very efficient law officer and Lloyd George always said that he was the most efficient of all the departmental Ministers. It was a difficult time because an immense number of war regulations had just come into effect. F. E. had been used to common law and statute law, but the new regulations were almost unknown to the Bar and to solicitors. He had an extremely difficult job to cope with them; he worked fantastically hard and was tremendously admired. Lloyd George said that in all the years he was Prime Minister, F. E.'s department was the only one that never had to be referred to the War Cabinet because there were problems.

I shall only give highlights of F. E.'s ministerial career, because you all know the political history of the disaster of the war and the appalling tragedies so that the job of a law officer, although extremely important, faded into absolute insignificance by comparison with what was happening elsewhere. A case that caused enormous controversy was that of Sir Roger Casement. People sometimes do not remember that Sir Roger Casement was already a famous figure – almost as famous as David Livingstone – for his work in the Congo, in effect as a missionary. Because of the Easter rebellion in Dublin, which had to be put down with great severity, and because he was a passionate Irish Sinn Féiner, Casement went to Germany and helped to recruit an Irish unit that was intended to fight against Britain. He had an English passport and English knighthood, so there is no doubt that he was a traitor, although even that has been challenged. Every aspect of the case is still a matter of deep controversy, particularly in Ireland where people have passionately conflicting views on it. I cannot be dogmatic about it as I have never seen the essential documents but, from all I have read about it over the years, there is absolutely no doubt that Casement committed treason under English law, like Joyce (Lord Haw-Haw) in the Second World War and John Amery – Julian's brother – who were both hanged for treason.

When Casement's flat in central London was seized, an extraordinary diary was found. Why he ever kept diaries and, above all, why he brought them to England at the time is a mystery. The diary contained scarifying accounts of his sex life when he went to the Amazon basin after the Congo; they were so horrifying that even Old Etonians could not read them – nor could George V who was a sailor. One civil servant actually fainted, so it must have been pretty hot stuff. I know a bit about it, but I do not think it appropriate in mixed company to go into detail.

In one sense, the diaries were irrelevant because there was no suggestion that Casement would be tried for his sexual activities; he was to be tried for treason. The Irish regarded him as a hero – they still do – and eighteen Irish bishops signed a petition asking that he should not be hanged. The Archbishop of Canterbury lobbied that he should not be hanged, although when he was invited to read the diary he said, 'No, thank you', and gave it to one of his priests to read instead. The diary was irrelevant to the prosecution but because of the build-up – and because we were desperate to get the Americans into the war, and the Irish in Massachusetts and Boston were up in arms about the prosecution, and some senators were bringing pressure to bear, particularly Senator Cabot Lodge who was chairman of the Senate Foreign Affairs Committee at the time – there was enormous pressure on the British government not to hang Casement. The diaries were undoubtedly shown around; Asquith showed them to the American ambassador and there is no doubt that F. E. showed them to a number of colleagues. He also offered to give them to the defence counsel, which is where criticism of him particularly arose. Nobody is quite sure why he offered the diaries to the defence counsel, unless it was to intimidate them into pleading guilty to the charge of treason, which would have been a disreputable thing for a prosecuting counsel to do.

Some people asked why F. E. was prosecuting. Was it just because he wanted publicity? However, that was nonsense, because in those days the Attorney-General – as he had become – always led major prosecutions, even in criminal cases, so there was no doubt he had to do it. The real explanation, I believe, for him wanting the defence counsel to see the diaries was that he hoped the defence would put up a plea of insanity so that Sir Roger Casement, instead of being hanged, could be sent to a criminal lunatic asylum. That, it was thought, would pacify the Archbishop of Canterbury, the Irish bishops and the American Irish, and bring the Americans into the war.

There is a myth that Home Secretaries take decisions about hanging on their own, but it was certainly not so in that case. The Cabinet met three times to discuss the case and, only two days before Casement was hanged, the Cabinet had a long meeting and a number of senior Cabinet ministers were in favour of him not being hanged. Unfortunately, they sent a psychiatrist to see him – it is always fatal to bring a psychiatrist into a case – and he told the Cabinet that Casement was undoubtedly sane. As the psychiatrist had been appointed because he was the most knowledgeable psychiatrist in Britain at the time, it would have been difficult for the Cabinet to say that Casement was insane, so they hanged him. To this day, some people feel that F. E. behaved shabbily, but I do not see what alternative he had. I strongly believe that his real incentive was to persuade the defence to plead criminal insanity.

The next step forward for F. E. was in 1919 when he was offered the post of Lord Chancellor. The decision must have been difficult for him. In those days the post of Lord Chancellor was vastly more important than it is today because now it has been dumbed down, like first-class honours degrees. Incidentally, F. E. was wholly opposed to having a Minister for Justice; he made a speech pouring scorn on the whole concept and said that nobody would ever have respect for a Ministry of Justice.

By taking the job of Lord Chancellor, F. E. was giving up the possibility of being Prime Minister. Immediately after the war, Lloyd George offered him the job because, as he said, 'As Attorney-General, you can't be in the Cabinet, but as Lord Chancellor you can.' There were many arguments against F. E. taking the job. First, he desperately needed to make some money, although the Lord Chancellor's salary was £10,000 a year, which was a large amount in 1919 – anybody in England except F. E. could have lived happily and in great comfort on £10,000 a year. There was much derision when he said he could not afford to take the job.

People said that once he became Lord Chancellor he could never go back to the Bar but, being F. E., he brushed that aside, saying that it was nonsense and an old-fashioned view and that there was no earthly reason why he should not be Lord Chancellor and go back to the Bar afterwards. Many pointed out to him that if he became Lord Chancellor he would never be Prime Minister, and that was one of the reasons why Lloyd George offered him the post; he did not want a rival in the Cabinet who might replace him. Again, F. E. brushed that aside, because Lord Salisbury had been Prime Minister for much of F. E.'s youth – and indeed Lord Curzon nearly became Prime Minister a few years later. F. E. obviously thought he could be Prime Minister while in the Lords, which was not a wholly unreasonable assumption in 1919. He discussed it through the night with Winston Churchill and eventually decided to take the Lord Chancellorship.

Many people thought Smith an unsuitable Lord Chancellor; the King was very opposed – he thought the chap was altogether too flashy. When he was Attorney-General, F. E. had a reputation for taking actresses to smart restaurants and for other things Attorney-Generals were not supposed to do. Many senior members of the legal profession thought he did not have the dignity to be Lord Chancellor, but he was a very good one. He put through some extremely important laws between 1919 and 1922. He completely reorganised the wholly antiquated property laws, which was a remarkable achievement at the time. One of the most interesting things he did was to try to change the divorce laws. In those days, a person could only be divorced on the grounds of adultery. There was great opposition to change on the Conservative side; all the bishops were against it. Smith supported the Matrimonial Causes Bill to widen the range of circumstances in which a woman could apply to divorce her husband. When he spoke in the Second Reading debate in the

House of Lords, L. G. Garvin, editor of *The Observer*, said of the speech that 'in its massive marshalling of facts, its force of good judgment and right feeling and its generous revolt against the horrible mass of suffering caused by existing conditions, it was the greatest speech Lord Birkenhead ever made'. That was from Garvin – perhaps one of the greatest editors of an English news-paper during the last century and someone who as a man of the left would not normally have been an admirer of F. E.

Although the speech was a triumph of reasoned argument, it was also charged with emotion. F. E. realised that no amount of reason could dislodge deep-seated religious conviction, but he spoke very much from the heart, not only to prove that the ecclesiastical view of marriage had been decisively rejected, but also to vanquish the uncompromising opponents of divorce who would have liked to put the clock back still further and whose arguments he described as the 'whisperings of the abandoned superstitions of the middle ages', and who did not, he said, 'live in this world'. Those who accepted adultery were much more at his mercy. On them – the bishops sitting in the House of Lords – he heaped his amazing oratory: '...that men of experience, men of affairs, men whose opinions and experience we respect should have concentrated on adultery as the one circumstance which ought to afford relief from the marriage tie'.[13] He argued that the moral and spiritual sides of marriage are incomparably more important than the physical side and cried shame on those who harped on an aspect of marriage that he claimed mattered less to decent people than its other blessings.

Because of the strength of F. E.'s oratory, the Bill passed in the House of Lords (by ninety-three votes to forty-five). He said: 'We are not formulating or dealing with a new heaven; we are dealing with an old world in which horrible sufferings are proceeding before our eyes.'[14] He invited the House of Lords to 'remove this great blot from our civilisation' and win 'unspeakable gratitude by thousands of the most unhappy of your fellow subjects and ... by generations yet to be ... for the wisdom and humanity of the decision taken to-night'.[15] The Bill was sent to the House of Commons who threw it out. The divorce laws were not changed until A. P. Herbert's Bill of 1937. That is just one of the examples that could be used to rebut the view of F. E. as a hard-faced opportunist with no concern for social matters.

In terms of statesmanship and ministerial skills, the Irish Treaty, following the civil war in Ireland, was the greatest achievement of F. E.'s life. F. E., who came from Liverpool, was strongly Orange; indeed, by an extraordinary coincidence, his birthday was the date of the battle of the Boyne. He had played a role in the crisis over Ulster in 1913–14, when Sir Edward Carson led the Protestants of Ulster in revolt, and F. E. gave him strong support in speeches. At one vast meeting on the anniversary of the battle of the Boyne, attended by 120,000 people, Sir Edward Carson – like F. E., a great barrister and orator – made a tremendous speech, while F. E. rode around passing messages for Sir Edward, which brought him the nickname Galloper Smith, a title he never liked.

Against that background, F. E. made the Irish Treaty possible through his tremendous skills of negotiation and persuasiveness. He managed to establish a close friendship with Michael Collins, who was much younger than him, but F. E. was wonderful with young people; he liked having young people around him and he liked playing violent physical games with them. F. E. drafted, single-handed – no parliamentary draftsmen were involved – the Oath of Allegiance that enabled the Irish side and the English side to sign the treaty, which was a critical part of the process. When they signed the treaty, F. E. said, 'I may be signing my political death warrant.' Michael Collins said as he signed it, 'I may be signing my actual death warrant.'[16] That was true in both cases: a few months later, Michael Collins was gunned down by extremist elements in his own party and F. E. enraged the back-benchers of the Conservative Party so much by agreeing to the Irish Free State that they lost all confidence in him, particularly because he had been such an ardent supporter of Carson in 1914. Carson, too, denounced F. E. in the strongest terms.

That led to the famous meeting of Conservative MPs at the Carlton Club in October 1922 – the year after the Irish Treaty. It was the treaty that led Conservative backbenchers to decide that they were no longer prepared to serve in the coalition. The Carlton Club was not at its present site in St James's Street; the great Carlton Club in Pall Mall was bombed during the war. It was a huge building so it was perfectly possible for the whole Parliamentary Conservative Party to meet there; indeed, it was not uncommon. The 1922 meeting was the most important political event in the twentieth century, because it completely changed history. By then F. E. was extremely unpopular with the backbenchers; he had become excessively arrogant and was beginning to drink heavily. He was given the job of talking to groups of Conservative backbenchers to try to rally their support for the coalition. We are coming into modern territory. The backbenchers were increasingly falling out of sympathy with the coalition; only its senior members really liked it.

F. E. was extremely bullying and angry with the backbenchers, who left meetings with him feeling very hostile. He created an atmosphere of hostility. The leaders of the coalition were by far the most distinguished group of statesmen who have ever led a British government – Lloyd George, Winston Churchill, Austen Chamberlain, Lord Curzon, F. E. Smith and others of great distinction – but the backbench Tories had had enough of the lot of them. To the absolute astonishment of the leadership of the party, following a speech by Baldwin attacking Lloyd George, the 1922 meeting voted by a large majority to leave the coalition. That ended Lloyd George's premiership and he never held office again although he lived until 1945. F. E. was also put out of office; so unpopular was he with Tory backbenchers at that point that, although he led the meeting, he was advised not to speak because he would be shouted down. He was booed and one of them shouted 'Judas' at him, which shows the degree to which the hero of the Tory Party had fallen out with his colleagues over the Irish Treaty.

Any historian would say that achieving the treaty was a great act of statesmanship. However, Carson – shortly afterwards to be made a Lord of Appeal in Ordinary; in those days they did not seem to mind making controversial people senior judges – made the most brutal speech ever heard in the Lords; he bludgeoned the government for their hypocrisy in surrendering to force and then claiming credit for statesmanship. Standing near F. E., who was sitting on the Woolsack, Carson said of the man who had been his close political and personal friend:

> ...of all the men in my experience that I think are the most loathsome it is those who will sell their friends for the purpose of conciliating their enemies and perhaps, still worse, the men who climb up a ladder into power ... and then when they have got into power, kick the ladder away without any concern for the pain, or injury, or mischief, or damage that they do to those who have helped them to gain power.[17]

F. E.'s reply to Carson was that his 'constructive effort at statecraft ... would be immature on the lips of a hysterical school girl'.[18] However, extraordinarily, in two or three years they were bosom chums again. That is the most amazing thing about politicians of that period.

One of the most famous of F. E.'s speeches was his rectorial address to the students of Glasgow University.[19] His two distinguished opponents were John Simon, his old Wadham contemporary, who was a highly paid barrister, and H. G. Wells. Nevertheless, F. E. was elected. The subject of his speech was idealism in international politics and in it he used the famous sentence: 'The world continues to offer glittering prizes to those who have stout hearts and sharp swords.'[20] As that was just after one million Englishmen had been killed in the trenches, it was thought to be a brutal, insensitive and thoroughly objectionable point of view, which summed up for many people F. E. Smith's heartless desire for merely material success. The speech was publicly denounced by a later Lord Chancellor,

Quintin Hogg, Lord Hailsham. However, I was captivated when I read the sentence; when I was ten I thought it was marvellous. Unfortunately, there are no glittering prizes now except that of Speaker of the House of Commons, and that post is occupied.

After 1922, F. E., with all the other nobs, sat with the Liberals on the other side of the House for the next two years, although he never joined them. He went on a lecture tour of America and when he returned to London he shocked the House of Lords in a speech that again shows the strength with which people spoke in those days, describing Salisbury and Selborne, two of the leading Tory peers, as the Dolly Sisters of the Conservative Party. He weighed into Curzon with the utmost venom:

> When I see sitting by him the noble Marquess, Lord Salisbury, who for four years pursued us with malignant criticism, who impeached us not merely with criticism as to whether we were right in a decision or wrong in it, but impeached our morality and for four years impeached the honesty of the Government of which the noble Marquess [Curzon] was a member, then I rejoice at the vicissitudes and paradoxes of politics.[21]

Nobody makes speeches like that nowadays.

In 1924, there was a short Labour government and then Baldwin came back as Prime Minister. He wanted to pull the Conservative Party back together after the serious divisions of the 1922 meeting, so he brought Winston Churchill back as Chancellor of the Exchequer and made F. E. Secretary of State for India. There are many things I should like to tell you about F. E.'s period as Secretary of State but I need to bring this talk to a halt.

I shall finish by reading some comments about F. E. by his contemporaries, as they are obviously much more to the point than my rambling remarks. The first, rather critical, one is by Lord Schuster who was for many years the senior legal member of the Lord Chancellor's department – he was made a lord only at the end of his career – when it was said of him that Lord

Chancellors reigned, but Schuster ruled. Once Birkenhead arrived, that changed; nobody ruled F. E., and Schuster may have had a chip on his shoulder about that. Schuster wrote the biography of Lord Birkenhead in the *Dictionary of National Biography*; the entry ran for seven pages.

Anyone who writes about F. E. tends to start by reading Schuster; it encourages the Lytton Strachey approach to political biography. Schuster said of F. E.:

> The brilliance of his first appearance, the rapidity of his wit and the ferocity of his attack caused men to take a false view of his character and of his attainments. He was regarded as a swashbuckler and courageous but headstrong and superficial in the courts, as the man for a crushing cross-examination or a speech to a jury rather than for a serious legal argument, and in the House for the brilliant raillery and rhetorical display of a partisan rather than the measured view and wise counsel of the statesman.[22]

His appearance and manner of life contributed to this view. He was strikingly handsome, six-foot one-inch in height and of a distinguished figure. His clothes, although not in any way particularly out of the ordinary, gave the impression that he was overdressed. The hat worn on the back of his head, the red flower in his buttonhole, the very long cigar he always carried in his mouth made him a ready subject for the caricaturist. The great houses in which he stayed, the late hours which he kept, his fondness for gaiety and for gay people (in the old sense of the word, you may be sure), for cards, for horses and for all the bright and expensive things of life confirmed the opinion that he was a reckless partisan, fighting hard for his own side, grasping at his own enjoyment and advantage, not a responsible or serious person, either as a lawyer or as a parliamentarian.

That is pretty damning. A very different view was formed by those who served with F. E. on equal terms. Lord Schuster was just a disgruntled civil servant, although one of great distinction.

In 1928, F. E. finally ran out of money. Since he became
a minister in 1915, he had lived on the money he earned as a
barrister when he was a young man, but he had continued to be
extravagant. He was heavily in debt and to increase his income
when he was Secretary of State for India he wrote newspaper
articles – as did Winston Churchill, who wrote for the *News of the
World* every Sunday; it was a Conservative paper in those days.
Churchill's articles were brilliant and many of them reappeared
– no doubt polished up a bit – in *Great Contemporaries*. He was one
of the most highly paid journalists in England throughout the
1930s. That is how he earned his living.

F. E. was not nearly as good at journalism although he was
paid about as much as Churchill, so it was an important income
for him. For a long time he was allowed to continue writing, but
there was a great hullabaloo about ministers writing newspaper
articles for money. It is not allowed these days, although ministers
no doubt get money in other ways. When Baldwin told F. E. that
he would have to stop writing articles, he resigned saying that he
must earn more money. By then, F. E. was not at all a well man;
he was drinking far too heavily, although everybody said that drink
did not go to his head but only to his feet. In his last years, he
apparently used to sway on the platform, but nevertheless brilliant
oratory flowed from him unaffected by the alcohol. However, it
eventually caught up with him and in 1930 he died of cirrhosis of
the liver at the age of fifty-eight, just after the 1929 crash.

I shall read some tributes from the people who worked
with him and knew him best – all of them distinguished men.
Although people always write in a courteous and friendly way –
at my age of eighty-one, one hopes they will – there is a degree
of sincerity in the comments about F. E. that is far more than
the conventional statements one hears in such circumstances. Mr
Baldwin wrote:

> I am very grieved to hear that Lord Birkenhead has died. I knew
> him as a political opponent and also as a personal friend. He was

truly a wonderful man. His great intellectual capacity is equalled by his deft command in debate of every weapon both of offence and of defence. To disagree with Lord Birkenhead in no way diminished the extraordinary respect which one had to pay to his powers. As a friend he was genial, loyal and reliable. It saddens me greatly to know that we shall never greet each other again.

Lloyd George's tribute:

There was no more brilliant mind consecrated to the service of the state during this generation. He had qualities of mind and of heart which were unique. The public knew the former and admired him; it was only his most intimate friends who understood the latter. His death at the time when his powers would naturally have mellowed is an incalculable loss. He had an unquenchable courage of a very high order. He had loyalty. He had also in public matters superb judgment. These are qualities the nation can ill afford to lose at a time that it is passing through its worst crisis.

Winston Churchill's tribute appeared in *The Times* on 1 October 1930:

Lord Birkenhead has been my greatest friend for nearly a quarter of a century. He was the most loyal, faithful, valiant friend any man could have and a wise, learned, delightful companion. He would not, I think, have wished to live except in his full health and vigour. All who knew him well mourn him and miss him often, but even more is our country the poorer. These are the times when he is needed most; his deeply found sagacity, his keen courageous mind, his experience and understanding, his massive system of conclusions, his intellectual independence, his knowledge of all grave issues now pending, make his death at this moment a national impoverishment. His happy, generous, brilliant, warm-hearted life is closed. It is closed in years when he might have made his greatest contribution to the fortunes of the England he loved so well.

1   2nd Earl of Birkenhead, *Frederick Edwin, Earl of Birkenhead: The First Phase* (London: Thornton Butterworth, 1933), p.136.
2   Earl of Birkenhead, *Law Life and Letters*, Vol. II (London: Hodder & Stoughton, 1927), p.213.
3   See, e.g., John Campbell, *F. E.: First Earl of Birkenhead* (London: Jonathan Cape, 1983), pp.172–5.
4   Winston Churchill, *Great Contemporaries* (London: Thornton Butterworth, 1937). The story also appears in Birkenhead, *Frederick Edwin, Earl of Birkenhead*, p.115.
5   Smith received 5,862 votes to 5,153 for his Liberal opponent.
6   Birkenhead, *Law Life and Letters*, pp.235–6.
7   Birkenhead, *Law Life and Letters*, pp.235–7.
8   House of Commons: Official Report (Hansard): 12 March 1906, Vol. 153, cols 1014–23. The speech is also reproduced in *The Speeches of Lord Birkenhead* (London: Cassell, 1929), pp.1–14.
9   See, e.g., John Charmley, *Churchill: The End of Glory* (London: Hodder & Stoughton, 1993), pp.44–5.
10 See Campbell, *F. E.: First Earl of Birkenhead*, pp.267–70.
11 Campbell, *F. E.: First Earl of Birkenhead*, pp.222–6.
12 He also expressed his enthusiasm in two letters to Austen Chamberlain. See Birkenhead, *Frederick Edwin, Earl of Birkenhead*, pp.205, 207.
13 House of Lords: Official Report (Hansard): 24 March 1920, Vol. 39, col. 669.
14 House of Lords: Official Report (Hansard): 24 March 1920, Vol. 39, col. 673.
15 House of Lords: Official Report (Hansard): 24 March 1920, Vol. 39, col. 679.
16 2nd Earl of Birkenhead, *Frederick Edwin, Earl of Birkenhead*, Vol. II (London: Thomas Butterworth, 1933), p.163.
17 House of Lords: Official Report (Hansard): 14 December 1921, Vol. 48, cols 44–5.
18 House of Lords: Official Report (Hansard): 16 December 1921, Vol. 48, col. 204.
19 'Idealism in International Politics', University of Glasgow, 7 November 1923, *The Speeches of Lord Birkenhead*, pp.204–17.
20 *The Speeches of Lord Birkenhead*, p.217.
21 House of Lords: Official Report (Hansard): 22 March 1923, Vol. 53, cols 578–9.
22 C. Schuster, 'Smith, Frederick Edwin', *Oxford Dictionary of National Biography* (Oxford: Oxford University Press, 1937). The most recent entry on Smith in the *Oxford Dictionary of National Biography* is by John Campbell.

Nancy Astor

Shirley Williams
Delivered on 28 March 2011

Biographical note

Nancy Astor

Nancy Witcher Langhorne, born 19 May 1879, daughter of C. D. Langhorne, of Virginia, and Nancy Witcher Keene. Educated at finishing school in New York City. Married first in 1897, R. G. Shaw (divorced 1903); second in 1906, Waldorf, 2nd Viscount Astor (died 1952). Lived at Cliveden. Involved in Milner's Kindergarten, advocating unity and equality among English-speaking peoples; favoured expansion of the British Empire. Elected Conservative MP for Plymouth Sutton in 1919, succeeding her husband on his succession to the peerage, and serving in the House of Commons until retiring, with reluctance, in 1945. She entered the history books as the first woman to take her seat in Parliament, which she did on 1 December 1919. Companion of Honour 1937. Honorary Freeman of Plymouth 1959. Died 2 May 1964.

Noted for her acerbic wit and barbed exchanges (not least with Winston Churchill), she was a devoted MP. A Christian Scientist, she was a noted critic of Roman Catholicism. She favoured prohibition, the subject of her maiden speech. She successfully pioneered a Bill through Parliament to prohibit the sale of alcohol to persons under the age of eighteen.

Nancy Astor, née Langhorne, was born in Virginia in 1879 and died in England in 1964. Her long life spanned a transformation in the lives of women in both the country of her birth and of the country she adopted. When she was a small child, the third of five daughters of an ambitious, dynamic and ruthless Virginian businessman and gambler, women had no right to vote and no right to stand for elective office. Few were highly educated and a large proportion was illiterate. Working-class women were employed in underpaid menial jobs, in the textile industry, in agriculture and as domestic servants. Middle-class women were not expected to work and if they did, would often have to leave their jobs on marriage. Women aspired to marry well, since their future status would depend on that of their husband. Things had not changed very much for them since Jane Austen elegantly described their lives a century before.

The Langhorne girls were beautiful, the passport to an early marriage. They were also lively and rebellious. Richmond, Virginia, close to where they grew up, was the capital of the Old Confederacy, to which many of its inhabitants remained loyal. It cherished a tradition of gracious living, gallantry and plantation farming established in the decades before the Civil War. To be a rebel was socially acceptable, for it was to be identified with the old ways.

In 1892, after many vicissitudes on his way up the social ladder, Chillie, Nancy's father, bought a neo-classical mansion near Charlottesville. It was called Mirador and was to be at the centre of Nancy's roseate recollections of her happy childhood. She attended a local school headed by a relative of the South's great hero, General Robert E. Lee, and then went to a finishing school for young ladies in New York. Her father, keen on gambling and drink, was a stern disciplinarian and, as far as his eight children were concerned, insisted on an austere, even Puritan upbringing for them.

Like other Southern belles, Nancy married early, falling in love with a handsome wild young Virginian she met in New York. Robert Shaw was dashing and attractive, but he came from a family with a history of alcoholism and mental instability. Against her father's advice, she married him at the age of eighteen, but by the second day of their marriage she had run back home. Her parents persuaded her to try to keep the marriage going. It lasted long enough for the couple to produce one son, Bobbie, a troubled and troublesome youth on whom his mother doted, but ended in divorce on the grounds of Robert's adultery. The marriage left Nancy with two legacies, a passionate hatred of alcohol and a strong aversion to sex other than for the purpose of procreation. Nancy's verve, beauty and quick mind made her hugely attractive to men, but her intense and romantic relationships with several of the outstanding men of her generation, Philip Kerr (later Lord Lothian), Hilaire Belloc, T. E. Lawrence and George Bernard Shaw, were not love affairs. It is unlikely she ever had any, other than with her adoring second husband Waldorf.

Following the breakdown of her marriage and the death of her quiet, calm and much loved mother, Nancy felt an obligation to become housekeeper of Mirador for her father, Chillie. But housekeeping did not come easily to Nancy. Hugely energetic and intellectually restless, she found herself bored and frustrated. Her father offered her a way out, a trip to England for the hunting season. Nancy was a fine horsewoman, bold and sometimes reckless. Being part of the hunting season would give her entry to England's exclusive social circles. She accepted with enthusiasm.

Edwardian England's social and political elites spent much of their time at dinner parties and weekend parties in the great houses to which they were invited. To be a society hostess was the aspiration of many wealthy women. It was at these parties that political friendships were formed, marriages arranged and business deals made. Reading some of the biographies of the politicians of the era, one is struck by the social engagements, the well-organised field sports from hunting to the shooting of grouse and quail, golf and steeple-chasing, and the time devoted to reading. Where did the time come from? Part of the answer was to be found in the limited, almost formal interaction with constituencies and with what were called 'the common people'.

Young men of aristocratic background were very welcome at these parties, and so were attractive young women. Nancy Shaw quickly became a popular guest, helped by the fact that her father now owned an impressive stud farm of racehorses in Virginia. She went back there after her first visit to England, but returned for another hunting season in 1905. On the ship she met Waldorf Astor, son of the reclusive and eccentric William Waldorf. Waldorf, born in America, had been brought up in the most exclusive traditional English upper-class style: an austere prep school, Eton and Oxford University. He was a fine sportsman, a good debater and a considerable scholar, but managed to combine these attributes with modesty and a strong sense of public service. It was this that led him into politics. He insisted on standing for a marginal seat, and was returned for Plymouth on his second attempt in 1910.

Waldorf fell in love with Nancy and they married auspiciously in 1906. Three Prime Ministers signed the register. Their wedding present from Waldorf's father was Cliveden, the lovely Thameside estate in Berkshire. Cliveden was a major undertaking for Nancy; there were twenty domestic staff and forty outdoor staff, gardeners and grooms. It became the hub of her immensely successful social circle, one that included leading politicians, writers, artists and many more. The secret of her success was that she left her guests with large amounts of free time and abundant space between the formal meals. At those meals, she served her guests with plenty of good wine and spirits, despite her own unbroken commitment to prohibition, a cause she was to espouse throughout her life.

During these pre-war years the cause of women's suffrage advanced. But it was indeed a slow progress. At the end of the eighteenth century, in 1792, Mary Wollstonecraft had published her remarkable pamphlet, *A Vindication of the Rights of Women*, but it had not inspired a revolution. The contemporaneous revolution was in France, where the year before, in 1791, Olympe de Gouges, a playwright and early feminist writer, had written *Declaration of the Rights of Woman and the Female Citizen*. A supporter of the French Revolution, she had taken her declaration to the National Assembly where the all-male members laughed her out of court. Two years later, in November 1793, this inconvenient woman was guillotined following a trial by the Revolutionary Tribunal.

Women's suffrage became a major political issue towards the end of the nineteenth century, led by Millicent Fawcett who argued for it on constitutional grounds. By 1905, impatience towards an unresponsive Parliament turned into militancy. In that year Christabel Pankhurst and Annie Kenny broke up a meeting addressed by Edward Grey, the Foreign Secretary, in Manchester. It was to be the first of many interventions by the suffragettes. Their activism embraced attacks on property, ranging from burning out post-boxes and breaking windows to the slashing of Velásquez's masterpiece, the *Rokeby Venus*. The Prime Minister, Herbert Henry Asquith, detested the whole business, and remained stonily opposed to women's suffrage. Attacks upon him, including one in Scotland where women attempted to rip off his clothes, confirmed him in that opposition. He did not regard women as suited to public life, dismissing the suffragettes as 'a hysterical sideshow' in a section of his memoirs entitled 'Miscellanea'.[1] He shared with *The Times*, in its editorial of 28 March 1912, the opinion that 'there is mixed up with the women's movement much mental disorder and he cannot conceal from himself the physiological exigencies that lie behind it'.

The paradox was that Asquith had, in his second wife, Margot Asquith, née Tennant, one of the most politically engaged and manipulative women in the modern history of England, a person who never hesitated to intervene in her husband's political affairs.[2] She shared her husband's antipathy to David Lloyd George, and encouraged friendly editors and journalists to denounce him. Lloyd George's strong support for women's suffrage did nothing to recommend him in her eyes. Why should it? She wielded power behind the scenes, exemplifying Milton's description of the proper relationship between men and women in *Paradise Lost*: 'He for God only, she for God in him.'

Margot and Nancy had a respectful relationship, in which Margot patronised Nancy. Berating her for some naive comment in a letter, Margot rebuked her: 'You add, "Don't let's ever, ever talk politics." My dear, I never talk politics with my own sex, for I've never met one nowadays with the smallest political knowledge.' But they had a good deal in common. Both were confident; both loved to be conspicuous, the centre of the scene. Both were good at repartee. The lionised film star, Jean Harlow, was once introduced to Mrs Asquith. 'Hi Margot!' she said. Mrs Asquith regarded her frostily. 'The 't' is silent,' she said, 'as in Harlow.'

Both women were courageous, taking on their enemies with delight. Mrs Asquith used to travel third-class on the railways, and would then berate her fellow passengers on political matters. Lady Astor would drive into the most hostile neighbourhoods in Plymouth to take on the hecklers and hooligans she found there. Both women found such encounters stimulating.

By 1911, the majority of the Asquith Cabinet had moved in support of a bill to enfranchise women. Private Members' Bills had not been successful, so it was suggested that an amendment on which there would be a free vote should be debated as part of the government's new Reform Bill, a Bill intended to extend the adult male franchise from 60 per cent to 100 per cent of the population. The Cabinet agreed to differ publicly on the issue, and that there would be no ministerial resignations whatever the outcome. But this eminently reasonable proposal was scuppered by the then Speaker, James Lowther (later Lord Ullswater) who decided that it made so much difference the entire Bill would have to be withdrawn and reintroduced later. It was to be six more years before the suffrage for women over thirty finally got passed by the Commons.[3]

This eventual and long-delayed achievement owed little to Nancy Astor. Neither financially nor politically had she contributed. From time to time she would utter pithy remarks, mainly dismissive of men, attributing the world's political ills to their leadership, and as a mistress of repartee once said, 'I married beneath me; all women do.' But her claim to a historical milestone as the first woman to take her seat in the House of Commons owed everything to political expediency and privilege, not to leadership.

The constituency of Plymouth had been fought twice by Waldorf Astor. To his credit, he did not want a safe Conservative seat, but he and Nancy bought a house there and moved in in 1909. A year later, Waldorf was defeated in the January election, but won in the subsequent election in December of the same year.[4] Waldorf and Nancy were devoted to Plymouth and felt themselves to be part of the town. The relationship was almost feudal, with the Astors supporting local charities and good works. It was therefore not surprising when Waldorf Astor was compelled to resign as an MP on his elevation to the peerage in 1919, following his father's death, that his political agent pleaded that Nancy should stand in his place. There was a real fear that the khaki election might lead to a Conservative defeat in Plymouth; the Astor name was worth a fair number of votes.[5] In October 1919, the local Plymouth Conservative Association duly selected Nancy Astor as its candidate.

She took to her own campaign like a duck to water. She campaigned in a carriage drawn by a pair of handsome sorrel horses driven by a top-hatted coachman. From this mobile platform Nancy would address passers-by and knots of interested voters. She was invariably well turned out and forceful, going from street to street to meet the people. She found this contact with ordinary men and women highly stimulating.

On 1 December 1919 Nancy Astor took her seat in Parliament,[6] supported by two Prime Ministers, David Lloyd George and Arthur Balfour. She was to devote much of her time in the early years to denunciation of drunkenness and the case for prohibition, something of an embarrassment to her party, which was close to the brewers. She also championed legislation on social justice. But she was an isolated figure until 1921 when she was joined by Mrs Wintringham, and in 1923 by six others.[7] She was resented by some male MPs, not least among them Winston Churchill. He famously compared her presence to an intrusion into his bathroom 'when I have nothing to defend myself with, not even a sponge'. He was not attractive enough to worry on that score, she acidly retorted.

In her long political career, Nancy made some serious misjudgements, the worst of them inspired by her social circle rather than her political party.

The many parties at Cliveden had spawned a political group dedicated to avoiding war with Germany, which became known as the Cliveden set. Many of its members, among the most prominent being Lord Halifax and Lord Lothian, had suffered serious bereavement during the First World War. Nancy, who had lost two of her dearest friends, Julian and Billy Grenfell, who were called by her 'the golden boys', was one of them. She also shared the sense that Germany had been shamefully treated in the Versailles Treaty, and that the country had legitimate grievances that had to be addressed. Yet another factor was a sneaking admiration in some quarters for Mussolini and for Hitler, new leaders who seemed to be tackling the mass unemployment and misery of the Great Depression. Rearmament was deeply unpopular, and there was little political reaction in Great Britain to Hitler's invasion of the Rhineland. It was only after Munich, when his troops marched into Czechoslovakia, that senior Conservative and Liberal politicians, with the exception of a vocal and angry Winston Churchill, began to change their minds.

During the Second World War, Nancy Astor distinguished herself for her dedication to helping her heavily bombed constituents, and for the second time making Cliveden available for war purposes, among them provision for wounded Canadian soldiers. But her political life had run its course. Even she could not defy the desire of her constituents for a new beginning after the long years of national government. Her devoted and loving husband, who had guided and protected her throughout her years in Parliament, felt obliged to advise her not to stand again.[8] She never forgave him.[9] The House of Commons was her life. Yet so was Cliveden. Her friend George Bernard Shaw had described Nancy Astor as 'a recklessly unladylike lady'. Her long-standing opponent, Winston Churchill, put it more subtly. 'She reigns in the old world and the new,' he told the *Sunday Pictorial* in 1931, 'at once a leader of smart society and of advanced feminist democracy.' It was, in the end, an uneasy combination.

1   Earl of Oxford and Asquith, *Memoirs and Reflections, 1852–1927*, 2 vols (London: Cassell, 1928).

2   See Daphne Bennett, *Margot* (London: Gollanz, 1984).

3   The Representation of the People Act 1918. A separate Act provided for women to be eligible to stand for election to the House of Commons.

4   He topped the poll in the two-Member constituency with 8,113 votes; the other Unionist, Arthur S. Benn, received 7,942. The Liberal candidates, C. E. Mallet and A. Williams, both of whom had sat in the previous Parliament, received 7,379 and 7,260 respectively. *The Times Guide to the House of Commons 1911* (London: The Times, 1911), p.50.

5   In the 1918 general election, in what had become the constituency of Plymouth Sutton, Waldorf had been returned with a majority of 11,757.

6   House of Commons: Official Report (Hansard): 1 December 1919, Vol. 122, col. 46.

7   See Melanie Phillips, *The Divided House* (London: Sidgwick & Jackson, 1980), pp.44–5.
8   Waldorf's perception of events was borne out in 1945: Nancy's 1935 majority of 6,097 was transformed into a Labour majority of 4,679.
9   Michael Foot, *Loyalists and Loners* (London: Collins, 1986), pp.230–31.

Winston Churchill

Nicholas Soames
Delivered on 26 April 2011

Biographical note

Winston Churchill

Winston Spencer Churchill, born 30 November 1874 at Blenheim Palace, son of Rt Hon. Lord Randolph Churchill MP. Educated at Harrow School and Sandhurst. Married 1908, Clementine, daughter of Col. Sir Henry Hosier KCB. Joined 4th Hussars 1895. Served with Spanish forces in Cuba, with the Malakand field force, the Tirah expedition, the Nile, and in South African War. Served in France 1916.

MP for Oldham 1900–06 (Conservative 1900–04, Liberal 1904–06); Liberal MP North-West Manchester 1906–08 and Dundee 1908–22; Constitutionalist, then Conservative, MP for Epping Forest 1924–45; Conservative MP for Woodford 1945–64. Under-Secretary of State for the Colonies 1905–08; President of the Board of Trade 1908–10; Home Secretary 1910–11; First Lord of the Admiralty 1911–15; Chancellor of the Duchy of Lancaster 1915; Minister of Munitions 1917–19; Secretary of State for War and Air 1919–21; Secretary of State for the Colonies 1921–22; Chancellor of the Exchequer 1924–29; First Lord of the Admiralty (War Cabinet) 1939–40; Prime Minister and Minister for Defence 1940–45; Leader of the Opposition 1945–51; Prime Minister 1951–55, Minister of Defence 1951–2.

Leader of the Conservative Party 1940–55. Father of the House of Commons 1959–64. Privy Counsellor 1907; Companion of Honour 1922; Lord Warden of the Cinque Ports 1941–65; Order of Merit 1946; Knight of the Garter 1953. Author. Died 24 January 1965 and accorded a state funeral. Frequently voted the Greatest Englishman, Churchill led the nation to victory in the Second World War.

In Churchill's first Parliament, I am rather afraid that he sorely tried Mr Speaker Gully. I wonder how you, Mr Speaker, would have handled his point of order of 19 November 1941 to Mr Speaker Fitzroy, whose portrait is behind me, on the then Speaker's golden wedding anniversary. Churchill said that he had searched without success for any Speaker so celebrating, back to Mr Speaker Rous in 1653, before which time the occupants of the Chair held their tenure for shorter and more precarious periods. This was his point of order, Mr Speaker, and I am not quite sure how you would have answered it:

> Mr Speaker, I rise to commit an irregularity, for which I venture to ask your indulgence and that of the House. The intervention which I make is without precedent, and the reason for the intervention is also without precedent, and the fact that the reason for my intervention is without precedent is the reason why I must ask for a precedent for my intervention.[1]

I am sure, Mr Speaker, that you would have batted it away very neatly.

I cannot pretend to you that what I am going to say about Winston Churchill is truly objective. I am sure that you will understand that the judgements of clever-dick hindsight of some of the revisionist historians are not for me. What I have to say is a grandfilial tribute, fortified by the deepest affection, admiration and profound respect.

There are so many different Churchills to speak of and there are so many different aspects of his rich and full life, but naturally for many people today it is Churchill's later life as Prime Minister, parliamentarian and war leader that he is remembered and, of course, for very good reason. Winston Churchill served for sixty-four years of almost uninterrupted membership of the House of Commons in various parties and for various constituencies, and for forty-seven years he sat in Cabinet, holding all but one of the great offices of state. He fought twenty-one elections between 1899 and 1959, of which he won sixteen, representing the seats of Oldham, Manchester North West, Dundee, Epping and, finally, the safe haven of Woodford.[2] He sat for the last time in the House on 28 July 1964. So it is that, for the paltry twenty-seven years that I have been a Member of Parliament, I am constantly reminded of and moved by his enduring presence in the daily life and ritual of the House of Commons, and by seeing what an inspiration he yet remains to so many of us here in Parliament, in the country and, of course, overseas.

Every day, we who are privileged to work and to have our being in this magnificent palace, when we arrive in Parliament Square, pass the Ivor Roberts-Jones statue of Churchill trudging doggedly forward into the future. On entering the Members' Lobby, there is the great Oscar Nemon statue, with his right toe that is often touched for luck by Members hoping to speak as they go through the Churchill Arch – still bearing upon it all its battle scars – into the chamber of the House. He stands opposite Mr Attlee, and across from his great friend and sometimes ally, David Lloyd George.

There is the plaque in Westminster Hall commemorating the lying in state before his state funeral. There is the brooding head of his remarkable father, my great-grandfather, Lord Randolph Churchill, who blazed like a meteor through the political firmament before dying tragically young. And there is the seat below the gangway in the chamber which was Winston Churchill's for the years that he was not in office. Of course, for anyone who has had the honour and great good fortune of doing it, there is the quite astonishing sensation of speaking from the same dispatch box in the chamber in the House of Commons as did Winston Churchill.

First elected to Parliament in October 1900 as the Conservative Member for Oldham, Churchill went on to become the radical and fiery Liberal politician of the early 1900s. He became a bold and reforming Home Secretary, in 1910 sharing the task of seeing through the House Lloyd George's National Insurance Act of 1911, the apogee of the Liberal government's social reforms. And – just as well for this speech – as a member of the government, he spoke in support of the Parliament Act 1911 but, incidentally, he opposed, as Leader of the Opposition, the additional restrictions of the 1949 Act.

Churchill was the First Lord of the Admiralty who, by a miracle of audacious good judgement, had the Fleet put to sea ready for war and the reserves called up and deployed in late July 1914. On 3 August, Germany declared war on France and invaded Belgium. At eleven o'clock on the night of 4 August, the British ultimatum to Germany expired – Great Britain was at war. As the first stroke of Big Ben sounded the dread hour, there flashed from the Admiralty to every British ship and naval establishment across the world the signal, 'Commence hostilities against Germany'. As Churchill wrote of that night in volume I of *The World Crisis*:

> We could at least see for ten days ahead. If war should come no one would know where to look for the British Fleet. Somewhere in the enormous waste of waters to the north of our islands, cruising now this way and now that, shrouded in mists and enveloped by storms, dwelt this mighty organization... The king's ships were at sea.[3]

Then, by a marvellous stroke of fate, after all that had befallen him in the previous years, Churchill was again appointed First Lord of the Admiralty on the very day that war was declared twenty-five years later, on 3 September 1939. He reported to the Admiralty at six o'clock that evening, a moment fraught with colliding emotions and memories, of which he wrote: 'And so it was that I came back into the same room I had quit in pain and sorrow almost a quarter of a century before.'[4] The Admiralty thrilled, of course, with the return of their favourite minister, saluted his arrival as First Lord in the famous signal to the Fleet, 'Winston is back'.

Twice Prime Minister – for the first time at the age of sixty-five in 1940 – Churchill left Downing Street for the last time on 6 April 1955, aged eighty. But what is very clear about Churchill's long and full life is that, despite his myriad occupations and pastimes, it was to the public service above all that Churchill devoted the greatest part of his life and which clearly most fascinated and absorbed him. Remember that Churchill lived his life astride two centuries, living through a period as cataclysmic as any in the history of the world.

After all, this is the story of the great panorama of the life of a 24-year-old cavalry subaltern, Lieutenant Churchill of the 4th Hussars, who armed with sword and pistol charged the Mahdi's men with the 21st Lancers at the Battle of Omdurman in 1898 in the last formal cavalry charge of the British Army. He lived through two world wars at a time of the most profound economic, social and technical change, but yet went on to usher in the nuclear age as Prime Minister in the 1950s.

It is indeed hard for us to grasp today when we remember that, in the course of his long public life, Churchill served six of the kings and queens of Great Britain. Commissioned from the Royal Military Academy, Sandhurst to the 4th Hussars, while Queen Victoria – the Queen Empress – was still on the throne, he soldiered in Cuba and Egypt; in India and on the north-west frontier of Pakistan, where British troops are engaged today; and in the Sudan and South Africa. He served Edward VII and George V as a Minister of the Crown as well as a soldier again serving, this time, in the trenches in France and Flanders. He served Edward VIII as one of his most senior privy counsellors;

served George VI as his wartime Prime Minister; and served the present Queen, whom he greatly revered and loved, as her first Prime Minister when she ascended the throne in 1952. It was indeed his profound understanding for the great landscape of the generations and their histories, and the events and circumstances that shaped them, that enabled him to bring to the conduct of public affairs a sense of proportion and experience that perhaps seem sometimes to be a little missing in our contemporary public life.

But really the most important point to understand about Churchill was that he was, above all, a very human, human being and, like all of us, he was entirely fallible. Indeed, it was his very humanity, his failures as well as his triumphs – his weaknesses as well as his phenomenal strengths – that make him so fascinating. But what always baffled Churchill's contemporaries and continues to engage and mystify his endless biographers was that he was, as a person, such a mass of contradictions in which, incidentally, he closely resembled someone with whom his relations were particularly stormy, but of the greatest importance – General Charles de Gaulle. Both were soldiers, men of action of great physical and moral courage. Each regarded himself as a man of destiny who, in their person, embodied their peoples. They read deeply of the histories of their nations and of others. Each seemed to others to be separate, aloof, utterly egotistical and even ruthless, but de Gaulle dedicated a great deal of time and sensitivity to his adored mentally handicapped daughter, and Churchill was of course deeply sentimental, easily moved to, and not at all ashamed of, tears.

There was a hardness in both of them, but also gentleness, understanding and compassion. Each of them wrote and spoke incomparably. There was, I was told by my late father, an unforgettable occasion when de Gaulle came to London on a state visit in 1959. In Westminster Hall, in front of a huge audience of Members of both Houses and others, all of whom had the text, he held the Hall enraptured with a faultless delivery, without notes and with a grand gesture that rolled away all the disputes, animosities and misunderstandings of the past, referred to 'Le Grand Churchill', upon which Churchill, of course, burst into tears. The entire audience trembled with emotion, knowing that they were present at a great reconciliation between two very great, yet very difficult, men.

Both of them were also rather lonely men, who preferred to march alone rather than in company and who, in old age, reflected rather more on what they had not achieved rather than on what they had. Both had a strong romantic streak, but also one of melancholy, and both were subject to periods of depression and unhappiness. This is perhaps the price that we today can now understand of genius and of greatness.

Both were great war leaders, but also in peacetime shared a vision of Europe. It was indeed a different vision, it is true – but a vision none the less. Both wanted desperately to be great leaders in peace as in war – and, in their way, they both succeeded. Where would Britain and France – indeed, Europe – be now, if Churchill and de Gaulle had not lived and not conveyed to their fellow countrymen their passionate faith in their own peoples?

I want to speak in particular of one aspect of Churchill's remarkable and complex character, although it reflects many others, and to talk of Churchill the orator and the parliamentarian. I do so as a Member of Parliament who, like my grandfather before me, reveres our British parliamentary system and, above all, the House of Commons and all it means, to this day, to the life of our country.

When Mr Attlee was asked if Churchill had been a great parliamentarian, he thought for a moment and replied, 'No, he was a great parliamentary figure.' To those outside politics, this might seem a fine distinction, somewhat ungenerous to so long-standing a Member and the author of some of the greatest speeches ever delivered in the long and ancient history of the House of Commons. But, as so often, Mr Attlee had made a wise comment, and nor was it in any way to Churchill's discredit.

Unlike his father, Churchill was not a natural speaker. Lord Randolph Churchill, in his very brief prime between 1880 and 1887, before the shadows fell over his meteoric career and extinguished his short life after a tragic illness, was the most brilliant and audacious platform speaker and parliamentary debater of the day. He could fill the largest halls in the land as well as the House of Commons. Lord Randolph was that relative rarity: a natural, spontaneous debater in the House of Commons – swift to pounce on an error by an opponent, quick to invoke the deadly weapons of mockery and irony, and acutely sensitive to the mood of the House.

But his son, Winston, had not inherited those gifts. For him, every speech, however brief, had to be carefully prepared – an agonising process for anyone involved. Indeed, there was much truth in the jibe of his greatest friend, F. E. Smith, who said, 'Winston has spent the best years of his life composing his impromptu speeches.'

People are always surprised that this most articulate of men was so dependent on detailed prior preparation, even for minor speeches. When he was Churchill's Parliamentary Private Secretary in the 1920s, Bob Boothby wrote of the prolonged nightmare of the preparation of a Churchill speech. It was a process that exhausted advisers, officials when in office, friends commanded to assist and very long-suffering and much put-upon secretaries.

Churchill never had a speech writer and however many people might have been involved in the preparation of his major speeches, the result was entirely his own. For Churchill, a speech was a work of art. He was one of the greatest of all modern essayists – his speeches were meticulously prepared literary and dramatic efforts. As Charles Masterman wrote of the young Churchill – and it could rightly have been said of him throughout his long career – 'He sets his ideas to rhetoric as musicians set theirs to music.'

But the laborious process of days and even weeks of thought

did not always mean that Churchill's speeches were successful. As with all politicians of the first rank, Churchill's career was littered with oratorical disasters, when he misjudged the audience or the occasion. When this happened, there could be no adjustment or change. On these occasions, his friends and admirers could only suffer as he ploughed on amid mounting tumult and hostility. The problem was sharply observed by Arthur Balfour after such a disaster in 1916, when he said, 'Anybody who knows my right hon. Friend is aware that when he makes one of these great speeches they are not the unpremeditated effusions of a hasty moment.'[5] Also, virtually all his books and articles were – in whole or in substantial part – dictated. In his own words, 'I live from mouth to hand.' In a very real sense, as Robert Rhodes James remarked, he wrote his speeches and he spoke his books.

Determined to succeed and openly and deeply ambitious, the young Churchill, in and out of Parliament, dedicated himself to acquiring the art of oratory. For it was to be an orator, and a parliamentary orator of the first rank, that he aspired, and by sheer diligence and hours and even days of preparation he achieved, as Sir Harold Nicolson marvellously described, 'that combination of great flights of oratory with sudden swoops to the intimate and conversational'.

Churchill's first major speech, in May 1901, took six weeks to prepare. It was a strong, vigorous and bold denunciation of his government's decision to increase the size of the army. It was a brave speech by a very new and young Member of Parliament, at a time of great imperial power and national self-confidence. It must have sent alarm bells ringing in the Chief Whip's office. As a matter of fact, they never stopped ringing until forty years later, when he became Prime Minister.

In opening his speech, speaking from the same place in the chamber as had his father in his later sad years, Churchill recalled that it was fifteen years since Lord Randolph had made for the cause of military economy, 'the greatest sacrifice of any Minister of modern times ... I am very glad the House has allowed me

... to lift again the tattered flag I found lying on a stricken field'. Thus he went on,

> Europe is now groaning beneath the weight of armies. There is scarcely a single important government whose finances are not embarrassed; there is not a parliament or people from whom the cry of weariness has not been wrung. What a pity it would be if, just at a moment when there is good hope of a change, our statesmen were to commit us to the old and vicious policy [instead of proclaiming] that the cruel and clanking struggle of armaments is drawing to a close and that with the new century has come a clearer and calmer sky.[6]

On 22 April 1904, Churchill had a parliamentary disaster. While pretending again to be making an impromptu speech, for once his memory let him down. He completely forgot what he was going to say next, and had to resume his seat in a shocked and stunned silence.[7] Many Members of the House had unforgettable and tragic memories of Lord Randolph's last speeches and wondered whether there was a fatal and hereditary weakness. Churchill never again made an important speech without copious notes to hand.

To an exceptional extent, Churchill's oratory mirrored the real man. As Lady Violet Bonham Carter, one of his greatest friends, wrote, 'There was nothing false, inflated or artificial in his eloquence. It was his natural idiom. His world was built and fashioned on heroic lines. He spoke its language.'[8] Indeed, his writings did reflect his life.

Much has been made of the simplicity of Churchill's oratory and the use of short words and short sentences. His great gift was to take a very complex theme, themes or topics, and reduce them not to simplicities and clichés, but to terms that others could understand without feeling or, indeed, being talked down to. The essence of that philosophy is captured in a remarkable and, I think, one of the most beautiful speeches that he ever made, in

1925, to mark the unveiling of the memorial to the Royal Navy Division of which he had been the founder and which he had raised when he was First Lord of the Admiralty in 1914. They had served with great gallantry and suffered unspeakable losses in the First World War.

His words to the relatives of the fallen and the survivors and their families are so contemporary that they could be made at the unveiling of any memorial to soldiers lost in the present conflict. It is a speech, incidentally, that I believe could only have been made by someone who had himself served in what Churchill called 'the place of honour'. He said:

> We are often tempted to ask ourselves what we gained by the enormous sacrifices made by those to whom this memorial is dedicated. But that was never the issue with those who marched away. No question of advantage presented itself to their minds. They only saw the light shining on the clear path to duty. They only saw their duty to resist oppression, to protect the weak, to vindicate the profound but unwritten Law of Nations, to testify to truth, justice and mercy among men. They never asked the question 'What shall we gain?' They asked only the question 'Where lies the right?' It was thus that they marched away for ever, and yet from the uncalculating exaltation and devotion, detached from all consideration of material gain, we may be sure that good will come to their countrymen and to this island they guarded in its reputation and safety so faithfully and so well.[9]

As all Members of Parliament know, the ease and flow of making a speech outside the House is not at all the same as that required in the chamber. The trouble with what then became Churchill's speaking technique in Parliament is that it is often quite impossible, even to this day, in a very different and much tamer House of Commons, to reliably gauge the mood of the chamber in advance, particularly on the big occasions. Indeed, the mood can still change from hour to hour, and in those days, almost from minute to minute. One moment, it is relaxed and good-humoured. At the next, it can be angry and querulous, and the House in that mood can be a formidable arena, especially for those on the receiving end of its displeasure. Churchill had not only to anticipate those varying moods, but to impose his views upon it with these very detailed, prepared speeches.

This was inevitably going to lead to some spectacular disasters, but ultimately also to his greatest triumphs. Mr Attlee's comment was indeed correct. Churchill could not have made the epic and spontaneous speech of David Lloyd George on 8 May 1940, in the Norway debate that subsequently led to Churchill becoming Prime Minister. However, politics are not about speaking techniques. As Lord Rosebery wrote of Lord Chatham's oratory: 'It is not merely the thing that is said, but the man who says it that counts, the character which breathes through the sentences.'

This was the problem, particularly in the early days in the House of Commons. Churchill's burning personal ambition was manifest. Even before he defected to the Liberal Party in 1904, he was deeply unpopular, even reviled, and much distrusted on the Unionist benches. An experienced political commentator, Henry Lucy, wrote tartly: 'Winston Churchill may be safely counted upon to make himself quite as disagreeable on the Liberal side as he did on the Unionist.' That was putting it mildly, and there was great pleasure, not confined in any way to the opposition benches, when his first ministerial speech in 1906 was a celebrated catastrophe. 'The harshness of utterance, which in its proper place is one of Winston's assets as a speaker, asserted itself out of season,' his new Private Secretary, the brilliant and devoted Eddie Marsh, sadly noted. The exultant Conservatives claimed that he was finished. They were destined to make the same claim on numerous other occasions. Fortunately, they were to find that he was, like Mr Gladstone, 'terrible on the rebound'. The truth is that they never liked him, and I am very much afraid that he never really liked them.

That is a classic example of Churchill's fundamental difficulty as a parliamentarian. If he got the mood wrong, he knew that he had got it wrong, but there was no escape from the carefully prepared text, as for me tonight. It was entirely characteristic, of course, that he recovered. Indeed, his next speech was a triumph and his outstanding qualities and energy as a minister became swiftly recognised. There was, however, always the lurking fear of a repetition, and repetitions inevitably there were in such a long parliamentary career.

The truth is that, for many people, it was all too obvious that Churchill's greatest interest was in office and in the exercise of power. That was his natural habitat. Furthermore, he did not make speeches to the House, but at the House. Also, if the division records for the exceptionally busy session of 1911 are any guide, he does not appear to have gone there very much, even though he was a senior minister. He certainly did little to try to woo or to seduce the House, that most jealous and, sometimes, self-important institution. Something, incidentally, that has not much changed down the years. It was the character, breathing through the sentences, that sometimes worried the House of Commons and his friends and colleagues. His extraordinary personal ambition was unconcealed and there seemed to be no controversy into which he would not plunge himself with partisan ardour, and the fact that his scathing speeches were known to have been carefully prepared in advance made them all the more difficult to take.

In 1904, Churchill, a backbencher of only two-and-a-half years' standing, delivered a bitter denunciation of the Prime Minister who, he said, had 'flouted the traditions of Parliament and dishonoured the service of the Crown'. Pretty rough stuff for a junior Member, even by Churchill's standards. Mr Balfour's reply inflicted more damage on Churchill than he himself had received from the attack. 'It is not, on the whole, desirable,' the Prime Minister said,

> to come down to this House with invective which is both prepared and violent … If there is preparation there should be more finish,

and if there is so much violence, there should certainly be more
obvious veracity of feeling.[10]

That was the victory of the rapier over the bludgeon.

Churchill's attitude to party did not help much, either. The
celebrated jibe that he regarded party rather as a rider regards
his horse – not minding much about it, provided that it carried
him safely and comfortably – had much truth to it. He was, after
all, in turn Conservative, Liberal, Lloyd George coalitionist,
constitutionalist and anti-socialist and Conservative again, without appearing to care very much which side he was on, provided
that it was the winning one.

There was just enough validity in that charge to harm
Churchill's sometimes flawed reputation. Churchill's tenure of
the Treasury, under Mr Baldwin, between 1924 and 1929, was
considered unsuccessful. Indeed, in Sir Martin Gilbert's view, in
his magnificent biography of Churchill, it was the only office
in forty-seven years that he did not adorn.[11] Further, some of
the campaigns engaged by him made him deeply unpopular and
mistrusted. His prolonged campaign on the Government of India
Act between 1931 and 1935 – an Act which proposed the grant-
ing of a modest degree of dominion status to India – which was
well described as Winston's six-year war, led him to use language
so offensive about the Indian leaders that, when he turned his
attention to the infinitely more real menace looming in Europe
and which he alone could see, very few were prepared to listen.
His opposition not only devalued the language of alarmism and
discredited his judgement, but, at the end of the day, it bored the
House of Commons.

Many of us here tonight know to our cost that the boredom
threshold of the House of Commons remains very low, and the
single-issue politician empties the chamber like a ferret in a rabbit-
hole. Also, those Conservatives who supported Churchill in his
largely futile Indian enterprise were from the extreme right and
agreed with him only on the India issue. As he was to find in the

terrible 1930s, rhetoric by itself is not enough. He simply did not arouse either affection or trust, and having forfeited those crucial assets, his political fortunes very nearly disintegrated.[12] Thus, when he began to deliver his warnings about Hitler and the need to re-arm, people ignored him, and his personal support was quite literally limited to Brendan Bracken, Bob Boothby and, from time to time, a very few others; he was almost totally isolated. Indeed, after he had been howled down by an enraged House of Commons over the abdication crisis in December 1936 – in itself a colossal but, in my view, entirely understandable personal misjudgement – his position was so hopeless that even his few supporters were in despair, as was he. Some looked elsewhere for their leadership against Chamberlain and appeasement.

The harsh truth is that Churchill was so widely distrusted and disliked by his parliamentary colleagues that they simply did not believe him, but at the end of the day, the true test of parliamentary oratory is less its quality and more its persuasive power – something that all Members of Parliament in this room have seen in our time. It was in this that, until 1939, as Robert Rhodes James rightly claimed, Churchill had failed,[13] for the days of the old oratory in the Commons had passed; the House was looking for something different. Thus, Churchill's magnificent and moving speech on Czechoslovakia – 'All is over. Silent, mournful, abandoned, broken, Czechoslovakia recedes into the darkness' – was not a success. Hardly anyone wanted to hear it, and when he described Munich as a total and unmitigated defeat, there was absolute uproar in the House.

It was only in March 1939 that the nation suddenly woke up to the grim fact that Churchill had been right and that the policy of sleepwalking and wishful thinking had led us to the verge of catastrophe but, even then, he did not convince the House of Commons – events had to do that for him. As he said to Anthony Eden in the Cabinet room at No. 10 in May 1940, 'Had it not been for Hitler, Anthony, neither of us would be in this room.' Indeed, Churchill's appointment as Prime Minister was not well received by the House. All contemporary accounts testify to the cold reception accorded to him on his first appearance in the chamber as Prime Minister on 13 May, compared with the warmth of the response to the deposed Neville Chamberlain.[14]

However, Parliament's distrust of Churchill was magnificently, totally and marvellously eclipsed by one speech: the brief and unforgettable 'Blood, sweat, toil and tears' speech.[15] The effect was electrifying, for here he was indeed imposing his views, his character and his resolve on the House of Commons, whether it liked it or not. There were to be many great parliamentary performances during the war, but that was the turning point. The poet and the patriot in him shone through. He was still speaking at the House of Commons, but it was now listening and warmly cheering, and its pulse, under his leadership, beat in time with the great unfolding events of those extraordinary days. He was later to write that, even at the height of the great crises of the war, he did not begrudge twelve hours preparing a speech to the House of Commons. The previous defect had become the most wonderful of virtues.

This is surely the whole point of the political importance of Churchill's oratory. His speeches were indeed his own; both Parliament and country heard the whole man. Speeches do not win wars, but Churchill's in the summer and autumn of 1940 galvanised the British people and broadcast to the free world that Hitler had not triumphed, that the British Empire would fight and that the real war had not ended, but had only just begun. Their impact was phenomenal; they made Hitler hesitate at a crucial moment, while transforming American public opinion.

General Ismay, the Chief of the Imperial General Staff, once found Churchill bemoaning the bother of preparing a speech for the Commons, and clearly apprehensive about its reception. The soldier said emolliently to my grandfather, 'Why don't you just tell them all to go to hell, Prime Minister?' Churchill rounded on him in a flash: 'You should never say such a thing to me, Pug. I am, above all else, the servant of the House.' I, for my part, truly think it a source of wonder and great pride that such a man led Britain through the war, genuinely believing this.

Indeed, it was Churchill's amazing achievement, as Max Hastings points out in his brilliant book *Finest Years*, to exercise the privileges of a dictator without ever casting off the mantle of a democrat.[16] Of course, Churchill did not command the confidence of all the British people all of the time, but the power of his words did enable millions to look beyond the horror and the havoc of the battlefield and the squalor of their circumstances amid privation and terrible bombardment, and to perceive a higher purpose in their struggles and sacrifices.

After the war, Churchill was generally considered to have been a poor Leader of the Opposition. It was not a chore that he relished, for understandable reasons, and his performance in the Commons was not highly rated by either side. There were many who wished that he had taken the advice of, among others, my grandmother and retired in glory in 1945. But in his second premiership, between 1951 and 1955, although the old advantages remained obvious, his mere arrival in the chamber caused not only a sensation in the galleries, but a ripple of excitement on the Floor of the House. His fluency in replying to questions and in major debates got better and better, and he had a marvellous Indian summer, while the nation greatly benefited from his stature and authority abroad.

Churchill's last major speech to the House of Commons was in the defence debate on 1 March 1955. Our world was in the grip of the cold war. Winston Churchill was in his eighty-first year, and it was less than a month before he would resign as Prime Minister for the last time. His secretary, Grace Hamblin, who was known in the Churchill family for generations as 'the Hambone', and who, after fifty years' service to my grandparents, later became the first curator of Chartwell, recalled that Churchill had spent a total of twenty hours preparing his last major speech on the Floor of the House. Every word of it he dictated himself.

Speaking in the debate, Churchill announced to Parliament and the world that Britain would build its own hydrogen bomb. He gave a dramatic and broad review of the tense and dangerous situation. He expressed the hope that 'safety will be the sturdy child of terror, and survival the twin brother of annihilation'. He ended thus:

> The day may yet dawn when fair play, love for one's fellow-man, respect for justice and freedom, will enable the tormented generations to march forth serene and triumphant from the hideous epoch in which we have to dwell. Meanwhile, never flinch, never weary, never despair.[17]

Two nights before he left No. 10 for the last time, on 4 April 1955, he and my grandmother gave a dinner for the Queen and Prince Philip, attended only by his family and his closest and dearest friends and colleagues. It had been agreed that there would be no speeches, but the Sovereign, greatly moved by the departure from office of her first Prime Minister, whom she had known since she was a child, proposed a most graceful toast to my grandfather, with the words, 'To my Prime Minister.' Churchill, dressed in the full evening dress of a knight of the garter, pulled himself to his feet and replied thus to the Queen:

> I propose the health of your Majesty – a toast I used to drink as a subaltern officer in the 4th Hussars at Bangalore in India in the reign of your Majesty's great-great-grandmother, Queen Victoria. I drink to the wise and kindly way of life of which your Majesty is the young and gleaming champion.

Churchill's last day in the House of Commons was 28 July 1964. It was probably too late a conclusion to his extraordinary political life. Whatever his ups and downs with the House, he greatly revered and loved our political institutions and understood better than most, from his profound knowledge as a historian,

their absolutely central place in our national life. In a speech at
Oxford in June 1930, he said of the House of Commons:

> I see the Houses of Parliament – and particularly the House of
> Commons – alone among the senates and chambers of the world
> a living and ruling entity; the swift vehicle of public opinion; the
> arena – perhaps fortunately the padded arena – of the inevitable
> class and social conflict; the College from which the Ministers of
> State are chosen, and hitherto the solid and unfailing foundation
> of ... executive power. I regard these parliamentary institutions as
> precious to us almost beyond compare. They seem to give by far
> the closest association yet achieved between the life of the people
> and the action of the State. They possess apparently an unlimited
> capacity of adaptiveness, and they stand an effective buffer against
> every form of revolutionary or reactionary violence. It should be
> the duty of all faithful subjects to preserve these institutions in their
> healthy vigour, to guard them against the encroachment of external
> forces, and to revivify them from one generation to another from
> the springs of national talent, interest, and esteem.[18]

Surely we can all say amen to that.

Isaiah Berlin, the great British philosopher, said of Churchill
in 1945 at the end of the war that he was:

> a man larger than life, composed of bigger and simpler elements
> than ordinary men, a gigantic historical figure during his own
> lifetime, superhumanly bold, strong and imaginative, one of the
> two greatest men of action his nation has produced, an orator
> of prodigious powers, the saviour of his country, a mythical hero
> who belongs to legend as much as to reality, the largest human
> being of our time.

Well, ladies and gentlemen, certainly he was one of the most
brilliant and gifted Englishmen of all time: parliamentarian,
statesman and war leader, a gallant soldier, a fearless early

aviator, the master of strategy, journalist, author of forty-three book-length works in seventy-two volumes – and the winner of the Nobel Prize for Literature – sage, historian, painter and visionary and, incidentally, a devoted and loving husband, father and grandfather.

These qualities shine for us today even brighter, when they march with great good humour and almost complete lack of side and pomposity and, most of all, a generous and full understanding of men and women, and what made them tick. So here indeed was a man for the difficult times – indeed, for all the times. Half-American and yet ever-ardent for closer bonds between North America and Europe; born in an English palace 136 years ago, buried in the tiny graveyard at Bladon at the entrance to the park at Blenheim, he was at one with all people of courage and good will, no matter what their rank, their race or their nation.

1   House of Commons: Official Report (Hansard): 19 November 1941, Vol. 376, col. 320.
2   On his association with the Essex seats, see David A. Thomas, *Churchill: The Member for Woodford* (London: Frank Cass, 1995).
3   Winston S. Churchill, *The World Crisis*, Vol. 1 (New York: Scribners, 1923).
4   Winston S. Churchill, *The Gathering Storm* (Harmondsworth: Penguin Books, 1960 edn), p.363.
5   House of Commons: Official Report (Hansard): 8 March 1916, Vol. 80, col. 1571.
6   House of Commons: Official Report (Hansard): 13 May 1901, Vol. 39, cols 1562–79. See also Winston S. Churchill, *My Early Life* (London: Odhams Press, 1930), pp.364–5.
7   House of Commons: Official Report (Hansard): 22 April 1904, Vol. 133, col. 1001.
8   See Violet Bonham Carter, *Winston Churchill as I Knew Him* (London: Eyre & Spottiswoode, 1965).
9   Unveiling and Dedication of War Memorial, Admiralty, London, 25 April 1925 (London: Royal Naval Division, 1925).
10   See Roy Jenkins, *Churchill* (London: Macmillan, 2001), p.95.
11   Martin Gilbert, *Churchill: A Life* (New York: Henry Holt, 1991).
12   See, e.g., Martin Gilbert, *Winston Churchill: The Wilderness Years* (London: Macmillan, 1981).
13   Robert Rhodes James, *Churchill: A Study in Failure* (London: Weidenfeld & Nicolson, 1970).

14 See, for example, Robert Rhodes James (ed.), *CHIPS: The Diaries of Sir Henry Channon* (London: Weidenfeld & Nicolson, 1967), p.252.

15 House of Commons: Official Report (Hansard): 13 May 1940, Vol. 360, cols 1501–5.

16 Max Hastings, *The Finest Years* (London: HarperPress, 2009).

17 House of Commons: Official Report (Hansard): 1 March 1955, Vol. 537, col. 1905.

18 Martin Gilbert, *Winston S. Churchill, Vol. V: 1922–1939* (London: Heinemann, 1976), p.361.

Aneurin Bevan

Gordon Marsden
Delivered on 17 May 2011

Biographical note

Aneurin Bevan

Born 15 November 1897, son of David Bevan, of Tredegar. Educated at Sirhowy Council School, Tredegar. Married 1934, Jennie Lee (Labour MP 1929–31, 1945–70). Miners' Agent. Urban District and County Councillor. Labour MP for Ebbw Vale from 1929 to 1960. (A leading rebel, he was expelled from the party 1939 and had the whip withdrawn March–April 1955.) Editor of *Tribune* 1942–45. Minister of Health 1945–51; Minister of Labour and National Service 1951. Resigned from the government in protest at the imposition of prescription charges.

Privy Counsellor 1945; Member of Labour National Executive Committee 1944–54, 1956–60; Treasurer of the Labour Party 1959–60; Deputy Leader of the Labour Party and Deputy Leader of the Opposition 1959–60. Died 6 July 1960.

A Welsh socialist who made a name in the House of Commons as a fiery, and partisan, debater, famously describing Tories as 'lower than vermin'. He was seen as the father of the National Health Service. A leader of the Labour left, he stunned some supporters when, as shadow Foreign Secretary in 1957, he spoke against unilateral nuclear disarmament. Elected Deputy Leader of the Labour Party in 1959, he died of cancer the following year.

One of the most over-used and degraded words in twenty-first century chatter – or twitter if you prefer – is the word 'iconic'. The pity of it is it risks trivialising those hailed as twentieth-century political icons – a socialist pantheon into which Nye Bevan has been enrolled, if not embalmed. And the danger of it is in wearing such a label – with all its embellishments – is that Bevan's liveliness and relevance for a new century can be squeezed out. This is a man whose life was bookended by the zenith of the British Empire – and by its collapse.

A life politically shaped by an industrial world and struggle in the Welsh valleys that no longer exists, and the impact of the First World War and the General Strike. Whose passion and arguments were honed in the Great Depression but who died before the social and cultural revolutions of the 1960s, and nearly thirty years before the collapse of Communism. What does such an icon, however venerated and admirable, have to say to our politics today – a world post-Iraq, 9/11 and 7/7 – a man whose very vividness of personality and oratory might seem to lock him into a grittier and wholly other time and space?

But icons, like well-loved paintings, can have the encrustations of their own and succeeding ages removed. And that's particularly valuable if the varnish has sometimes darkened and obscured some of their essential essence. In inviting myself and others to contribute to this series of lectures on great twentieth-century parliamentarians, you, Mr Speaker, urged us to take on board their relevance for Parliament and politics today. I have taken you at your word, Mr Speaker, and so emboldened I want to do a bit of stripping away – looking at those aspects of Nye Bevan that speak particularly to our contemporary world.

Very few great political figures are as two-dimensional as commentators of their times – or even their admirers – sometimes make them appear. And in this and his paradoxes Bevan was no exception. The Greeks have a word for it – *poikilos* (brightly or many-coloured) – and in my lecture today I want to look at some of the colours that shine brighter on Bevan's canvas when the darkened varnish gets stripped away. Bevan the communitarian and big society man but also Bevan the individualist. Bevan the modernist but also passionate conserver of environmental and built heritages – Green Bevan, if you like. Bevan the man of dialectic and Marxist analysis but also Bevan the passionate anti-materialist. Bevan the man of sharp aesthetics and tastes, even Bevan the sensualist. A man who was the relentless pursuer and shining example of Denis Healey's famous dictum that 'all politicians should have a hinterland'.

All of these characteristics were integrated and woven into a thirty-year parliamentary career where almost from the start he came to dominate and devastate, not just in his own party but also in many of the great debates – in peace and war – that took place here in Parliament in that period. A period, 1929–60, beginning in economic and financial crisis, slump, depression, mass unemployment, and ending in the consumer society and 'you've never had it so good' nostrums of Harold Macmillan. It was centre-pieced by a world war with Britain's very survival at stake – followed by Cold War and a debate about the nuclear deterrent.

The latter was one that in its time was as divisive in the Labour Party and the British left as Iraq has been in the twenty-first century – and to which of course in the last years of his life Nye Bevan supplied his own paradoxical coda – one that shook his faithful Bevanites to the core and which remains enigmatic even today. Whether it was shocking those supporters at the 1957 Labour Party conference in Brighton when he referred to

unilateralism as an 'emotional spasm', enraging Middle Britain
with his infamous 'lower than vermin' jibe at the Tories in his
July 1948 speech in Manchester or in his persistent strategy
throughout the Second World War of using his articles in *Tribune*
and speeches in the Commons to call Churchill to account and
frequently cut him down to size from the demi-god national
saviour status he had assumed, Bevan, as both politician and
parliamentarian, fully lived out Jesus's famous admonition
in the New Testament, 'think not that I have come to bring
peace, but a sword'. To some of course, especially among his
own party colleagues, first in the wartime coalition and then
in government from 1945–51 and opposition thereafter – men
like Ernie Bevin, Morrison, Dalton, Gaitskell – and from time
to time 'like some exasperated headmaster' Attlee himself, the
analogy was less biblical. It must have seemed more like Marlon
Brando's famed retort when his character in his 1953 film *The
Wild One* was asked what he was rebelling against and replied
'whaddya got?'

   That sense of struggle and the sword constantly being *engarde*
– using his wit as a rapier but not afraid to bludgeon, sometimes
with collateral damage, if necessary – suffused and seldom
waned in Bevan's writing and speeches. That was true whether
on public platforms, at party conferences or in the Commons
chamber, from his first days as a young MP for Ebbw Vale
thrust into the 1929–31 parliament and the traumatic economic
crisis which brought about Ramsay MacDonald's collapse
into a national coalition government. And Michael Foot in his
majestic two-volume biography of Bevan, which remains a central
tract for understanding the man and his complexities, is right to
underline how Bevan's socialism was rooted in the Marxist ideas
and analysis he had absorbed as a young miner, self-taught agitator and union official in the valleys of 1920s South Wales – analysis
which remained a constant throughout his life.[1]

   Here was one Labour parliamentary figure who deviated from
the adage that it was a party who in its rise had owed more to

Methodism than to Marx – for all that the cultural influence of his family's Free Church roots remained an important penumbra around Bevan. That Marxist analysis was a central influence on the language Bevan used when talking and thinking about Parliament and the British parliamentary tradition. But instead of that analysis sidelining Parliament in the political and industrial struggle as it did for others, Bevan elevated parliamentary activity to the core of his purpose and strategy.

I think it's true that at times in his career, especially in his struggles against economic orthodoxy in the 1930s, Bevan saw Parliament as a pragmatic but crucial conduit for going over the heads of Labour Party or trade union bosses to appeal directly to British workers and the British people. But Parliament was also central to his philosophy of political progress. And he puts it right at the start of his only book, *In Place of Fear* written in 1952:

> the function of parliamentary democracy, under universal franchise, historically considered, is to expose wealth-privilege to the attack of the people. It is a sword pointed at the heart of property power. The arena where the issues are joined is Parliament.[2]

In Place of Fear comes as close as anything to summing up his credo as Labour politician and parliamentarian, and his historical perspective on both. His detailed observations in that book on Parliament – its physical surroundings and psychological impact – are not only key in understanding him but remain relevant tracts for our times as well as his. He comments on the atmosphere of Parliament, 'its physical arrangements, procedure, its semi-ecclesiastical ritual',[3] where the new Member comes hoping to be a 'tribune of the people and is instead expected to worship – and the most conservative of all religions – ancestor worship'.[4] He is sardonic about how what he sees as the convoluted verbal conventions of the House can stymie that tribune's maiden speech: 'the stone he thought he had thrown turned out to be a sponge'.[5]

He criticises the inadequacy of the facilities of the 1950s parliament, not on account of the intimate post-war chamber – faithfully reconstructed after bomb damage and still too small to seat all MPs – but in terms of the arrangements outside the chamber. These he saw as 'steeped in class bias' and based on the assumption that 'Members of Parliament are well-to-do and possess houses within easy reach of the House of Commons'.[6] Bevan was an ardent early advocate of the need for 'men and women of moderate means' to have clerical and office facilities put at their disposal. It is intriguing to hear Bevan's *raison d'être* for doing so in the wake of Parliament's recent expenses controversies.

> It is nonsense to complain of an immense and tendentiously all-powerful civil service and at the same time cavil at the small expenditure required to equip elected representatives responsible for controlling its actions with the means to do so adequately.[7]

Bevan was no knee-jerk demoniser of the civil service and the whole apparatus of Whitehall; he didn't brand them as *Yes Minister*-style impediments to political progress. The civil servants who toiled closest with him in his epic battles to set up the National Health Service were full of surprised praise for the administrative skills he showed as rebel turned Cabinet minister, who worked with them smoothly as midwife to that iconic British institution – and here the epithet *is* justified – the NHS. 'He sold himself to the Ministry within a fortnight,' as the Chief Medical Officer of Health said at the time.

But Bevan remained constantly on the alert for rival structures that could threaten to emasculate his vision of an empowering Parliament serving the people. As Foot points out, 'throughout his life Bevan became suspicious and jealous of bodies set up by Parliament to remove power from Parliament … and when he established the NHS, he insisted the minister in charge be directly answerable for everything connected with the service across the floor of the House of Commons.'[8] Well, there's an interesting two penn'orth to some of the current Sturm und Drang about bonfires of the quangos – and with the Localism Bill being debated on the floor of the Commons as I speak.[9]

For Bevan, though, his motivation was not to uphold the quasi-mystical sovereign Parliament of Enoch Powell and the High-Tory tradition, but his pragmatic determination to use and hold the institution accountable to the people via its representatives.[10] This was something he spoke up for very early on in his parliamentary career and from which he never wavered. Here he is on the Insurance Bill debates of 1933 and 1934: 'If you close the avenue of appeal between the citizen and state between elections then human beings are not going to have the patience to sit down in resignation for five years until they have another chance.'[11]

That continual rejuvenating connection was for him what gave legitimacy to a Parliament which constantly needed to be taking the lead in the long march of everyman – and every woman. Hence the righteous anger when he felt they were being side-lined – as in his outburst in the Commons in November 1936 over the national government's Unemployment Assistance Board: 'The House of Commons has reduced my people to such impotence ... You have established 7,000 officials without the slightest responsibility to the people and we cannot control them here.'[12]

The well-spring of that was Bevan's life experience as advocate and agitator in the valleys as a young miner. As he says in *In Place of Fear*,

> my concern was with the one practical question: where does power lie ... and how can it be attained by the workers. It was no abstract question for us. The circumstances of our lives made it a burning, luminous mark of interrogation.[13]

Time and again Bevan came back to that interrogation in his parliamentary career – and time and again he rooted it in his constituents and his origins. Again I quote from *In Place of Fear*:

the first function of a political leader is advocacy and that only becomes full representation if the elected person speaks with the authentic accents of those who elected him. That does not mean he need be provincial, nor that he speaks in the local vernacular. It does mean he should share their values and realities.[14]

That, I suggest, hints at an elegant synthesis in the age-old tussle between the Burkean representative and the Chartists' delegate views of Members of Parliament. It is a question made even sharper for us now in the age of interactive blogging, online lobbying and a 24/7 commentariat no longer restricted to a media elite. Advocacy for Bevan meant being constantly prepared to challenge and to make the smooth places rough.

Foot points to the famous NHS debate in Parliament of 9 February 1948 – a time when the whole NHS project seemed to totter on the edge, running up against the July deadline for the Act setting it up to come into completion and facing implacable opposition from the BMA.[15] Not for Bevan as for his current beleaguered successor as Health Secretary (Andrew Lansley) the luxury of a moment of pause.[16] Instead Bevan used coruscating oratory pillorying the BMA to raise the scarlet standard even higher at a time when the conventional approach might have been to lower the political temperature. For him, as Foot says, 'Parliament was not only a prize to be defended; it was a weapon to be used ... used positively to retain the initiative in the hands of a reforming administration.'[17] And part of making the smooth places rough was the way Bevan was prepared in committee and in major debates to elevate trivial disputes into serious controversies, always striving to transmute the small change of politics into large principles.

For Bevan, men and women needed constantly to be stirred by a doing philosophy. And if the price of liberty is eternal vigilance, Bevan's price of democracy was constant interrogation, even during the height of the war when his challenges and questioning of Churchill had many of his own side participating in the wartime coalition baying for his blood. This included – as

Bevan put it – preventing Parliament becoming a 'Reichstag', rubber-stamping the Great Leader's conduct of war,[18] defending the *Daily Worker* when Herbert Morrison wanted to close them down for sniping at the war effort and resisting the attempts to gag Labour MPs or ministerial critics by closed meetings of the PLP and whips. He provocatively proclaimed: 'In this fashion political parties become the enemies of parliamentary democracy. It is better that ministers should be embarrassed than that Parliament should die.'[19]

For all his often high-wire rhetoric, Bevan was no mere bull in the parliamentary china shop. He was quite prepared to be feline, to use his considerable and roguish charm, and to surprise potential adversaries whether inside the House or elsewhere, by listening – as he famously did in the long strategic haul with local authorities, hospitals and the medical profession in developing the detailed blueprint for the NHS in 1946–7. For Bevan, these qualities were not antipathetic to conviction and determination in a politician. All of these weapons of war had constantly to be validated by the politics of connection – between the high ground of Parliament and the common ground that had nurtured him and the people he represents, 'an MP on Monday, fresh from his constituency was a better being than the one who had escaped from (Parliament's) foetid corridors on Friday'.[20] Bevan was not precious about the role of the legislator as that of high priest, as his comments on the chapter from *In Place of Fear* on 'The Role of Parliament: Active or Passive' show:

> It is the finished work, not the tools of his craft that excites the love of the artist... The student of politics must therefore seek neither universality nor immortality for his ideas and institutions but integrity and vitality ... his holy grail is the living truth, knowing that being alive the truth must change.[21]

I think this explains why for all Bevan's commitment to collectivist struggle, to holding the ring for public ownership and even

extending it in his epic struggle with Gaitskell and his social democratic revisionists throughout the 1950s, and indeed to drawing
his strength from the mass of constituency activists who increasingly lionised him from the 1940s onwards, he felt comfortable in
proclaiming a confident and sometimes wilful individualism. His
personal duels with Herbert Morrison and Ernie Bevin doubtless
strengthened Bevan's distrust for the union block vote, the whips
and any notion of the party, right or wrong. It's why, perhaps,
Bevan found Tito's Yugoslav model of socialism and defiance of
Stalin attractive in the 1950s – until he had a rude awakening with
Tito's suppression of his great friend Milovan Đjilas.

But Bevan's defence of individualism was not just based on
his political experience, innate and philosophical. Foot puts it
nicely when he said his lifelong conviction was that 'standing
orders were made for man, not man for standing orders'. It's
why Bevan even in his most antagonistic moments with Churchill
could recognise a kindred rogue spirit – as in his revealing aside
commenting on Churchill in *Tribune* August 1940: 'against the
dull weight of party organisation the most dynamic personalities fight in vain'.[22] It's why he attacked the use of the whips
and NEC as attempted muzzles, as he and others increasingly
argued, from 1943 onwards, for a more semi-detached approach
to the Churchill coalition – a thought for the day for the Deputy
Prime Minister perhaps.

During the wartime parliamentary sessions, Bevan consistently
pressed for more free votes, worried that Labour would be black-
mailed into silence. He was convinced that the over-regulation of
freedom of association and press control, even in the darkest hours
of 1940 and 1941, would do lasting damage to the body politic.
For him the psychological impact of the war, however traumatic,
could be transformative in the political education of the British
people. Foot rightly draws attention to Bevan's astonishing
prophecy in early 1940 – at the height of the phoney war – about
how its intellectual ferment among the young especially would
lead to victory for the left after the conflict. Thus emboldened

he was quite prepared to take on, almost single-handed, the Home Secretary, Anderson, for the latter's undue repression of civil liberties in emergency legislation.

Again some may wish to find in this contemporary resonance with Parliament's post-9/11 and -7/7 terrorism debates around the 28-day detention proposals. Foot emphasises in his biography that while for Bevan 'liberal economics had been exposed as sterile and self-defeating, the liberal virtues, protecting the right to heresy, and free debate, retained an eternal validity'.[23] Bevan writes in his concluding chapter on 'Democratic Socialism' from *In Place of Fear* as fiercely as Edmund Burke ever did about the pitfalls of utilitarianism for the individual. 'Not even the apparently enlightened principle of the greatest good for the greatest number can excuse indifference to individual suffering. There is no test for progress other than its impact on the individual.'[24] Here Bevan adds sardonically 'it is this preoccupation with the needs of the individual that has caused Democratic socialism to be called dull'.[25] But Bevan is happy to flaunt that alleged dullness. He says, 'The philosophy of Democratic Socialism is essentially cool in temper. It sees the individual in his context with society and is therefore compassionate and tolerant.'

On the back of that assertion Bevan took positions that could not be more of the moment. He always believed that, for example, alongside all the other rights of human beings should be enshrined the right of privacy. And what contemporary prophet of empathy could better Bevan, who begins his chapter on Democratic Socialism quoting Dylan Thomas's poem on a child victim of a London bombing-raid, 'after the first death, there is no other', and then says poignantly 'the capacity for emotional concern for individual life is the most significant quality of a civilised human being. It is not achieved when limited to people of a certain colour, race, religion, nation or class.'[26]

Alongside that sensitivity went others – concern for the environments and the contexts in which people, his people, had to live. I am not going to play the parlour game of what Bevan's

position would have been on renewables, low carbon targets or
the Green Investment Bank, but what we can be confident about
is that he would have been engaged and would have recognised
the centrality of the green debate to the ordinary citizen. As a
keen admirer of the progressive planner Lewis Munford, Bevan
stuck out for the idea of natural beauty and recreation not arti-
ficially constrained, asking, 'why are there so many paths in the
park ... let the people stroll where they wish without all those
petty rules prescribed by those with comfortable gardens of
their own'. His view of the spread in the 1930s of the suburbs
and metroland was trenchantly judgemental: 'an architectural
leprosy ... devastating areas once green and lovely.' In his
comments on planning and growth policy in 1935, he attacked
the imbalance between derelict and stagnant areas in South
Wales, the Midlands and the North, and the over-concentrated,
overheated London and the Home Counties – all contexts being
echoed in the current debate about rebalancing our economy.
For Bevan 'this great concentration of population in two or
three large centres of the country is not a tendency we can view
with complacency'.

Far from being a class warrior wanting to pit industrial
Britain against its less politically dependable countryside, Bevan
espoused the view – to coin a phrase – that we were all in it
together, 'unless country and town move together in recipro-
cal activity, civilisation will limp on one foot'. Indeed, while
Bevan has sometimes been portrayed as a centralising and
prescriptive Marxist, his comments in an early draft of *In Place
of Fear* reveal a much more nuanced, one might almost say
'localist', outlook:

> Social science has not yet decided the optimum limit for a town.
> For myself I should judge that the sight of the Civic Centre
> should be an almost daily experience of its citizens... There is no
> conflict between a wide cosmopolitanism and a rich local life –
> the one gives meaning and particularity to the other.[27]

Foot is right to remind us also of the influences of Bevan's reading on his outlook:

> He was profoundly critical of many of the most spectacular developments in modern industrial civilisation and critical in terms rarely employed by socialists who have forgotten or never read William Morris.[28]

In their own home life away from Westminster, first in the 1930s in a ramshackle Tudor Cottage, on Brimpton Common in Berkshire, and latterly at Asheridge Farm in Buckinghamshire, Nye and his wife and political soulmate Jennie Lee continually sought out that balance.[29] It was perhaps also a reflection of Bevan's plea for more 'serenity' in modern man's relations with society and his 'passion to escape from an all-pervading restlessness' – the sort of vision that we might more readily associate with the 1960s counter-culture or Zen Buddhism than with an apostle of the dialectic struggle. Foot gives a list of 'room 101' objects that Jennie and Nye would not have in their domestic retreats – they included reproduction furniture, bric-a-brac, imitation antique china or electric fires with imitation coal. 'They both had strong views on taste and would not tolerate anything bogus … anything modern was selected for its simplicity of taste.'[30] Jennie Lee herself underlined Bevan's three-line whip on shoptalk by these hearths and homes: 'Nye was an adept at escaping to his cabbages… Often in the evening we would ban any talk about politics and he would simply read to me.'

Wherever he found himself in company, whether in his own home or elsewhere, Bevan exuberantly fulfilled Healey's injunction that all politicians should have a hinterland. His glorying in the good things of life – wine, food and the arts, written and visual – were natural outcrops from that sentiment. It's significant that *In Place of Fear* highlights with pride his 1948 Local Government Act, which 'enables municipal authorities to spend public monies on education, artistic and other allied activities'.

Bevan sees them as organic inheritors of the expenditure on the arts of the previous 'Popes, Kings, Dukes and Princes'.[31] But for him it is the nobler instincts in patronage that should prevail where the 'glories of art were produced for social and not for private consumption'. He scorned the rich collector 'who makes us a legacy of his accumulated treasures where we can catch only a small glimpse of their beauty'.[32]

Confident in his own origins and comfortable in his own skin, Bevan was happy to associate and joust with such diverse and eclectic characters as H. G. Wells, Beaverbrook and Churchill's *confidant* and wartime Minister of Information, Brendan Bracken, in what Foot calls 'his forays into proletarian espionage'. None of this in any way undercut Bevan's convictions or diluted his trenchant political assaults on those with whom he might break a lance in gleeful mockery. In his own London house at Cliveden Place he promoted the same eclecticism, hosting American writers, trade unionists, playwrights, actors, artists and journalists, men like Walt Lippmann and Ed Murrow[33] – despite the caricatures of Bevan as anti-American. Foot remarks that 'only on rare occasions were visitors invited for a political purpose ... the preference was for the company of those who did not know the latest manoeuvres at Westminster'.[34]

The life of the intellect but not one divorced from the senses or emotion was pure oxygen for Bevan. It was intensified by his autodidact background on which he was balanced and thoughtful in his own writing and analysis. 'Trained instruction often makes for a wider mobility in thought and action ... but what the self-educated learn they hold and what they hold is an illumination of their own experience.'[35] In Bevan's case this had included adolescent reading as diverse as Eugene Debs and Jack London courtesy of Tredegar's Workmen's Library – 'everything I could lay my hands on'.[36] In Bevan there was a balance, perfectly poised but rare in a front-rank politician, of a man fascinated and refreshed by the continued interface between concept and ideals and pragmatic action. That creative tension is elegantly described by Foot: 'He knew that his real treasure was his mind; he was resolved to keep it fresh and young and never to bury it in a cemetery of blue books and committee meetings.'

Arguably part of the price Bevan had to pay for that balance was never leading the party he loved and captivated. But I feel it was one he would have been happy to render rather than to be seen as one of those whom the poet C. Day Lewis characterised in the 1930s – 'consider these, for we have condemned them […] who steer by no star, whose moon means nothing'.

I'm conscious that in exploring some of the less familiar aspects of Bevan's political and inner life I have not been able to cover in detail the set pieces and narrative controversies of his career. And I wish I had room to say more about his remarkable partnership with Jennie Lee – an extraordinary meeting of minds and souls that brought forward not just one but two great institutional and cultural legacies to contemporary Britain: the NHS and the Open University. But as I worked in preparing this lecture and looked at some of the other, perhaps lesser commented on, elements of his make-up as a politician and parliamentarian, I found them not only intriguing in their own right but also speaking powerfully to us in our own times. The details of conflicts about rearming post-war Germany, frenzied debates about the future of nationalisation, the internecine conflicts between Bevanites and Gaitskellites at party conferences and in the NEC inevitably risk – with the passage of time – for many of today's generation resembling Milton's weariness of history that has to chronicle the wars of 'kites and crows fighting in the air'.

But because Bevan's political philosophy was so powerfully embedded in his understanding of human beings as individuals, hopes, fears and aspirations, so much of what he says in those areas still cuts to the heart of our preoccupations today. Here is his observation on political and economic crisis from *In Place of Fear*.

There is one situation fatal for a democratic Parliament – that is helplessness in face of economic difficulties. Parliament does not

keep the ring – Parliament is one of the contestants in the ring
... autarky we cannot achieve, especially in Britain, we cannot
insulate ourselves but we can cushion the shocks.[37]

How the Nye Bevan who wrote of how 'the fashionable maga-
zines and newspapers neon-light the petty foibles of the well to do'
might have smiled and engaged, as while we sit here, Parliament,
politicians and the judiciary find themselves enmeshed with
footballers and TV celebrities in a merry-go-round of tweet-
ing, super-injunctions and fierce debates about privacy and
public interest.

Yet for all that, I am still speaking about a man born in the year
of Victoria's Diamond Jubilee and sent down the pit as a four-
teen-year-old in the same year as the game-changing Parliament
Act which your Centenary Lectures, Mr Speaker, are marking.
Meanwhile we here in our twenty-first-century Parliament wres-
tle with our own challenges: how we regain trust and reconnect
our institutions with the public. As we excavate the very bedrock
of our society to see if it is or can be big, good or otherwise, we
fret about whether our new virtual and digital worlds coarsen or
empower our relationships, public and private. We count the cost
of skewed values in banking and business, and the economic and
social dislocation they have brought both in Britain and globally,
as they did in 1929 when Nye Bevan entered Parliament as MP
for Ebbw Vale. Who in such a context would lightly ignore the
challenging words from his final conference speech to Labour at
Blackpool in November 1959 – just months before his terminal
cancer laid him low, in Foot's poignant phrase, 'like a great tree
hacked down wantonly in, full leaf'? Here *are* the words Bevan
uttered in my constituency just over half a century ago:

What is the lesson for us? It is that we must enlarge and expand
our personalities... This so-called affluent society is an ugly society still. It is a vulgar society. It is a meretricious society. It is a
society in which priorities have gone all wrong.[38]

There he goes again – making the smooth place rough. It was a quality Bevan's contemporaries recognised and admired in the assessments that followed his death in July 1960. Let me, as a former editor of *History Today*, quote what the commentator Henry Fairlie wrote of him in the magazine's obituary piece on Bevan in October that year:

> I know of no politician of his generation by nature so inclined to treat the British people as adults. Bevan's true genius was as the perpetual enemy of the complacency that affects free and apparently prosperous societies.

At the start of this lecture, I sought to dissociate Bevan from the false glitter of the overused word 'icon'. But in that word's original Greek meaning – simply being an image – he is a true icon, a true image, not a false god. He points us to an image of the politician, the public figure, the parliamentarian who does need to have a hinterland, to care passionately about human sensitivities and values, about the individual as well as the institution, about the local as well as the national, about the politics of connection.

Those are lights for all times – not least ours – and for all in this Parliament, whatever their political persuasions. And they continue to make Nye Bevan the great and relevant man for all seasons that he was – and still is.

1   Michael Foot, *Aneurin Bevan*, Vol. I: *1897–1945* (London: MacGibbon & Kee, 1962), *Aneurin Bevan*, Vol. 2: *1945–1960* (London: Davis-Poynter, 1973, Paladin 1975).
2   Aneurin Bevan, *In Place of Fear* (London: Heinemann, 1952), p.5.
3   Bevan, *In Place of Fear*, p.5.
4   Bevan, *In Place of Fear*, p.6.
5   Bevan, *In Place of Fear*, p.7.
6   Bevan, *In Place of Fear*, p.10.
7   Bevan, *In Place of Fear*, p.11.
8   Foot, *Aneurin Bevan*, Vol. I: *1897–1945* (London: Paladin edn, 1975), p.164.
9   Now the Localism Act 2011.

10   See John Campbell, *Nye Bevan: A Biography* (London: Hodder & Stoughton, 1994), p.56.

11   Quoted in Foot, *Aneurin Bevan*, Vol. I: *1897–1945*, p.164.

12   Foot, *Aneurin Bevan*, Vol. I: *1897–1945*, p.239.

13   Bevan, *In Place of Fear*, p.1.

14   Bevan, *In Place of Fear*, p.14.

15   Foot, *Aneurin Bevan*, Vol. 2: *1945–60*, pp.177–91.

16   The Health and Social Care Bill introduced in 2010 encountered significant parliamentary opposition and was subject to an unprecedented 'natural break' during its passage.

17   Foot, *Aneurin Bevan*, Vol. 2: *1945–60*, p.176.

18   Foot, *Aneurin Bevan*, Vol. I: *1897–1945*, p.324.

19   Foot, *Aneurin Bevan*, Vol. I: *1897–1945*, p.330.

20   Foot, *Aneurin Bevan*, Vol. I: *1897–1945*, p.263.

21   Bevan, *In Place of Fear*, p.13.

22   Quoted in Foot, *Aneurin Bevan*, Vol. I: *1897–1945*, p.322.

23   Foot, *Aneurin Bevan*, Vol. 2: *1945–60*, p.22.

24   Bevan, *In Place of Fear*, pp.166–7.

25   Bevan, *In Place of Fear*, p.168.

26   Bevan, *In Place of Fear*, p.167.

27   Reproduced in Foot, *Aneurin Bevan*, Vol. 2: *1945–60*, p.368, n.1.

28   Foot, *Aneurin Bevan*, Vol. I: *1897–1945*, p.195.

29   On their life together, see Jennie Lee, *My Life with Nye* (London: Jonathan Cape, 1980).

30   Foot, *Aneurin Bevan*, Vol. I: *1897–1945*, p.193.

31   Bevan, *In Place of Fear*, p.51.

32   Bevan, *In Place of Fear*, p.50.

33   Foot, *Aneurin Bevan*, Vol. I: *1897–1945*, p.465.

34   Foot, *Aneurin Bevan*, Vol. I: *1897–1945*, p.192.

35   Bevan, *In Place of Fear*, p.18.

36   Bevan, *In Place of Fear*, p.17.

37   Bevan, *In Place of Fear*, p.29.

38   Labour Party Conference 1959. Quoted in Foot, *Aneurin Bevan*, Vol. 2: *1945–60*, pp.644–5. See also Campbell, *Nye Bevan: A Biography*, p.362.

Enoch Powell

Philip Norton
Delivered on 14 June 2011

Biographical note

Enoch Powell

John Enoch Powell, born 16 June 1912, son of Albert Enoch Powell, of Stechford. Educated at King Edward's School, Birmingham, Trinity College, Cambridge. Married Margaret Pamela (Pam), daughter of Lt-Col. L. K. E. Wilson. Fellow of Trinity College, Cambridge, 1934–38; Professor of Greek, University of Sydney, 1937–39; Served 1939–45, Royal Warwickshire Regiment and General Staff; rose from Private to Brigadier. Conservative Research Department 1945–50. Conservative MP for Wolverhampton South-West 1950–74; Ulster Unionist MP for South Down 1974–87. Director, London Municipal Society 1952–55. Parliamentary Secretary, Ministry of Housing and Local Government 1955–57; Financial Secretary to the Treasury 1957–58; Minister of Health 1960–63 (in Cabinet 1962–63). MBE 1943, Privy Counsellor 1960. Died 8 February 1998.

A distinguished academic and soldier, Powell was an outstanding debater. With Iain Macleod, he refused in 1963 to serve in the Cabinet under Alec Douglas-Home. He was noted for taking an independent line, even when in the shadow Cabinet. He shot to national fame with a speech on immigration in 1968, using a classical allusion ('the River Tiber foaming with much blood') to warn of the danger of continuing immigration, a speech that triggered his dismissal from the shadow Cabinet and mass marches in support of his views. He combined being a controversial figure nationally with a devotion to the House of Commons. He refused to seek re-election as a Conservative in 1974 and served as an Ulster Unionist from 1974 until defeated in 1987.

T here are many here who knew Enoch Powell better than I did. Although I first met him, very briefly, at a party conference when I was a young schoolboy, I got to know him towards the end of his period in the House of Commons. He spoke regularly to my students: indeed, he was something of an annual fixture. I cannot recall an occasion when he declined an invitation to speak and, once he made a commitment, he stuck to it. He was, as Michael Foot observed, the soul of honour and loyalty.[1]

There were arguably two Enoch Powells. There was the public figure and the private man, neatly illustrated in a recollection of Jeremy Paxman of his first encounter with Powell:

'Are you frightened of my husband?' his wife asked me when I was sent as a very young and inexperienced reporter, to interview him. Yes, I replied, aware, like all of my generation, that this was the man who had stabbed his party leader, Edward Heath, in the back in the 1974 elections, and, most notoriously, had prophesied race war in a speech talking of 'the River Tiber foaming with much blood'. 'Oh dear,' she said, 'everyone is. And he's such a sweetie.' And when we came to sit down and talk, indeed he was – courteous, charming and thoughtful.[2]

All those who knew him would agree that Enoch Powell was a remarkable individual. Born in Stechford, Birmingham, on 16 June 1912, he was the only child of schoolteachers Albert and Ellen Powell. His mother was an amazing woman: she taught herself Greek and gave up teaching in order to devote herself to her son. The young John Enoch – Jack as he was known in the family – was soon learning Greek and proved an insular and studious pupil. A parallel is sometimes drawn with John Stuart Mill, but Powell was a willing student and happy in his home life. His parents were devoted to him and he to them.

Educated at King Edward's High School, Birmingham, and Trinity College, Cambridge, he gained all the prizes available as he went through school and university. He picked up sufficient scholarships for him to cover all the costs of his education and to have something left over.

He had a stellar career or rather careers. I begin with the career that he did not pursue. He did contemplate pursuing a career in music but then decided against it. Had he pursued it, then Jack Powell may have become this country's leading clarinettist.

In the event, his formal career, by which I mean his paid employment, had three stages. Before the war, he was a classics scholar, during the war he was a soldier and after it he was a politician. He excelled in all three, though formally his achievements were greater in the first two than the third. As a scholar and a soldier, he set records in a way that he did not do in politics.

After graduation, he remained at Cambridge, having accepted a fellowship at Trinity College. Not letting his age get in the way, he applied for chairs. Though his age counted against him in England, it was not a barrier to being offered a chair at the University of Sydney, where in 1937 he became Professor of Greek, making him, at the age of twenty-five, the youngest professor in the Empire. He was subsequently offered a chair at Durham, but the war intervened.

He was a classics scholar of some distinction. His acclaimed *Lexicon to Herodotus* was commenced before he graduated. He revised Stuart-Jones's edition of Thucydides's *Historiae* for Oxford University Press. It was his early study of Thucydides that led to the use of his middle name. Because there was an established scholar, John U. Powell, who was a specialist on Thucydides, Jack decided that in order to avoid confusion he would henceforth no longer sign himself as J. E. Powell but as J. Enoch Powell.

His *Lexicon* was published in 1938 and his *History of Herodotus* in 1939, both by Cambridge University Press. However, he was not defined solely by his formal studies. He was much more than a classics scholar; he was also a poet, historian and biblical scholar. Indeed, he defined himself as much as a poet as a scholar. He published two volumes of poetry before the war and two more after. Historical works came later in life. He co-authored *The House of Lords in the Middle Ages*, published in 1968, the result of two decades of research, and penned a biography of Joseph Chamberlain, published in 1977. After he left the House of Commons, he returned to an early interest in the St Matthew Gospel – his controversial *The Evolution of the Gospel* was published in 1994 – and in St John's Gospel.

His studies were facilitated by the fact that he was a linguist. When he turned his studies to a subject that required or would benefit from command of a particular language, he learned the language. He spoke eight languages but by the end of his life he had reportedly learned twelve.

His classics career came to an end on the outbreak of war. He had recognised for some time that war was inevitable and had prepared for it. When war was declared, he returned to England to enlist in the Royal Warwickshire Regiment. When denied the opportunity to enlist as an Englishman, because he had no previous military training, he joined as an Australian.

Throughout the war, he was keen to see combat, but he was always denied the opportunity. His intellectual and language skills meant that he was too valuable to intelligence to be let loose on the front. He did push for a combat role, on one occasion rushing to see Orde Wingate when he was in Cairo, but was used instead to assess intelligence reports and contribute to military planning. In North Africa, he was astute in his assessment of Rommel's capabilities. His task, as he recalled, 'was to try to see the situation as Rommel saw it'.[3] Such was his role in contributing to Allied success that he was awarded the military MBE 'for gallant and distinguished services in the Middle East'. It was while in the Middle East that he developed his lifelong scepticism of the United States and its intentions towards Britain, becoming convinced that the destruction of the British Empire was a clear American goal.

He was then posted to India where he served on the South-East Asia Command planning staff and helped craft the plans for invading Burma. He became committed to India. As Simon Heffer records of his stay in the country, by 1944

> he had begun to feel a massive affinity with the Indian people, and a deep sense that Britain and India were made to be together, to extend civilisation together. India had begun to humanise him, to take him out of himself.[4]

In order to facilitate his understanding of the country, he promptly set about learning Urdu. He also saw a major role for himself in the future of India, wishing to become Viceroy.

Powell, though, is best remembered for his rapid promotion, all the more remarkable because at times he was prepared to decline promotion in order to undertake a task that he preferred. His willingness to decline a post is something to which we shall return. Having started as a Private, he rose through the ranks. By the end of 1942 he was already a Lieutenant-Colonel and in March 1944 was promoted Colonel as Assistant Director of Military Intelligence. He was thirty-one. He then achieved the rank of Brigadier, aged thirty-two. He had predicted that the war would last ten years and that he would end it as a General. Had it lasted ten, one suspects he would indeed have become General Powell.

There is no doubt as to Powell's phenomenal achievement, not least given that he had no military background. He was exceptional though not unique in rising through the ranks in wartime from Private to Brigadier. Another who did so was Fitzroy Maclean, who also saw parliamentary service; indeed was already, from

1941, a Conservative MP. Maclean, incidentally, did see combat, of a rather clandestine variety, and is thought by some to be the person on whom Ian Fleming modelled James Bond.

With his promotion, Powell also became one of the youngest Brigadiers in the British Army. He was beaten to the accolade of being the youngest by Michael Calvert, an apparently fearless soldier who was known as 'Mad Mike', who fought in Burma under Wingate. He was a year younger than Powell but achieved promotion to acting Brigadier in 1943, aged thirty, and Brigadier in March 1944.[5]

Maclean and Calvert achieved promotion because of their exceptional fighting skills. Powell was on his own in being promoted because of his intelligence skills. All three had in common that they were unconventional and free-thinking individuals.

Powell was thus a remarkable academic and a remarkable soldier. Once war was over, the third phase of his career began. Having been a professor and Brigadier, he now set about the task of becoming a parliamentarian. He saw himself instinctively as a Tory. Having looked up Conservative Central Office in the telephone directory, he turned up in full uniform to offer his services to the party. He was appointed to the parliamentary secretariat and then the research department, where he worked alongside Reginald Maudling and Iain Macleod. He contested the safe Labour seat of Normanton in a by-election in 1947 but had difficulty in then being adopted for a winnable seat, his background and his rather austere manner counting against him.[6] After nineteen unsuccessful bids for other seats, he was adopted for the new, notionally Labour but winnable seat of Wolverhampton South-West, which he duly won in the general election of 1950 with a majority of 691.

His start was somewhat inauspicious: *The Times Guide to the House of Commons* got his details right but published someone else's photograph. He also had an early spat with some members of the local party, his rather military approach to organisation clashing with the norms of a voluntary association. The dispute was soon resolved and he was to represent the constituency until February 1974, when he declined to seek re-election. His majority at the 1970 general election had been 14,467. A committed Unionist, he returned to the Commons in the October 1974 election as Ulster Unionist MP for South Down, serving until losing the seat by 731 votes in 1987.

During his time in the House, he achieved ministerial office but relative to his earlier careers, his achievements were modest. The reasons for this I shall explore later. He served as Parliamentary Secretary at the Ministry of Housing and Local Government, from 1955 to 1957, as Financial Secretary to the Treasury from 1957 to 1958 and as Minister of Health from 1960 to 1963. He held no ministerial office after the age of fifty-one.

On the face of it, he was not a politician of the front rank, yet he proved to be one of the most controversial politicians of his generation as well as an outstanding parliamentarian.

To the public, he was a politician who made his name through his 'rivers of blood' speech on immigration – or rather against immigration, warning in dire terms of the consequences of unchecked immigration. Delivered in Birmingham on Saturday 20 April 1968, it was a speech that both made him and destroyed him – he became a national figure and a political pariah in the course of a few sentences. A classical allusion to Virgil, saying that the Tiber would foam with much blood, both gave the press a distinctive peg on which to hang the story and the party leader, Edward Heath, a reason to dismiss him from the shadow Cabinet. To those within Westminster, he was an assiduous Member of the House, willing to engage with anyone who sought him out, and one of the finest debaters of his generation.

What I propose to do in the time available is to focus on one part of his career – the third – but the one most in keeping with this series of lectures. Enoch Powell was a man of passion and firm beliefs. He had a particular attachment to institutions as the basis of authority, but there were two in particular that he loved. Indeed, unusually for him, he used the same phrase about both, saying that he took to each like a duck to water. He said it on a BBC *Panorama* programme in 1968 of his time in the army, and in an interview on Radio Clyde in 1977 on the House of Commons.[7]

His love of the Commons was not born of some early attachment. His desire to become an MP was essentially instrumental. He wanted to be elected to Parliament to fight for the Empire and especially India. Burke had said that the keys to India were to be found not in Calcutta or Delhi but on the dispatch box of the House of Commons, so Powell headed in the direction of Westminster. However, as he set out on his quest, the cause for which he wished to fight was lost. But by then, he was already attending debates in the House of Commons – albeit then meeting in the chamber of the House of Lords – and his love affair with the institution began. When he entered the Commons he was already thirty-seven but he was to become one of the outstanding parliamentarians of the latter half of the twentieth century.

But why is that? Powell, as I have indicated, never held any of the great offices of state. He never led his party. Though he was Minister of Health for three years, only one of those was spent in the Cabinet. From his curriculum vitae, one would have difficulty discerning why he gained an outstanding parliamentary reputation. Indeed, his entries in *Dod's Parliamentary Companion* – right up until 1987, the last edition in which he had an entry – were short and gave little away. Perhaps his entry was most revealing for the fact that, unlike many, he published his home address and telephone number even though, more than most, he had good cause not to do so. A good number of Members had longer entries, and some – not least those who held high ministerial office – ostensibly more impressive entries, yet many, unlike Powell, are no longer remembered.

Nicholas Soames, in his outstanding lecture on his grandfather, recalls the observation of Clement Attlee who, when asked if Churchill had been a great parliamentarian, replied: 'No, he was a great parliamentary figure.' There have been some great parliamentary figures. There have been some distinguished parliamentarians. Edward Heath I would put in this category. He was a great performer from below the gangway in his later years, but he used the House of Commons rather than embraced it. He was not alone.

Heath, like a number of others over the years, could deliver powerful speeches in the House and draw Members to the chamber, but they did not quite match Powell. Powell could hold the Commons. As Michael Foot – who also deserves the accolade of a great parliamentarian – wrote of Powell in 1986:

> in the House of Commons, he can compel attention, even from those who detest what he appears to say or stand for, as no one else has done since Aneurin Bevan, almost alone, faced the all-powerful Winston Churchill with the wartime parliament at his back. To elevate Enoch Powell into such company may at first seem a sacrilege, but most of those who have sat in the parliaments of the past two decades would not dissent.[8]

My contention is that Powell was a great parliamentarian but not necessarily a great politician. He achieved some political successes but one of the very attributes that put him among the parliamentary greats meant that he was not going to be among those who achieved their principal political aims. He had some tactical victories, he had a notable influence on others (not least Margaret Thatcher), but he never won, or was not directly and solely responsible for winning, any of his major political wars.

What is it, then, that makes Enoch Powell, or indeed anyone, a great parliamentarian? I suggest that there are three essential attributes, each of which is necessary but not sufficient. Many eminent parliamentarians have one or two of these attributes, but Enoch Powell, I shall argue, embraced all three.

Love of Parliament

The first attribute is a sheer commitment to, indeed a love of, Parliament.

In an interview in 1977, Powell spoke of his election to the Commons in 1950 and his discovery that debate in the House was congenial. 'It was', he said,

> an environment so attractive, an environment so congenial to me that I remember distinctly the sensation which I had on each of the three occasions when I refused government office... I remember on each occasion the sensation when I re-entered the House of Commons after notifying my decision. It was like coming home to one's mother. It was as though I said, 'I am back again; I am back where I belong, I have not gone away, I am back.'[9]

As a parliamentarian, he immersed himself in the history of the institution and its procedures. He was a scholar of Parliament and a deft user of its procedures. It is remarkable how few parliamentarians steep themselves in the pages of *Erskine May*. Powell knew the institution. He may have had an idealised view of it, but he knew its rules.

He was a great believer in the House, which to him meant the chamber. This was the place where the government spoke to the people and the people, through their representatives, spoke to government.[10] It was the arena in which government was tested and where the great debates of the nation took place. It was where government was both sustained and challenged. Ministers were tested in the chamber. The government had to persuade the House and maintain its confidence.

With Michael Foot, he was wary of anything that could be seen to take Members away from the chamber. To him, select committees were a way of keeping Members occupied on the detail, focusing on the means rather than the ends. If he were a Prime Minister who wanted to deprive the House of political effectiveness, 'I would,' he said, 'encourage the House of Commons to set up as many committees as possible. My object would be, especially in the afternoons and evenings, to have hon. Members busily and I am sure happily employed upstairs.'[11]

He was none too keen either on Members having their own offices, seeing them also as a means of distracting Members from attendance in the chamber. He declined to have an office. For him, a seat in the Library was adequate for when he was not in the chamber. He was rarely to be found other than in the chamber or the Library, or striding between the two.

The chamber was the beating heart of the Commons and its effectiveness rested on the will of its Members and their capacity to employ its procedures. Powell did not simply proclaim the importance of procedure: he used it to effect. One of the most notable occasions was when he joined with Michael Foot and other Members to scupper the Parliament (No. 2) Bill, introduced in 1968 to reform the House of Lords.[12] For Powell, attached to the existing institution and steeped in its history, it went too far and for Foot, an abolitionist, it did not go far enough. The measure was introduced after earlier cross-party talks had been discontinued. It was not opposed by the opposition, which permitted a free vote. However, as a measure of constitutional significance committee stage was taken on the floor of the House. Fearing they could lose, the government did not seek to impose a guillotine. It was thus at the mercy of Powell and Foot and their supporters. As Alexander and Watkins recorded, they 'employed brilliant tactics'.[13]

Powell's contributions were erudite and frequent. He argued that the hereditary House could be replaced only by a House of nomination or election. On an elected House, he raised an objection that has resonated since. 'How can the same electorate,' he asked, 'be represented in two ways so that the two sets of representatives can conflict and disagree with one another?' In debating an amendment to Clause Two of the Bill, he argued that the government had set out to create a chamber that was both independent and subservient. He later attacked the calculations for attendance requirements for voting peers, arguing that the government had made a mistake in their own arithmetic.

Government MPs grew increasingly resentful at having to sit late and take part in frequent divisions.[14] After thirteen days in committee and having only just completed five clauses, the government failed to mobilise 100 MPs to carry a closure motion.[15] The Cabinet took the decision not to proceed with the Bill.

'The destruction of the Parliament (No. 2) Bill,' declared Simon Heffer, 'was perhaps the greatest triumph of Powell's political career, and it served to rehabilitate him in the Commons.'[16] Notably, though, as Powell conceded, it was a team effort. The Bill was not particularly wanted by MPs and this, Powell recorded, made it possible, as he put it,

> for a relatively small number of Members, who constituted them-selves the spokesmen of that general feeling, to use – not to abuse, but use legitimately – the proper procedures of the House so as to render progress so slow that the government had to conclude that the game was not on.[17]

The key point, as Powell recognised, is that knowledge and use of procedure are essential weapons in the armoury of backbench-ers. The Parliament (No. 2) Bill was not proceeded with even though the government never lost a division.

His love of the institution encompassed his commitment to his constituency and hence his constituents. He was an assiduous constituency Member. Unlike many MPs in the 1950s, he took a flat in the constituency and, after his marriage, bought a house. Dealing with constituency correspondence became part of his daily routine. He became entrenched in Wolverhampton. When he became the Member for South Down, he applied himself assiduously to the constituency. Though there were tensions with others in the Ulster Unionist Party – he supported integration, not devolution – he worked hard as a constituency Member, visiting usually at least every other weekend, and gaining the respect of people throughout the constituency.

This experience also points to another requirement for anyone wishing to make their mark in Westminster: that is, secure your base. The constituency holds the ultimate power of political life and death. Goodwill is an enormously valuable resource at times of trouble. Powell's frequent rebellions under the Heath government led to the withdrawal of the whip being contemplated. This was not pursued not least because it was recognised it would serve little purpose: it would give him even greater publicity and he was secure in his constituency.

Over-riding commitment to one's beliefs

A great parliamentarian is one who has a clear belief or set of beliefs and is prepared to express them, indeed fight for them, even at the expense of office and in the face of a baying mob. Powell expressed his beliefs, firmly and unflinchingly, even if they were unpalatable to his audience. As Minister of Health, he faced down a pay claim from nurses. As Patrick Cosgrave observed, 'This was the first evidence the general public had of his flint-like capacity to defy received opinion.'[18] He declined to hold a public inquiry into the effects of the thalidomide drug. He faced the wrath of his fellow MPs in arguing against a rise in MPs' pay. He opposed increases until electors had an opportunity to express their views and he never accepted an increase until a general election had intervened. In 1978, as Roy Lewis noted, 'He debated this principle singlehandedly against the entire House when it moved for large increases of salaries and expenses on the plea of rising living and professional costs.'[19] Powell was having none of it, and for good measure was also against full-time secretaries and researchers.

He faced the wrath of his own party in 1974 when he declined to stand again as a Conservative MP, denouncing the basis for the premature election as 'essentially fraudulent' and recommending that electors vote for the party committed to renegotiating the treaty of Brussels and submitting it to the British people, in effect the Labour Party. He regarded the issue of the European Community as on a higher plane than loyalty to the party and Labour were offering a referendum on continued membership. Having been credited with facilitating a Conservative victory in 1970, he now had the dubious distinction of having contributed to the return of a Labour government. It was not the first time he provided some support to the Labour Party: he voted Labour in 1945, at least by proxy, in protest at the Munich agreement:[20] he had been vehemently anti-Chamberlain. Nor was it the last. He and Ulster Unionist leader Jim Molyneaux negotiated with Jim Callaghan over parliamentary votes, achieving in return an increase in the number of Members returned from Northern Ireland, and in 1987 he advocated voting Labour because of the party's policy on unilateral nuclear disarmament;[21] he was a longstanding critic of holding nuclear weapons, not being able to conceive an occasion when the UK would be prepared to use them.

He was prepared to fight for his beliefs. They came first. As Tony Blair recorded, 'There was no doubting the strength of his convictions or their sincerity, or his tenacity in pursuing them, regardless of his own political self-interest.'[22] The career came second. He would have liked to have got further up the greasy pole of ministerial office. He would have liked to lead his party. He stood in the party leadership election in 1965, garnering a modest fifteen votes. But his beliefs came before ambition. He was not prepared to pursue office if it meant sacrificing what he stood for. He was not, as has been suggested, a natural resigner. As he pointed out, he only resigned once, though he did decline office on three occasions. The resignation and one of his refusals to serve were major political events.

The resignation came in 1958. Unlike his refusals to accept office, this was on an issue of policy. As Financial Secretary to the Treasury, Powell had pursued the need to reduce government expenditure, a pursuit endorsed by the Chancellor Peter Thorneycroft. When the Cabinet failed to agree to the necessary cuts, all three Treasury ministers – Thorneycroft, Powell and the Economic Secretary Nigel Birch – resigned. Powell is sometimes seen as the guiding hand behind Thorneycroft, but the Chancellor appeared to require little persuading. The Treasury ministers, unlike their officials, were convinced of the need to act and, faced by a Prime Minister unwilling to take the steps they regarded as necessary, were prepared to leave government. Macmillan weathered the storm, but the incident was perhaps the first clear indication of Powell's willingness to put principles before ambition, but one masked by association with two equally principled colleagues.

The following year, Macmillan offered him a junior post in the education ministry. Powell declined it because Thorneycroft was not being offered anything. Powell eventually returned to government in 1960, when he was made Minister of Health outside the Cabinet. He joined the Cabinet in 1962, but his place at the Cabinet table proved short-lived. Macmillan's resignation in 1963 created a political crisis in government and a moral crisis for Powell. He regarded the way in which Macmillan handled the succession as wholly dishonest. He was no great adherent to Butskellism but he felt 'Rab' Butler was entitled to the leadership. A group of pro-Butler ministers met at Powell's house and made their views known to the Chief Whip. However, their efforts were frustrated by Macmillan, who moved with some speed to advise the sovereign to send for Lord Home, and by Butler's agreement to serve under Home. Though harbouring no personal animosity to Home, both Powell and Iain Macleod declined on principle to serve in his Cabinet.

Again, Powell was not alone in taking a stand, but he was clearly exceptional in his willingness to give up or decline office on grounds of policy and honour. At different points, what otherwise may have been a glowing ministerial career was deflected by an unwillingness to compromise and to put career first. There was no equivalent here of a rapid rise from Private to Brigadier, not because he was not qualified for such a trajectory but because he prevented it by his own decisions.

He expressed his views regardless of their consequences. Some believe his 'rivers of blood' speech in 1968 was a calculated bid for the party leadership. He denied this. 'You don't calculate,' he said. 'Politicians are like seeds and can't control where the

wind will take them.'[23] Similarly, his speeches in the general election campaign of 1970 have been seen by some as designed to
position him ready to challenge for the party leadership in the
event of the party losing the election. If he did calculate, as T. E.
Utley believed he did, then at times he got it very wrong. He was
operating on a very different plane to others.

As Norman Shrapnel observed, 'He was indeed a hard
man to understand, and harder still to fit into current political
categories.'[24] His body of beliefs was distinctive. He was not a
Thatcherite. Thatcherism blended economic liberalism with
social conservatism. Thatcher followed Powell in the economic
sphere but not in the social. He was an opponent of capital
punishment and supported reform of the law on homosexuality. A number of commentators argue that Powell generated an
eponymous philosophy. He had supporters – Powellites for want
of a better phrase – but not, I would argue, an 'ism' – there was no
Powellism. He had beliefs which in their totality did not cohere in
an over-arching philosophy and certainly not one to which others
subscribed. He had a core set of beliefs which were shared by a
number of Conservatives, but they did not necessarily follow him
in all his beliefs. Iain Macleod put it rather pithily: 'He does not fit
into any political slot. He is just Enoch Powell.'[25]

He was, in essence, a Tory neo-liberal. He had a Tory attachment, a passionate attachment, to institutions; they bestow
authority and are the product of prescription. They are greater
than the conceit of individuals who believe they know best and
have some grand design to achieve change. His attachment to
institutions and procedures was profound. He regarded his best
parliamentary speech as that he made on the Royal Titles Bill
in 1953, describing as 'evil' changes to the style of the United
Kingdom,[26] and one of the most bitter exchanges he had with
Edward Heath when he was in his shadow Cabinet was over
Black Rod interrupting the Commons to summon the Members
to hear the declaration of Royal Assent. Heath wanted to end
what he called 'ceremonial and mummery'. Powell apparently

pointed out that the formula of words Black Rod used went back to the Parliament of Carlisle of 1307 and were ancient even then.[27]

His scepticism as to man's reason extended to the economic sphere. To Powell, the market was the result of forces beyond the control of man. To him, a prices and incomes policy was the attempt, a futile attempt, to impose some grand design. He described the Macmillan era as:

the age of Franco-Macmillanite planning, it was the age (the early age) of prices and incomes policy. I had found this profoundly repugnant, because it jarred with another Tory prejudice that, upon the whole, things are wiser than people, that institutions are wiser than their members and that the nation is wiser than those who comprise it at any specific moment. The notion that there could be vested in ascertainable individuals in government wisdom sufficient to lay out and dispose the effort and resources of society as they expressed themselves in prices, was to me deeply repugnant.

He went on: 'So there started a period in which I was formulating to my fellow countrymen the doctrine of the market and following that doctrine as far as it would go in all directions.'[28] It was a doctrine that not only brought him into conflict with Macmillan but also later Edward Heath.

He was driven also by a belief in Empire and nation, in effect British greatness. He opposed the demise of Empire – but once it had gone he realised there was little scope for retaining its vestigial elements – and he was vehemently opposed to moves toward European integration. He wanted to defend the unity of the United Kingdom and protect it from the encroachment of the European Community. He had not initially opposed the application for membership, seeing it as a means of facilitating free trade, but he soon came to the view that there was more to it than economics. The European Community was a threat to national identity and independence. For him, it was pre-eminently a political and not an economic issue. He did not believe that the United Kingdom should be subservient to the European Community or, for that matter, to the United States or any other external power.

His enunciation of his beliefs, or at least some of them, acted as a clarion call to others. He was a leader, but by voice and not by organisation. He did not draw around him anything approaching an organised body of believers. During his time in the Conservative Research Department, he was described by Iain Macleod as 'memorably unapproachable'.[29] (That, though, did not apply to the secretary, who became Mrs Powell.) In developing his arguments, he was, in the words of John Biffen, 'self-contained'.[30] Michael Foot characterised him as a 'loner', which he meant in a descriptive and not a pejorative sense, denoting people who act alone and who in the last resort make up their own minds on great questions.[31]

Powell argued his case and variously carried some parliamentary colleagues with him. In the 1970–74 parliament, he led by voice and his vote followed the voice. He was a vehement critic of the European Communities Bill, the government's U-turns on industry and the economy, and its policies on Northern Ireland. He also opposed the government on Rhodesian sanctions and on the 1972 immigration rules, on which the government suffered the most important of its six defeats.

The Parliament witnessed a sea-change in Members' voting behaviour. Contrary to some claims, the 1950s were not a period of the independent Member willing to stand up to the whips. Rather, they constituted the high point of parliamentary cohesion.[32] When Powell abstained in the vote on the Schuman Plan in 1950, shortly after entering the House, his action was somewhat exceptional for a backbench MP. That changed, especially in the 1970s, with Powell to the fore. He was the leading Tory rebel of the Parliament. He voted against the Heath government on no fewer than 115 occasions.[33] Though no one else came close to matching that figure, in all bar six of the divisions he was joined by one or more colleagues on the Conservative benches. Indeed, the Powellites were the principal but by no means the only rebels in that Parliament. The Parliament set a post-war record for intra-party dissent in the division lobbies, though recent Parliaments have matched or surpassed it.

Powell was one of fifteen Conservative MPs to vote against the government on the Second Reading of the European Communities Bill in 1972, which Heath had made a vote of confidence, the first time in post-war history that Conservative MPs had voted against their own government in a vote of confidence. Five others abstained. The government – which had achieved a majority of 112 in the vote on the principle of entry the previous October – survived with a majority of eight, courtesy of six Liberal MPs and abstentions by four Labour Members.

It was not just the policies that the government pursued that attracted the unprecedented level of backbench opposition but the intransigent manner in which Heath pursued them.[34] The period was exceptional because of the combination of Heath's premiership and Powell's presence on the Conservative benches. Heath ceased to be Prime Minister in 1974 and party leader in 1975 but by then Powell had left the Conservative benches. The Powellite era was over.

Furthermore, although Powell was rarely alone in his frequent opposition, there were few Tory MPs who followed him consistently in not supporting the government in the division lobbies. I analysed every vote in the Parliament, but I focused especially on eight issues on which Powell opposed the government by vote or abstention, covering the economy, home affairs, foreign policy, the European Community and two free-standing issues. Not a single MP followed him in his stance on all eight and only fourteen followed him on six or seven of them. The party remained a party of tendencies rather than factions.[35] Nonetheless, forty-four could be classified as Powellites in following him on four or more of the issues.[36]

Powell's commitment – his unswerving commitment – to his

beliefs was what denied him the accolade of a great politician. He applied his logical mind to issues and pursued the logic wherever it took him. Paradoxically, he was very un-British in his approach to problem-solving. Britons characteristically take an empirical approach to problem-solving. The rationalist approach is regarded far more as a continental approach. According to Robert Dahl, 'While the empirical approach takes the attitude that if a program does not work in practice there must be something wrong about the theory, the rationalist will retort that what is true in theory must also be true in practice – that it is the practice, not the theory that is wrong.'[37]

Powell adopted the rationalist approach. He fought Nazism but he had a great admiration for German culture and indeed German intellectual rigour. His logic had him pursuing arguments that left others behind. What was right in logic was not necessarily acceptable politically. Macleod famously observed: 'I am a fellow-traveller but I prefer to get out one or two stops before the train crashes into the buffers at the terminus.'[38] Powell was well aware of his inability to temporise. There was no way he could have followed Butler in titling his memoirs *The Art of the Possible*, as he would readily have acknowledged. His would more likely have been *The Pursuit of Logic*.

Love of language
The third attribute is a love of language or at least a remarkable dexterity or superiority in the use of language. This can take three forms (or a combination of the three): humour, the telling phrase or the beautifully crafted speech.

It has been notable that the parliamentarians covered in this series have tended to employ humour. Churchill, Lloyd George, F. E. Smith and Aneurin Bevan were brilliant in their use of wit. They were also great wordsmiths – producing wonderful phrases which have entered the language – and could deliver memorable speeches, some from well-prepared scripts and others improvised.

Enoch Powell was distinctive in that he normally eschewed the use of wit. He certainly had a sense of humour and on occasion parts of a speech could evoke laughter, but he was not one to employ wit as a matter of course. This is borne out by a study of *The Oxford Dictionary of Humorous Quotations*. He rates only one entry. This contrasts notably with the parliamentarians covered in the preceding lectures. Even Nancy Astor rates two entries (both in the section on 'insults'). Nye Bevan, F. E. Smith, Lloyd George and Churchill each have entries in double figures.[39] Even Powell's entry appears almost for the sake of having one.

Contrast this with the number of entries he is accorded in *The Oxford Dictionary of Political Quotations*. Here he has twenty-one entries, way ahead of F. E. Smith and Nancy Astor, and not that far behind Bevan (with twenty-three) and Lloyd George (with thirty-one). Churchill is in a class of his own with 105. The essential point is that Powell was far more prone to deploy the telling phrase than he was a riveting and memorable witticism.

The point was picked up by *The Economist* in its obituary: 'There were not many jokes in a Powell speech,' it said, 'but the audience was held by its taut language delivered with passion.'[40] Powell chose his words to impact on the intellect. The memorable phrase was deployed often in the course of developing a beautifully crafted speech, compelling logic being expressed in precise and direct terms. 'There will never be anybody else so compelling as Enoch Powell,' declared Margaret Thatcher. 'He was magnetic. Listening to his speeches was an unforgettable privilege.'[41]

He was a fine parliamentary debater. He relished debate. In this respect he was like Churchill – but Lord Randolph rather than Winston. As Nicholas Soames said, Lord Randolph was the most brilliant platform speaker and parliamentary debater of the day. Powell was a latter-day Lord Randolph Churchill. He followed Churchill in being a persistent and telling critic of his party's leadership.

His speeches were normally delivered without notes. As John Biffen observed in his funeral oration, they needed no correction. The sentences came out perfectly formed. 'He was,' Biffen declared, 'a Hansard reporter's dream.'[42] His use of language was well captured by the *Daily Telegraph* which, in a leading article on Powell's death, emphasised his 'precision of language' and 'agility in debate' and continued:

> Powell will survive more surely than any other British politician of the twentieth century except Winston Churchill. His speeches and writings will be read so long as there exists a political and parliamentary culture in which speaking and writing matter. And if there comes a time when such a culture is all but destroyed, those brave few who wish to restore it will find in the thoughts of Enoch Powell something approaching their Bible.[43]

Some of his memorable phrases also are revealing about the man. When pressed on *Desert Island Discs* in 1989 as to how he would like to be remembered, he replied, 'I should like to have been killed in the war'. I put this alongside his more quoted observation, from his biography of Chamberlain, that 'all political careers, unless they are cut-off at some happy juncture, end in failure'. He would have preferred the death of a warrior (a not unprecedented theme among poets and indeed is to be found in one of his own poems), to go at the height of his powers, rather than endure the sunset of the ageing politician. Though not a fan of Macmillan's, he shared with him a sense of guilt at having survived a war – in Macmillan's case the First World War – when others of their generation had perished.

His beliefs and his capacity to express them so brilliantly led to some of the best speeches in the House of Commons in the latter half of the twentieth century. By common consent (though, as I have touched upon, not his own) his most compelling speech was that delivered in the early hours of 28 July 1959 on what happened in the Hola Camp in Kenya, where eleven Mau Mau detainees had been killed after refusing to work. The debate took place late at night. Powell was called shortly after 1.00 am but

there was a good attendance and his speech was devastating.
Denis Healey described it as 'the greatest parliamentary speech I
have ever heard'.[44] Responding to a Member who had described
those who died as sub-human, Powell declared: 'In general, I
would say that it is a fearful doctrine … to stand in judgement
on a fellow human being and to say, "Because he was such-and-
such, therefore the consequences which would otherwise flow
from his death should not flow."'[45] He attacked the argument that
because it was in Africa then different methods were acceptable:

> Nor can we ourselves pick and choose where and in what parts
> of the world we shall use this or that kind of stand. We cannot
> say, 'We will have African standards in Africa, Asian standards in
> Asia and perhaps British standards here at home.' We have not
> that choice to make. We must be consistent with ourselves every-
> where. All government, all influence of man upon man, rests
> upon opinion. What we can do in Africa, where we still govern
> and where we no longer govern, depends upon the opinion which
> is entertained of the way in which this country acts and the way
> in which Englishmen act. We cannot, we dare not, in Africa of
> all places, fall below our own highest standards in the acceptance
> of responsibility.[46]

The speech encapsulated the high standards that he maintained
and his outstanding capacity to express them. Many may share
his views but not have his ability to express them to such effect.

His capacity to express himself forcefully, however, also created
problems. He could not empathise with those who lacked his
capacity to reach logically the same conclusions or to distinguish
between the person and the beliefs. He tore into Heath over
European integration and Thatcher over Northern Ireland,
using vituperative language that caused great offence, yet failed
to recognise the impact his words had. He used wounding words
even though harbouring no personal animosity.

Conclusion

What, then, to make of this remarkable man? As Patrick, now Lord, Cormack observed in his funeral oration, 'Enoch was a complex man if ever there was one. There was something of both the Cavalier and the Calvinist in his make-up.'[47]

One thing is clear. He had an outstanding intellect. 'He was brilliant,' declared *The Economist*. 'Everyone said that, even those who loathed his ideas.'[48] Indeed, at times his brilliance was such that his speeches went over the heads of his listeners. On occasion this may have been deliberate. One commentator observed following his 1965 conference speech as shadow Defence Secretary that he had 'just withdrawn us from East of Suez and received an enormous ovation because no one understood what he was talking about'.[49] The Americans did, though, and did not appreciate it.

His 'rivers of blood' speech in 1968 gave rise to claims, including from his own leader, that he was embracing racism. I take the view that he was a nationalist rather than a racist. I thought *The Economist* put it especially well in its obituary, when it observed that Powell was more akin to a British de Gaulle than a British Le Pen.[50] Powell himself contended that his views on immigration had nothing to do with race. Michael Foot was among those who believed that he was not a racist. Indeed, it is worth recalling that in 1944 Powell had refused to stay at a club because it would not admit a colleague who was Indian.[51] In his dealings with others, he treated each the same, regardless of creed or colour. Powell declared that his stance was determined by politics and not race. He believed that the nation flourished by having a sense of self-identification and that this would be lost in large conurbations if there was a large influx of those who would see themselves without that identity. The distinction was perhaps best expressed by his parliamentary ally, Richard Body, who argued that England was multiracial, and always had been, but that the problem lay in trying to make it multicultural.[52]

Just as his Birmingham speech both made and destroyed him politically, his capacity for developing and expressing intense lines of logic helped make his reputation as an outstanding orator but blunted his impact as a politician. He could win an argument but not necessarily persuade his audience to act. One could imagine Margaret Thatcher agreeing with him but recognising that, even for her, implementing what he said would be a step too far. As one of her ministerial colleagues put it to me, 'she could recognise a brick wall when she saw one'. Enoch Powell would probably explain why logically it was not a brick wall and therefore not an obstacle.

It was a distinction that Powell himself recognised. He acknowledged that one of Margaret Thatcher's remarkable characteristics, as he put it,

> is her ability to put up with things and go along with them, even though she doesn't agree with them, until the time comes when they can be dealt with. Now not possessing that quality myself – having the loquacity which always impels me to say: 'I don't agree' – I admire this.

It made Thatcher, in his view, a superb politician. That was the key difference. As Simon Heffer observed, Powell occupied the place of a philosopher rather than a practitioner, 'a role for which', as Heffer put it, 'baser skills are required'.[53]

As a philosopher, Powell was not one to temporise or compromise. As Norman Shrapnel observed,

> Powell was not the first or the last politician to be caught between the concept and the act, the purity of the idea and the twist and turns of real life, but in his case the gift for abstraction was so advanced that the gap yawned wider than for most.[54]

He tended to argue in terms of absolutes and this led to him being seen by some as extreme. As I have said, his approach to problem-solving was remarkably un-British, as was his embrace at times of conspiracy theories: his extreme distrust of the United States led him to see the hand of the CIA in such things as the death of Lord

Mountbatten. His embrace of such theories was not confined to matters affecting the USA. He was among those who believed that the works of Shakespeare were penned by the Earl of Oxford.

Once he had formed a view, he pursued it with intensity. He was a man of very determined views, but not necessarily fixed views. He could change, but once he had changed he pursued his new position with the same intensity as the old. This is perhaps most apparent in his approach to faith. For a period, he was a convinced atheist but ended his life as a devout Anglican.

Above all else, though, he adored the House of Commons. He was largely a lost soul when he was defeated in the general election of 1987. His sense of purpose, as well as an established daily routine, was gone. He had an idealised view of the House of Commons, but when he spoke in the House that view was the reality. The chamber was packed, ready to listen, and with some Members prepared to engage. For the humble backbencher of whom no one had heard, the reality was different.

Powell was a great parliamentarian, dedicated to the institution and by his actions contributing, like Michael Foot, to its reputation. Powell and Foot recognised in one another romantics who saw the House of Commons as being at the heart of the nation and being the bastion for the independence of the nation. They united, not only in their opposition to Lords reform and to the European Community, but in their defence of the House of Commons and the chamber of the House; that, to them, was the place where the ultimate power should and did reside and it was that for which they fought.

Michael Foot recognised in Powell, as Powell recognised in Foot, a great parliamentarian. That, to me, is Enoch Powell's enduring legacy.

1   Michael Foot, *Loyalists and Loners* (London: Collins, 1986), p.186.
2   Jeremy Paxman, *The Political Animal* (London: Michael Joseph, 2002), p.16.
3   Robert Shepherd, *Enoch Powell* (London: Hutchinson, 1996), p.43.
4   Simon Heffer, *Like the Roman* (London: Phoenix, 1999), p.92.

5   British Army Officers, 1939–1945: http://www.unithistories.com/
    officers/Army_officers_Co1.html. See also 'Obituary: Enoch Powell',
    The Independent, 11 February 1998.

6   Shepherd, *Enoch Powell*, pp.72–3.

7   'Panorama', BBC TV, in *Reflections of a Statesman* (London: Bellew
    Publishing, 1991), p.9; 'Towards 2000', in *Reflections of a Statesman*, p.26.

8   Foot, *Loyalists and Loners*, p.187.

9   'Theory and Practice', in *Reflections of a Statesman*, pp.56–7.

10 Enoch Powell, 'Parliament and the Question of Reform', *Teaching Politics*,
    Vol. 11 (2), 1982, p.169.

11 'The State of the Nation', Granada TV, 1973, in *Reflections of a Statesman*,
    p.249. For some justification of this view, see Andrew Alexander and Alan
    Watkins, *The Making of the Prime Minister 1970* (London: Macdonald Unit
    75, 1970), pp.100–101.

12 See Janet Morgan, *The House of Lords and the Labour Government 1964–1970*
    (Oxford: Clarendon Press, 1975), Chs 7 and 8.

13 Alexander and Watkins, *The Making of the Prime Minister 1970*, p.62.

14 Alexander and Watkins, *The Making of the Prime Minister 1970*, p.63.

15 Philip Norton, *Dissension in the House of Commons 1945–74* (London:
    Macmillan, 1975), pp.353–4.

16 Heffer, *Like the Roman*, p.521.

17 Quoted in Heffer, *Like the Roman*, p.521.

18 *The Independent*, 9 February 1998.

19 Roy Lewis, *Enoch Powell: Principle in Politics* (London: Cassell, 1979), p.233.

20 Andrew Roth, *Enoch Powell: Tory Tribune* (London: Macdonald, 1970),
    pp.50–53.

21 Shepherd, *Enoch Powell*, p.496.

22 *The Independent*, 9 February 1998.

23 Quoted in Denis Kavanagh, 'Obituary: Enoch Powell', *The Independent*, 9
    February 1998.

24 *The Guardian*, 9 February 1998.

25 Heffer, *Like the Roman*, p.380.

26 House of Commons: Official Report (Hansard): 3 March 1953, Vol. 512,
    col. 242. See also 'Royal Titles Bill', in *Reflections of a Statesman*, pp.195–202.

27 Alexander and Watkins, *The Making of the Prime Minister 1970*, p.83.

28 'Theory and Practice', *Reflections of a Statesman*, p.58.

29 Patrick Cosgrave, *The Independent*, 9 February 1998.

30 *BBC News Online*, 18 February 1998.

31 Foot, *Loyalists and Loners*, p.186.

32 See Norton, *Dissension in the House of Commons 1945–74*.

33 Philip Norton, *Conservative Dissidents* (London: Temple Smith, 1978), p.252.

34 See Norton, *Conservative Dissidents*.

35 See Richard Rose, 'Parties, Factions and Tendencies in Britain', *Political
    Studies*, Vol. 12, 1964, pp.33–46.

36 Norton, *Conservative Dissidents*, pp.250–51.

37 Robert Dahl, 'Some Explanations', in Robert A. Dahl (ed.), *Political Opposition in Western Democracies* (New Haven, CT: Yale University Press, 1966), p.355.

38 Nigel Fisher, *Iain Macleod* (London: Andre Deutsch, 1973), p.17.

39 Churchill has twenty-six, Lloyd George eleven, F. E. Smith ten, and Bevan ten.

40 'Enoch Powell', *The Economist*, 12 February 1998.

41 *The Independent*, 9 February 1998.

42 Quoted in 'Politicians say farewell to Enoch Powell', *BBC News Online*, 18 February 1998.

43 Cited in Heffer, *Like the Roman*, p.952.

44 Heffer, *Like the Roman*, p.252.

45 House of Commons: Official Report (Hansard): 27 July 1959, Vol. 610, col. 236.

46 House of Commons: Official Report (Hansard): 27 July 1959, Vol. 610, col. 237.

47 Sir Patrick Cormack, Address for the Rt Hon. Enoch Powell, Warwick Parish Church, 18 February 1998.

48 *The Economist*, 12 February 1998.

49 Quoted in Heffer, *Like the Roman*, p.391.

50 *The Economist*, 12 February 1998.

51 Shepherd, *Enoch Powell*, p.55.

52 Richard Body, *England for the English* (London: New European Publications, 2001).

53 Heffer, *Like the Roman*, p.958.

54 *The Guardian*, 9 February 1998.

Michael Foot

Neil Kinnock
Delivered on 12 July 2011

Biographical note

Michael Foot

Michael Mackintosh Foot, born 23 July 1913, son of Rt Hon. Sir Isaac Foot MP, Liberal MP for Bodmin. Educated at Leighton Park School, Reading, and Wadham College, Oxford. (President of the Oxford Union 1933.) Married 1949 Jill Craigie. Journalist. Editor of the *Evening Standard* 1942–43, political columnist, *Daily Herald*, 1944–64, managing director, *Tribune*, 1945–74, editor 1948–52 and 1955–60. Labour MP for Plymouth Devonport 1945–55, Ebbw Vale 1960–83 (Labour whip withdrawn 1961–63), and Blaenau Gwent 1983–92. Secretary of State for Employment 1974–76; Leader of the House of Commons and Lord President of the Council 1976–79. Deputy Leader of the Labour Party 1976–80, Leader 1980–83.

Member of Labour Party National Executive Committee 1947–50, 1972–83. Member of Parliamentary Labour Party Parliamentary Committee 1970–74. Privy Counsellor 1974. Died 3 March 2010.

A brilliant debater and literary figure, Foot was a leading figure on the British left, variously at odds with the Labour Party leadership and for a period the leading rebel in the ranks of the Parliamentary Labour Party. He was a leading supporter of the Campaign for Nuclear Disarmament. He served in Cabinet during the Labour Government of 1974–79 and was Party Leader from 1980 to 1983. He was recognised as having led the party in a disastrous election campaign in 1983. He was more at home on the back benches than on the front bench, the back benches providing him with the freedom to express his views, which he did with a passion and a wonderful command of English literature.

H. L. Mencken wrote of Senator Robert La Follete:

> I shall vote for him unhesitatingly, and for a plain reason: he is the best man in the running, as a man. There is no ring in his nose. Nobody owns him. Nobody bosses him. Nobody even advises him. Right or wrong, he has stood on his own firmly – battling for his ideas in good weather and bad, facing great odds gladly, going against his followers as well as with his followers … Suppose all politicians were like him? Suppose trimming went out of fashion, and there were an end to skulkers, dodgers and safe men? … What a country it would be!

Michael Foot certainly belongs in any pantheon of modern parliamentarians, as many obituaries reaffirmed. From the extreme left, to which he never belonged, to the Tory right, which he fought throughout his life, came almost unanimous agreement that he was a 'great House of Commons man'. In those tributes was recognition of the strength of his commitment to this place, of how he used it and why he believed so profoundly in its powers and potential.

They all knew of Michael Foot that, first, he loved the House of Commons – not as a place of trappings and tradition, but as an irreplaceable, incomparable weapon in the enduring battles for care, justice, peace, security and emancipation for individuals and communities and countries and cultures. To him, this place was the supreme implement for bringing the powerful to account, for gaining redress for the powerless, and for persuading a free people to guard their freedoms, enlarge those freedoms, and extend them to others who are not free.

Second, his politics was propelled by big ideas, chief among which were his convictions that, for the great majority of human beings, accountable collective organisation is indispensible for the achievement and maintenance of individual freedom; and that individual liberty under just law is not simply the most desirable but the *only* tolerable human condition and, therefore, worthy of incessant struggle.

Third, equipped with those pieces of progressive armour, he was willing to take personal political risks – risks which were sometimes so audacious that they made the bravest spirits falter under the weight of conventional opinion, orthodox interests and, not least, the lash of whips.

Michael Foot came to Parliament with those instincts, purposes and attributes already evident – if not complete – in his journalism and pamphleteering. It was powerful preparation. Throughout his political life he spoke as he wrote.

Once his youthful shyness was conquered – or at least subdued – Michael showed confidence and vitality in his public speaking. Like Aneurin Bevan but very few others, he was unusual in his ability to impress and inspire from the conference rostrum, on platforms of mass demonstrations and – above all – in the unique arena of the House of Commons. Whether it was packed for great, tense debates or sparsely attended for the conversational prying and poking and particularising of the committee stage, Michael Foot was in his element there.

Apart from using a document that was being debated, or picking up on what opponents on the other side (or foes on his own side) had said or had printed elsewhere, he used no speaking notes. When, as a Minister, he was obliged to read official statements he did it badly and with bewildering changes of spectacles that provided metaphorical quotation marks around the staid language of civil service-ese.

Of course, he never came alone to any speech. He was always

accompanied by an array of drafters, wordsmiths and – in the modern term – 'Special Advisors', all of whom were available at any time, none of whom cost a penny from the public purse. They included: Byron, Burke, Blake, Brailsford and the Bible; Churchill and Fox; Hazlitt and Heine; Keats and Kafka; Montaigne, Milton and Michelet; George Orwell and Tom Paine; Bertrand Russell and Rousseau; Shakespeare, Swift, Shelley, Sterne, Stendhal and Silone; Wordsworth, Rebecca West – and H. G. Wells, the subject of a well reviewed biography which Michael wrote in his eighties.

His references to these and many more writers were used to *mobilise* their thoughts and words, not to prove his erudition. Michael Foot was free of vanity. He was never an intellectual exhibitionist any more than he was a sartorial show-off – although it must be acknowledged that his words were always more elegant than his appearance (it could hardly have been otherwise).

These geniuses were his inspiration and his feedstock. They were his friends and counsellors – on pre-speech strolls around Hampstead Heath or St James's Park, at the desk in his study, on the top of the Number 24 bus. He must have been the only man ever to take *Paradise Lost* to a Plymouth Argyle away match. Most powerfully and publicly of all, of course, they supplied the projectiles that he lobbed gently or hurled ferociously from the green benches.

He rose to speak for the first time in the Commons on 20 August 1945 and finished his final intervention on 5 March 1992. Between those two dates, with a five-year gap from his defeat in Plymouth in 1955 to his victory in the Ebbw Vale by-election in 1960, he appeared in the official record 12,141 times.

His first words as an MP were spoken in the foreign affairs debate on the King's Speech – and they were dissident:

> I feel that a maiden speaker taking part in this debate has a special
> claim upon the indulgence which it is the custom of the House to

extend to maiden speakers.... We have been told from both sides today that controversy should be avoided on matters of foreign policy and we might imagine, from those appeals for unanimity, that – wherever else British policy may have failed in the past ten years – in the matter of foreign policy it has been a glittering and matchless success... Unhappily, I cannot subscribe to that view and, therefore, I may possibly sink from that high level of pure affability which we're supposed to attain in our maiden speeches.[1]

It was a good illustration, from the outset, of Foot's ability to be light with words yet heavy with meaning. He continued the speech with jabs at Churchill, and – separately – at appeasers of the Nazis, and he condemned the spreading Soviet oppression in Eastern Europe. Then, less than two weeks after the USA's nuclear bombs devastated Hiroshima and Nagasaki, he concluded by saying:

The invention of the atomic bomb should impel us to assume the position of leadership among the nations with all the courage we can muster. At the end of this war and after this election, the British people can play as conspicuous a part before the gaze of all mankind as they played in 1940. Hitler left behind him terrible legacies – racial hatred, love of violence, hunger, homelessness, famine and death. Surely it is the duty of our great country not to be content with some secondary role, but rather to seek the abatement of those evils by the assertion and example of a much more positive democracy. As we look out across this stricken Continent and as we see new hope struggling to be born across this wilderness of shattered faiths, may it not be our destiny – as the freest and most democratic nation, and a Socialist Power – to stand between the living and the dead and stay the flames?[2]

The speech was fluent, radical, perceptive, patriotic and unapologetically political with hints of sardonic humour. It was a foretaste of the parliamentary Foot who spoke in the Commons through forty-two of the next forty-seven years. The House, said the *New Statesman*, 'liked this first-rate verbal pamphleteer'. Other commentators joined in the praise.

Throughout the following ten years, Foot's frenetic campaigning as a diligent constituency MP, Bevanite champion, waspish columnist and inveterate nuclear disarmer brought him the title of a 'Robespierre, a febrile, class-conscious agitator'. Like most denigrations of Michael it was volleyed from the safe distance of a newspaper column. And while it was a ridiculous distortion it was still an insult to be proud of.

The conscientious constituency commitment was not quite enough to save him. In the 1955 general election, Michael was defeated by a hundred votes.

In the Labour Party, the years after 1955 were, almost entirely, a continuation of the civil war between the conflicting philosophies, purposes and personalities of Aneurin Bevan and Hugh Gaitskell and their partisan supporters. Most anguished of all, however, was the schism over the possession and potential use of nuclear weapons. And, in this case, Bevan and Foot diverged bitterly as Nye confronted the Labour movement with the *realpolitik* of deterrence strategy and Michael argued with remorseless passion for unilateral nuclear disarmament. Friendship between the soul mates eventually returned, but division over the issue still smouldered until the two were separated by Bevan's death in 1960.

Out of the House of Commons, Foot helped to establish CND, wrote an acclaimed biography of Jonathan Swift,[3] and continued his journalism – frequently showing that while he was not *in* Parliament, he was certainly *of* Parliament. He was greatly exercised, for instance, by the growth of consensualist politics and – even more blazingly – by the subordination of MPs by whips and authoritarian parliamentary party meetings.[4] On that subject, he 'unsheathed his pen', as he said of Swift, and wrote: 'The higher the Party meeting rises on the seesaw, the lower sinks the Commons.' Control by leaders and apparatchiks had 'turned the voting lobby into a corridor of humiliation where the MP must wear the badge of his tribe instead of carrying the banner of his convictions'.

In Foot's view, it all threatened to 'make the major parties more and more monolithically united to fight about less and less' – and that was 'an infallible recipe for deepening public boredom', which, of course, menaces the vitality of democracy in any age. The theme of resistance to deference and imposed conformity was always part of Michael Foot's inexhaustible dedication to his ideal of a House of Commons that is supreme and composed of politically aligned but independently minded Members. Indeed, he thought the two were interdependent. When he was back in the House after November 1960, he discomforted some with a speech that referred to Churchill and Bevan as heroes who 'were in perpetual quarrels with their party machines' and he scorned 'hon. Members who prefer to be herded'.

In the same parliamentarian spirit, he never veered from the conviction that, while the freedom to demonstrate peacefully (which Foot exercised frequently) must be inviolable, since the achievement of universal suffrage, parliamentary advocacy and action were in every way superior to what was fashionably called 'extra-parliamentary activity' or 'direct action'. He thought that press and political misrepresentation of genuine extra-parlia- mentary action as *anti*-parliamentary action was scandalous. But he frequently emphasised his certainty that those on the left who were contemptuous of parliamentary methods were 'casting aside the best implement for progress they are ever going to get, and defaming our cause'. Twenty years later, he had to make that case with his greatest vehemence as an anti-parliamentarian fad seized parts of the Labour movement and invited disrepute.

In the 1959 general election, Michael was again – foreseeably and much more heavily – defeated in Plymouth Devonport. Dispiriting though that was, much worse was to come. As 1960 opened, Nye Bevan was diagnosed as having a serious cancer. Realising, after months of treatment, that it was terminal, Bevan said to Michael, 'You'd better look for another seat. Perhaps you needn't look further than Ebbw Vale.'

Nye Bevan died on 6 July 1960. Michael Foot was selected by the Ebbw Vale Constituency Labour Party on 24 September and, for me as a fervent Young Socialist in Tredegar, the weeks between then and the by-election on 17 November were some of the most rumbustiously enjoyable I've ever had in politics.

A two-thirds share of the 76 per cent turnout produced a 17,000 Labour majority, rebuffed vindictive media coverage and was seen as something of a mixed blessing for the Labour establishment. On the front page of my parents' *News Chronicle*, Vicky, the greatest political cartoonist of the era and Foot's bosom friend, depicted a glum-faced Hugh Gaitskell reading the result and saying 'Oh dear, we've won.'

The victor's thoughts, published in the *Daily Herald* days after the by-election, defined his stance then and always:

> Against the rock of working-class pride, all the prissy values preached by the BBC, all the tinsel tuppenny-ha'penny ideas filtered through television, all the snobbery and smug complacency associated with a Tory-directed society beat in vain … The Ebbw Vale by-election was for me more exhilarating than any political experience in my life precisely because it revealed how strong and indestructible are the sinews of British democracy.

His words were unblushingly heady. But they were also a hammering declaration of intense respect and loyalty for the place and the people he was elected to represent. There could be no more fitting equipment for a zealous advocate who used Parliament as a battlefield for enlightenment and emancipation.

For Michael Foot, re-entry to the Commons meant, of course, resumption of combat – especially with the Labour leadership and particularly over defence policy. The unilateralist decision of Labour Party conference still stood and, while Michael Foot never subscribed to the myth that such decisions were sovereign over Labour Party members inside or outside Parliament, he did argue that they should not be contemptuously ignored. That, however, is what the Gaitskell leadership did, and the battle over The Bomb was therefore waged viciously and very publicly. When Michael and four other Labour MPs ignored an instruction to abstain and voted against the Army and Air Force estimates in March 1961,[5] they were all deprived of the party whip. It was not restored to them until May 1963.

Nineteen-sixty-three also saw huge changes in the political landscape and in Michael's life: in January, Hugh Gaitskell died and was succeeded by Harold Wilson. On 10 October, a seriously ill Harold Macmillan resigned as Prime Minister and was succeeded a week later by Lord Home. Four days after that, Michael and Jill were involved in a terrible motor collision which badly injured her and left him fighting to survive. His recovery to the point where he was able to walk took over three months, but, almost miraculously, by May 1964, he was back on the campaign trail – unbowed, but with a lifelong limp.

In October 1964, the election of the Labour government with a minuscule majority brought its own difficulties and divergences over economic policy, Vietnam, and over the postponement of the steel nationalisation that was so vital for Ebbw Vale. All three issues – and more – were severe aggravations but, in the Commons and elsewhere, Foot fulfilled an undertaking volunteered to Wilson that he would be restrained. By mid-1965, the Prime Minister – presumably hoping to turn restraint into obedience – offered Foot a ministerial post. He declined in writing and, typically, made no public reference to the invitation for decades afterwards. In addition, when multiple anxieties in the Labour Party threatened to erupt, Michael – despite deep concerns himself – memorably argued against divisive words or actions that would make the Labour left look as if it was 'turning away from power' and 'tearing itself to pieces for the convenience of the Tory enemy'. Happily for Labour, disunity was kept at bay and the reward for that came with the 97-seat majority in the March 1966 general election.

Almost immediately, the government was plunged into a series of economic, industrial, immigration legislation, and foreign policy divisions and crises. In addition, when Employment Secretary, Barbara Castle, made proposals for legal regulations to reduce strikes, the effects were shattering. Indeed, the government never really recovered from the impact.

Within months, another unsolicited source of contention came when proposals were made for Lords reform which would mean a House of Peers appointed in proportion to parties' numbers in the Commons, and a group of non-aligned Lords big enough to prevent an automatic government majority. Michael and others revolted furiously against the massive use of patronage which would be inevitable and the unthinkable possibility of a House of Lords that would compete with the Commons for public respect and power. He was joined in resistance by the brilliantly redoubtable Enoch Powell (whose fear was that constitutional disruption would damage the monarchy) and, with support mainly from the Labour left, they mercilessly filibustered the Bill to a standstill with what Jim Callaghan – the Home Secretary who was reluctantly responsible for the Bill – later called 'witty, logical and devastating oratory'.

Here, I must digress briefly on the subject of Michael's repeated alliances with Enoch Powell. They fascinated some but infuriated those who considered Powell to be a racist with excessively right-wing opinions on economic policy. When challenged, Michael responded by referring to what he saw as Powell's innate humanity and dedication to democracy. His explanations didn't convince me or many others but – much more important – they were resilient evidence of the high value that Michael gave to those qualities in anyone. As Ken Morgan makes clear in his masterful biography of Michael, 'For all his vehement socialism, the disciple of Lloyd George, the protégé of Beaverbrook and the good friend of Enoch Powell was hardly tribal in his political associations.'⁶ Indeed, Michael was so confident in his convictions that he thought it ridiculous and insulting that anyone should think him guilty of deviation because of his association with those three or many other non- – and anti- – socialists. The Bill, of course, was talked to unmourned death in April 1969.

In the next year, Harold Wilson called a general election nine months earlier than necessary and Labour slumped out of power. Like all of my Labour colleagues, I was deeply miserable about that – but my gloom was frankly lightened somewhat by the fact that I had been elected to the new House of Commons.

In opposition, appointment to the fuel and power portfolio in the shadow Cabinet was comfortable for the Member for Ebbw Vale and then, in 1971, it was followed by the position of shadow Leader of the House – a role that permitted him to speak on just about every subject, including UK membership of the European Community. Then, and for twenty years afterwards until he was persuaded otherwise, Michael was a leading voice against British engagement mainly – and emphatically – because he believed that membership would mean a theft of parliamentary sover-eignty, 'taking away', as he put it, 'powers that this House has had ever since it was founded, indeed almost since the Witanagemot'. Michael was never one for understatement.

His hostility to the government's European Communities Bill was characteristically relentless but, despite his opposition then and in the 1975 referendum, he used to become very agitated – as I saw for myself – when he was described as 'anti-European' or when Labour colleagues expressed nationalistic or chauvin-istic sentiments. In addition – and also typically – he actively extended his protection to Labour MPs whose pro-European convictions (and consequent help to the Heath government's legislation) provoked the wrath of their constituency parties. He did it, he explained, to defend their right to make conscientious judgements *as parliamentarians*.

A year after UK entry into the Community, British politics

went through one of those shudders of change that can only really be explained by Macmillan's urbane phrase, 'events, dear boy'.

The February 1974 election, and the Tory defeat, came out of an avalanche of international and domestic crises. Harold Wilson formed a minority government and his choice for the vital post of Secretary of State for Employment was Michael Foot. I sent a telegram of congratulation to Michael in which I added 'BEWARE' to Hazlitt's maxim that 'rules and models destroy genius and art'. He responded with a phone message, scrupulously recorded by my constituency party secretary. Quoting Hazlitt, he said: 'We never do anything well 'til we cease to think about the *manner* of doing it,' and then added, 'Now bugger off, you cheeky sod.'

When Michael became a Cabinet minister there were many – including friends – who thought he would be miserably disabled by the constrictions of office. He resoundingly proved them wrong with a social contract with the unions that worked for two years, and with a comprehensive programme of conciliation, anti-discrimination, and industrial health and safety laws that was shoehorned through a Commons in which Labour rarely enjoyed any secure majority.

He began his term of office with a speech in one of the debates on the Loyal Address which I, like others, recall as his finest. Made without notes, it mixed a battering of the Tories' industrial laws and policies with uproarious mockery and then, in a passage which brought loud and prolonged Labour applause, he said:

> To the wealthy threatening sanctions, or preaching sermons to people who have to fight every day of their lives to keep their heads above the inflationary flood, I say nothing can be more absurd than the spectacle of a few fat men exhorting all thin ones to tighten their belts... Relativities *must* be concerned with the East End and the West End, with rich and poor, with Disraeli's two nations.[7]

It was a maiden ministerial speech that, in the most testing parliamentary conditions, brought resounding praise from all quarters and sent Labour spirits soaring. In the desperate struggles of the coming years, Michael's bold ability to do ferocious parliamentary battle with the broadsword of conviction and the rapier of humour was vital to the survival of the government as it slogged through what seemed to be perpetual crisis.

In March 1976, Harold Wilson resigned as Labour leader and, as acknowledged leader of the parliamentary left, Michael was obliged to fight the ensuing Labour Party election. Jim Callaghan won by about forty votes, and sensibly made Michael Lord President and Leader of the House. In October, Michael was elected Deputy Leader of the Labour Party.

For an MP who is a parliamentarian in every fibre, being Leader of the House with a dependable government majority must be somewhere close to paradise. For the same chromosomal Commons man, holding that position without a majority is adjacent to purgatory. That, however, was the fate of Michael Foot. A government nearly wrecked by economic turmoil fought for wage restraint and public spending cuts and had to seek the assistance of the IMF. In the immediate wake of that earthquake, Leader of the House Foot – a sulphurous critic of timetable motions throughout his parliamentary career – had to propose five guillotines within a few months. That provoked vitriolic attacks from some on his own side and, from the Tories, came taunting reminders of his previous opposition to Timetable Motions. When Francis Pym criticised him Michael counterthrusted by recalling the number of Tory guillotines and saying: 'If I am St Just, he is Robespierre. Indeed, I think he might have had the decency to bring along Mme Defarge.'[8]

By March 1977, the stock of the government, and the morale of its supporters, was abysmal and when Margaret Thatcher tabled a no-confidence motion it became clear that only an unprecedented agreement with non-Labour parties could save the government. Along with the chairman of the PLP, the endlessly canny Cledwyn

Hughes, Michael Foot was, therefore, asked by Callaghan to make contact with David Steel's Liberals. After a frenzied four days, agreement to a government-saving pact was reached and then announced in the censure debate on 23 March.

Michael became, effectively, the Labour 'Keeper of the Pact' and fulfilled that time-eating and energy-swallowing function along with what seemed like endless other duties. Throughout it all, to the surprise of some, Michael manifested prodigious skills as a parliamentary fixer – wheeling and dealing, cajoling and conniving to sustain a Labour government. What could not be organised away, however, was Labour's election commitment to introduce devolution to Scotland and Wales.

In a Commons where several Labour MPs – emphatically including me – were irreconcilably opposed to the Bill, and the Conservatives, as the Unionist Party, were naturally against, it was never going to be possible to enact the Bill without accepting amendments that would effectively kill it. From December 1976 to July 1978 legislating, therefore, took a tortured path. The tolerance which Michael Foot showed to me as a leading campaigner for referendums and against his proposals was almost beyond human. Our arguments were sharp and rowdy, but we kept the nastiest private. One memorable supper at Michael and Jill's came to a rather abrupt conclusion with Michael throwing a tray at me – an action which sent another guest, Spike Milligan, diving under the dining table.

On the way home, my wife – who adored Michael – said, 'You know I'm against the Bill and Michael is totally wrong. But if you upset him like that again, I'll pick up the tray and give him a second try.'

Defeat of the government in the referendums on 1 March 1979 made a no-confidence motion certain. By the time the debate came on 28 March it was clear that the Liberals and Nationalists would join the Conservatives and Ulster Unionists to defeat the government.

Winding up that debate in a House that was tense and

tumultuous, Michael was brave and brilliant, partly with rollick-
ing mockery, partly with sombre defiance. Anyone who values
the Commons as a place of great political tournament that
affects the fate of the nation should listen to a recording of
that speech and rejoice at its fun and its force.

Even that could not, however, win the day. The no-confidence
motion was carried by one vote. The ensuing election was mainly
fought on the memory – real and manufactured – of the Winter
of Discontent, the minority government's escapology and the
Tory promise to sell council houses. The outcome was inevitable.
Margaret Thatcher gained an overall majority of forty-three.

When parties lose power, there is a morbid instinct to become
introspective and to engage in recriminations. The malady has
particularly afflicted Labour and in 1979 it was potentially lethal.
Parts of the Labour Party were seized by a poisonous delirium
that made many observers – some in sorrow, others ecstatically –
think that political death was a serious probability.

After more than a year in which the Labour Party resembled
an inward-facing circular firing squad, a weary Jim Callaghan
resigned as Leader in October 1980.

Michael Foot most certainly did not want to be Leader of the
Labour Party. He had no ambition or appetite for it and his self-
appraisal was surgically honest – 'I do not have the necessary
appeal to voters,' he said.

When I told Michael that my very careful assessment of
members of the PLP showed that he would lose against Denis
Healey by at least nine, and possibly as many as twenty-one,
votes, he responded very cheerily: 'That's what I thought. Nice
to have figures to prove it. This calls for a drink.'

I shared that feeling. I did not want Michael to endure the unnec-
essary pressures of a campaign and defeat – and I was certain that,
if by some chance he won, he would be submitting himself to
endless, fruitless torture. Other friends believed, however, that his
capacity to inspire would pull a faction-riven Labour movement
back to sanity and coherence. They intensely urged him to stand

and, eventually, he agreed to do it. Never was a sense of obligation more abused. Never was selflessness more betrayed.

In the thirty months that followed, he was subjected to agony. The infinite self-indulgence of some on the left (including people who had begged him to stand) combined explosively with desertion by some on the right (including people who had benefited from Michael's personal protection against vengeful activists). The aggregate effect enfeebled Labour, gave measureless comfort to the Tories, generated devastating treatment by the press, bewildered and alienated the public – and crucified Michael Foot.

Even Michael's gigantic capacity for forgiveness was stretched beyond snapping point by the rampant disregard for realities that swept the movement like the plague. Nineteen-eighty-one, he said, 'could and should have been the year in which Labour applied all its energies to concerted and united vengeance for the wounds inflicted on our people and destroying the Tory government. Instead it was turned into a period of futility and shame.'

He justifiably declared that 'the responsibility for transmitting every controversy of the time into an internal Labour Party dispute rested entirely with Tony Benn'. Benn's decision to challenge Denis Healey for the deputy leadership (bizarrely announced at 3.30 am on 2 April 1981), was – said Michael – a perfect gift to 'the scavenger Tory press and the vulturous television cameras'. Within weeks, Michael challenged Benn to fight him, not Healey.

At the time, I called the absence of a response from Benn 'revealing and cowardly'. It had a similar effect on others. In the election I and eleven of my PLP colleagues – 1.2 per cent of the electoral college – abstained. Denis Healey was re-elected with a majority of 0.852 per cent.

In the wake of that episode, Michael – typically – sought to promote reconciliation and common purpose. He was instantly rebuffed by Benn who declared, with the grandiosity that was becoming his stock in trade, 'I am not prepared to accept that in the shadow Cabinet you should be asked to abandon the policies of the Labour Party.' Michael's riposte was fully Footite:

The doctrine of shadow-Cabinet collective responsibility, a looser copy of the full-dress Cabinet cloak, is not some old, musty constitutional suit of armour. It is much more concerned with common sense, good faith and comradeship among those who must act together in Parliament if they are to give effective leadership to the Labour Party. No substitute for that good faith exists; Tony Benn has not discovered one.

The defeat of Benn in the deputy leadership and shadow Cabinet elections brought no respite: every National Executive meeting was a wrestling match that attracted appalling news coverage; in by-elections, Labour candidates were butchered by SDP and Tory victors; rumours of plots to overthrow Michael abounded. It is only fair to say that the constant pressure did push him into errors that made him rage against himself. But a lesser man than Foot would have crumbled completely. Instead, he inaugurated the first effective action against Militant, began to claw support away from the Bennites at Labour Party conference and the NEC, and sometimes regained admiration in the Commons. His January 1981 attack on the takeover of *The Times* and *Sunday Times* by Rupert Murdoch, and the decision of the Thatcher government not to refer it to the Monopolies Commission, brought him widespread support, and a searingly effective speech at the beginning of the Falklands War was loudly praised. It even had Tories saying 'he spoke for Britain'. But he could never have done enough. The festival of fools in the party that Michael led ensured that no striving would have ever been sufficient to repair the ceaseless damage.

Labour went into the 1983 general election in a state of shambolic disorganisation with a manifesto that was originally written as a rambling compendium of wish lists to make up a 'Party Programme'. It was retained simply because of the divisive uproar that would have accompanied any attempt to amend it significantly.

In what passed for a Labour campaign, Michael was – as ever – valiant and voluble. At sixty-nine, the age I am now, he visited eighty constituencies, appeared at the daily press conferences, spoke at as many as six public meetings a day. The election result was, however, a foregone conclusion. The Tories won 187 seats more than Labour. It was, as Michael said on the morning after the election 'a verdict of the electorate not only on our campaign but also on the whole period prior to it'. He then quickly announced his intention to resign as Leader (so catapulting me into my mid-life crisis as his successor).

In the years that followed, he remained an active and combative backbencher, wrote books, literary criticisms and polemics, gave libertarian defence to Salman Rushdie and others who were accused of offending various orthodoxies; ecstatically celebrated the end of Soviet Communism and the liberating opportunities that he hoped it would bring; lectured on Peterloo, Thomas Paine and Jonathan Swift; won large damages from the *Sunday Times* which had preposterously libelled him as a Communist fellow-traveller; chaired the Booker Committee and everywhere sustained his case that the central issue before humanity was 'how to destroy injustice without the World destroying itself'.

Most important of all, before and after his retirement in 1992, he brought his full emphatic attention to bear on the cataclysm raging in the Balkans as civil war and genocide smashed Yugoslavia, a country that he knew and loved. His final speech in the House of Commons on 5 March 1992 voiced his grave concern and his demand for effective peacekeeping.

'I was present as a reporter in 1945 at the establishment of the United Nations in San Francisco', he said:

[Pre-war conflicts] similar to these [in Yugoslavia] led people to say that we must have an international authority with the power and capacity to send in troops speedily to settle disputes. To some of us, that was almost the first lesson to be learned from the failures between 1918 and 1945. We wanted a real United Nations to act strongly, and the backing of a Security Council to carry through what it wanted to do. If the United Nations refrained from acting

[now], it would be a disaster for the world at large … I hope there will be no such holding back [in former Yugoslavia] because, for the solution to this problem and for the future of the world, we must hope that this United Nations force will have full backing for as long as is necessary to try to establish real peace in the area.[9]

Michael Foot's last sentences in the House of Commons asked for the tuition of history to be heeded, called for just force to be used in the cause of enduring peace, and – with tragically accurate foresight of evil – warned of the grievous results that would arise from less than assertive engagement by the United Nations. All that was fitting – indeed natural – for a man who had articulated those causes for a lifetime and would continue to do so into his nineties.

Michael Foot is recalled – by foes as well as friends – as a brilliant writer and a great parliamentary and platform orator. He was certainly those and more. But he was also a brave man – sometimes audacious in his irreverence, sometimes valiant in persisting with unpopular causes.

Most crucially, he was tenacious. He showed it in the consistency of his democratic socialist convictions, in his unconditional defence of liberty, and in his unrelenting dedication to the sovereignty and utility of Parliament. More tangibly, he applied it with the defiant dexterity that sustained a Labour government for two years longer than mere lobby arithmetic would have seemed to make feasible. Above all, he proved his mettle when duty compelled him to become Labour leader at a time that suicidally infantile leftism was inflicting absurdity and irrelevance on the party. In those hideous conditions, his resilience and spirit then showed – in Kenneth Morgan's words – 'that his kind of socialism was a faith worth fighting for'.

Those qualities also impelled him, in repeated public confrontations and in endless committee trench warfare, to resist and rally beyond exhaustion and (if I may borrow a phrase), to save the party that he loved.

By such dour, debilitating means – far from the dashing campaigning and sparkling creativity on which he thrived – Michael Foot enabled Labour to avoid terminal division and dissolution and to survive as a political entity.

When his greatly admired friend, H. G. Wells, died in 1946, Michael wrote:

...we shall hear no more of that splendid scorn and soaring imagination ... Let us recall his great qualities – courage which was shining and indomitable, humanity and patriotism. Not, of course, the vulgar flag-wagging variety but a deep, abiding love for the best spirit of (Britain) and all it has given to the World ... Our country should honour him more than the other nations which he sought – without thought for colour, race or creed – to join in allegiance to his Rights of Man. He belongs to them all, but first to us.

A 33-year-old Michael Foot could not have intended to write his own obituary. But, with those words, he did.

1   House of Commons: Official Report (Hansard): 20 August 1945, Vol. 413, col. 336.
2   House of Commons: Official Report (Hansard): 20 August 1945, Vol. 413, col. 341.
3   Michael Foot, *The Pen and the Sword: Jonathan Swift and the Power of the Press* (London: MacGibbon & Kee, 1957).
4   See Michael Foot, *Parliament in Danger!* (London: Pall Mall Press, 1959).
5   Philip Norton, *Dissension in the House of Commons 1945–74* (London: Macmillan, 1975), pp.160–61.
6   Kenneth O. Morgan, *Michael Foot: A Life* (London: HarperPress, 2007).
7   House of Commons: Official Report (Hansard): 18 March 1974, Vol. 870, col. 702.
8   House of Commons: Official Report (Hansard): 16 November 1977, Vol. 939, col. 702.
9   House of Commons: Official Report (Hansard): 5 March 1992, Vol. 205, col. 475–6.

Iain Macleod

Douglas Hurd
Delivered on 6 September 2011

Biographical note

Iain Macleod

Iain Norman Macleod, born 11 November 1913, son of Dr Norman Macleod, of Skipton. Educated at Fettes College, Gonville and Caius College, Cambridge. Married 1941 Evelyn Hester. Army service 1939–45. Head of Home Affairs, Conservative Research Department 1948–50. Author. Conservative MP for Enfield West 1950–70. Minister of Health 1952–55; Minister of Labour and National Service 1955–59; Secretary of State for the Colonies 1959–61; Chancellor of the Duchy of Lancaster, Leader of the House of Commons and Chairman of the Conservative Party 1961–63. Editor, *The Spectator* 1963–65. Opposition Shadow Cabinet 1964–70. Chancellor of the Exchequer 1970. Privy Counsellor 1952. Died 20 July 1970.

Hunched because of a wartime injury, Macleod was renowned as a debater – he was promoted to government in 1952 on the basis of a brilliant speech in response to Aneurin Bevan – and for having a sharp mind; famously described by the Marquess of Salisbury as being 'too clever by half'. With Enoch Powell, he refused to serve in Cabinet in 1963 under Sir Alec Douglas-Home. Appointed Chancellor of the Exchequer in June 1970, he died in No. 11 Downing Street the following month at the age of fifty-six.

I did not serve in the Commons with Iain Macleod because he died in 1970 and I was elected in 1974. But I was very conscious of him because in those days I was an innocent and enthusiastic attender at party conferences. He was the star. He had an extraordinary voice. Some of you can remember what it was like. I have been trying to analyse it for this purpose today. It was not exactly bell-like, but it was sonorous. He talked with great emphasis and force. A lot of it was witty and funny and he got a laugh out of every speech. But there was more to it than ordinary wit or ordinary fun. There was a clear sense of commitment. Whatever he was talking about, he spoke because he actually believed in it and that feeling of commitment came through in his speeches.

You have this extraordinary contrast between this amazingly effective voice and this harassed and often quite miserable body. A tank drove over him during the war and he suffered acute pain during much of his political life from a series of diseases that are not very clearly analysed by the doctors, but they included, certainly, a liability to heart failure combined with a certain feebleness of the other bits and pieces that are important to human life. So he suffered a good deal, as indeed did his wife, Eve. They were in physical pain, which kept them together.

He was a playboy as a young man. He believed in pleasure, and above all he believed in playing bridge and winning money at bridge. He could have made quite a substantial income out of winnings at bridge. He used to go to White's; he played quite often there. He had a remarkably quick, clear mind, which he needed and deployed for the purposes of bridge. That aptitude actually did him good, but it also opened him up for criticism.

He was the last and one of the greatest Colonial Secretaries. He was one of the most eloquent exponents of the doctrine of One Nation, and I will come on to that in a minute. He allowed himself to be outmanoeuvred and outwitted by people much older than himself during the dramas of the Tory leadership in 1963, and he never entirely recovered from that. He died within a month or so of becoming Chancellor of the Exchequer in 1970. I want to spend a little time before I close on the what-ifs of that.

Iain Macleod had clearly taken no interest in foreign affairs or colonial matters before his appointment to succeed Alan Lennox-Boyd. He just did not appear to be interested; he was overwhelmingly interested in the social services and the National Health Service, which was his centrepiece, his focus. But it soon became clear that he was going to be a different Colonial Secretary. He succeeded two highly intelligent and distinguished holders of that office – Oliver Lyttelton and Alan Lennox-Boyd.

I do not know whether any of you remember Alan Lennox-Boyd.[1] He was a magical person. He had more charm to the acre, if you see what I mean – he was a great big man – than anyone I have ever known. Going to speak in an election campaign in those days, the candidate was accompanied by a small cloud of speakers whose duty it was to keep the hall quiet while we waited for the candidate to arrive, which was sometimes a bit late. I did that for Alan Lennox-Boyd. Then he arrived, and a hush fell on the hall – Bedfordshire brick workers in those days – in not at all a safe seat. The magic that Alan Lennox-Boyd deployed has been something that stays in my mind, which I have never succeeded in imitating.

That is a side issue, but Macleod was succeeding a man who was not negligible – who was, indeed, a remarkable member of his own generation. It immediately became clear to the officials at the Colonial Office that there was going to be a change. The change that occurred with the arrival of Macleod was one of acceleration; he wanted to get on with things. He was absolutely committed in principle to the idea of independence for the colonies, and he explained the reasoning behind that in speech after speech to a rather reluctant Tory audience. He believed that speed was crucial, and that the big mistake would be to go too slowly. That was partly a matter of shrewd political calculation, and it was partly a matter of commitment. He believed in the commitment to transform the British Empire into a Commonwealth of countries that ruled themselves.

Macleod had a difficulty which came out of the machinery of government. He was the Colonial Secretary, but he did not deal with the Sudan or with Cyprus – those were Foreign Office matters; he did not deal with the countries of the central African federation that we were trying to create, because that was a matter for the Commonwealth Office. In addition to the Prime Minister, therefore, he had two other colleagues of the same weight as himself – indeed, politically they probably carried rather greater weight – and there was a continuing argument and battle in Whitehall over the things that Iain Macleod wanted to do.

Macleod genuinely believed in what he said. His most famous speech, and one of his last, was about the principle that lay under the Commonwealth. He said: 'This is the last thing I shall say as Colonial Secretary' – people already knew he was going:

> I believe quite simply in the brotherhood of man – men of all races, of all colours, of all creeds. I think it is this that must be in the centre of our thinking… It is perhaps strange to an English and to a Welsh audience to quote the greatest of our Scottish native poets, but no one has put this in simpler or finer words than Burns: 'It is coming yet for a' that, That man to man the whole world o'er, Shall brothers be for a' that.'[2]

He would have put everything he had into that quotation, and into making it stick. It had a sort of electrifying effect on an audience that was not naturally, by instinct, in favour of what was being said. He continued:

> And this is coming. There are foolish men who will deny it, but they will be swept away; but if we are wise then indeed the task of bringing these countries towards their destiny of free and equal partners and friends with us in the Commonwealth of Nations can be a task as exciting, as inspiring and as noble as the creation of empire itself.

I think that Macleod felt that. It was a brilliant piece of eloquent prose, but beyond that, he actually felt that. He looked at the argument, which was very frequent in those days, that it was all a matter of timing and the trouble was that he was moving far too fast. He took that on by saying:

> Well, look at the alternative around us. The French are attempting the alternative in Algeria, and de Gaulle, however many troops he deploys, is not able, in fact, to contain it. We have huge forces deployed in Cyprus – silly little Cyprus, as it were – which has a big problem that we are not able to solve, however many troops we send there.

Therefore, the thought that you can actually let these things rest – that in some way they will resolve themselves and there is a natural force in these problems, which is self-liquidating, that will actually solve the problems – is just wrong. Remember that he did not have any great experience of this and, in a way, he prided himself on that. He thought that he brought a fresh and unbiased mind to it, and that anyone looking at it from outside, as he did, must conclude that it must be quick. He was very much influenced by what happened in the colonial empires alongside our own.

There were a whole series of conferences and negotiations of all kinds, but one thing common to almost all of them was that you were dealing in East Africa with white settlers. His predecessors as Colonial Secretary had regarded them as the chaps who knew; they were on the ground and their advice should, on the whole, prevail. He did not think that at all. He was not a kith-and-kin man. He did not believe that. On the contrary, he believed that they were part of the game and were certainly not equipped with particular wisdom or foresight. They were just pieces on the board. He had to be polite to them as best he could and limit the quarrelsome meetings to a minimum, but they were basically blocks in the way. They were hindrances in his path – in the path of the colonial policy in which he believed.

It was a complete change. He got himself moving much faster than had been expected. He got himself involved quickly in highly detailed, technical negotiations in Kenya, Northern Rhodesia and Nyasaland. All the time he was aiming for African progress, negotiating with the leaders – some of them very unsatisfactory – of would-be African countries, and also negotiating with white settlers in a defensive posture. That was what he believed in and was the way he wished to handle it. Having read Robert Shepherd's book, I think that that is an absolutely convincing argument.[3]

The alternative would have been to get ourselves bogged down, as the French did in Indochina and then in Algeria, as, of course, the Russians have done in Chechnya, and as we did in Cyprus and other places. Although of course we are discomfited and unhappy about some things that the modern Commonwealth does and does not do – we are impatient that it should be more clearly in our own image than it is – nevertheless, I think that the right path was the Macleod path, not the gradualist path that would have been followed had the Colonial Secretary been a new Lennox-Boyd or a new Oliver Lyttelton. On that point, he clearly had the right of the argument.

In the party, of course, it was controversial, and it became particularly controversial when Lord Salisbury, speaking in the

House of Lords, coined the phrase, 'too clever by half'. What Lord Salisbury said was actually in the context of bridge. He said that we had a Colonial Secretary who was very good at bridge. This is Lord Salisbury speaking:

> In bridge, as I understand it, it is not at all disgraceful, if you estimate your opponent correctly, to play your cards in order to destroy him. This process of analysing your enemy and defeating him is what is correct and fine in bridge, but the trouble with the Colonial Secretary is that he has transferred to the Colonial Office the techniques of the bridge table. The result is that his critics [Salisbury was thinking entirely of the white settlers, particularly in Rhodesia] are bemused by this and feel that they are being outwitted, and that a man is there not to get the best answer for Britain but to do them down and reduce them to some kind of impotence.[4]

That is what he meant by Macleod being 'too clever by half'. It was a hurtful phrase. It was one of those phrases which, if analysed, is not particularly potent, but in its context at that time, and with that audience in the House of Lords, it was powerful. In a way, it haunted Macleod, because everyone could remember that phrase. Everyone would think of that phrase when he got up to speak, and there is no doubt that it did him harm.

He came to be outwitted, at a crucial point in his own political career and in the life of the Tory party, by people who were older and more cunning than himself. That is to say, he was outwitted by Harold Macmillan in 1963 over the leadership of the party.[5] He believed – genuinely, and with some substance – that Alec Home had said in the Cabinet that he would not be a candidate. The situation then changed. I always thought it was understandable that Alec should come forward. He was pressed to come forward, and did, but Macleod simply hung on to the fact that he had heard Alec say that he would not be a candidate. When people said to him during those very tense days in 1963 surrounding the party conference, 'You must get yourself organised, Iain. Where are your troops? You've got to be out and about talking to people,' and so on, he said, 'My troops are about. They're fully in action, but it's not necessary, because I know that this is all going to be decided by Cabinet, and I know that Alec – whom I have difficulty with, because he is basically right-wing and, on the whole, rather soft in his attitude towards white settlers in Africa – has ruled himself out, so he's not in the game. That leaves the others,' who were well known, particularly Rab Butler.[6]

Then it gradually dawned on him that Macmillan was sewing it up in the background. The Redmayne exercise, the Chief Whip's exercise – going around asking people in the Cabinet and on the back benches what they thought – was designed to have the effect of playing into the hands of Alec Home. I knew Alec well; some of you did, too. He was not a man of thrusting ambition. People knew that, but that made him, in a curious Tory way, a rather attractive candidate. He did not terribly care. He was not going to go shoot himself if he did not get permission.

That is, of course, what Macmillan explained to the Queen. It was part of the backdrop of the whole thing. Here was a man who was not ruthlessly ambitious and who would have to be dragged to the altar, to some extent. That was exactly the sort of person whom the Tory party needed in 1963. All the time, of course, Macmillan was greatly exaggerating his own ill health. We all know that he could have gone on as Prime Minister reasonably successfully – adequately, anyway – for some time to come, but he decided to go, and the rest followed. In that way, not just Macleod, but also Reggie Maudling and others such as Ted Heath were outwitted and outclassed by people who had had a good deal more experience of politics than they did. The Tory party only just lost the 1964 election, but it did lose the 1964 election. Sir Alec became Prime Minister, but only for a short time, and he was narrowly defeated in that poll.

If you read about Macleod and about that period, you see a good deal of emphasis on the commitment of him and people like him to One Nation. The One Nation group actually came to be in 1950, which was the year in which Iain Macleod entered the House of Commons. He was one of the founding members.[7] He was a very good speaker, but he was a very good journalist and was very good at putting things together and creating a pamphlet or a manifesto. His mind worked quickly and neatly in *good* prose, as it were. This was very useful to the Tory party in this period of the early 1960s.

I happen to be writing a book on the life of Disraeli at the moment and what I say now will be mildly shocking to one or two of you, but Disraeli was not the inventor of One Nation. Disraeli's point, which he made absolutely emphatically in the novel *Sybil* and elsewhere, is that there were two nations. The Queen had two sets of subjects that were irreconcilable. They talked different languages. They had different habits. They worked in different ways and they were for ever – my words – going to be separate. Now, Disraeli believed that you should behave decently to farm labourers. He believed that the aristocrats had obligations to the people, but the idea of fusing them, which is the hallmark of the modern One Nation, never occurred to him. They were irreconcilable, and you had to keep the peace between them to stop them killing each other, but the idea that you could actually fuse them and bring them together under one heading was not, in his view, realistic.

When Disraeli died, the next one to take up the mantle was Lord Randolph Churchill, and he carried the argument a good deal further. He talked about Tory democracy in a way in which Disraeli would not have done, and he elevated it into a great principle. The first mention of the phrase 'One Nation' that I have come across is, unsurprisingly, by Stanley Baldwin, who was a One-Nation man and who believed in One Nation. In the early 1930s, when he was Prime Minister, he made a speech that included that phrase. That is the first time, as far as I can discover, that that phrase was used as a symbol or emblem of what the Tory party should be about.

I am not here arguing the merits of the case. I am simply pointing out in a slightly pedantic way that it is part of the Disraeli
myth that he invented 'One Nation'. All leaders of the Tory
party scurry to their cupboards to get quotations about it from
Disraeli. Disraeli has 114 quotations in the *Oxford Dictionary of
Quotations*, Gladstone has nine and Peel has one.[8] That just illustrates, for the moment, the kind of contrast.

Disraeli was unique in creating a myth. A myth is not necessarily a lie and it is not necessarily false; a myth is something
that is not actually justified by the hard facts. Disraeli created
this myth, a noble myth, that had various bits and pieces in it.
Eventually it had free trade in it, although it certainly did not
start as a free-trade myth – quite the opposite. It had empire in
it, and it had a great respect for the monarchy. The amazing flat-
tery of Queen Victoria that Disraeli undertook was part of that,
but it was all part of the myth. He believed in it, as he believed
in the other myths, but it was an artificial thing that he created –
that he blew up around him, as it were. It is interesting that the
cartoons of that time often portrayed Disraeli as a magician, as
a conjuror. That was, of course, partly connected with being a
Jew, but it illustrates that they saw relatively clearly that this was
a myth, not a strict account of reality.

I want to end on the question, 'What if?' What happened – now
we come to a time that I know about because I was Ted Heath's
Political Secretary throughout this time – was that the Tories
won the general election of 1970 against Harold Wilson. They
were greatly surprised that they won. It was a great surprise. All
the polls were adverse until the very last minute. It was generally
thought that we had fought a feeble campaign and the leader's
heart really was not in it, and then we won. In a way it was the
most amazing single day in my political experience, because it
was just so splendid. I remember being immensely pleased, not
because Harold Wilson had been defeated – I have no particular views about Harold Wilson – but because all the know-alls,
all the people who went around with us, the journalists already

writing books and having written books about how we had lost
and why, suddenly had to do a minor adjustment because we had
actually won. My feeling was one of great satisfaction.

Iain Macleod was, of course, a crucial part of that. He did away,
as it were, with the Disraeli concept, and his was straightforward
One-Nation stuff as we know it today. It linked in his mind with the
transformation of the Empire into a Commonwealth, it linked in his
mind with entry into Europe, which he favoured, and it linked in
his mind with a whole number of things. It was basically a kind of
Toryism that the Tory Reform Group now, on the whole, espouses.

Macleod was passionate to prove that point. Among the main
weapons at his disposal was the Beveridge report. Of course,
Beveridge was a Liberal, but the Tory left – the Tory One-Nation
people – seized on the Beveridge report, on the whole concept of
social security, as proof of One Nation. Then there was the 1944
White Paper on employment, which was a coalition White Paper
but did set out in general terms the aim of full employment as
the aim of every decent future government. Finally, there was
Rab Butler's 1944 Education Act, which put down in statute
a modern system of education that was substantially different
from that which people had been brought up on.

Those three things – Beveridge, full employment and
the Butler Act – were seized on by Macleod, and people like
Macleod, as the keystone for future Conservative success. They
were very impatient with people like Harry Crookshank and
Oliver Stanley, who had considerable weight and ability but did
not share that kind of conviction as to what politics was about.

Then Macleod fell ill, had a stroke and died in July 1970. He
died, therefore, just three or four weeks after Ted Heath had
taken office as Prime Minister, and he was already in action as
Chancellor of the Exchequer. What would the result have been
had he survived and been in good health? He was quite different
from the rest of Ted's Cabinet, all of whom were people I knew
and worked with well. He was quite different from the Jim Priors
of this world. He had a much sharper mind and a much sharper

tongue, and he thought much more clearly than Ted himself, who had great gifts but was not actually an intellectual or a clear thinker. Macleod raced along the intellectual path from one stepping-stone to another, and greatly enjoyed the process.

I think different things could have happened. He and Ted could have had a row. They were not easy together. It was very difficult to be easy alongside Ted Heath, but a lot of people managed it. Iain Macleod was not one of them. They were not, therefore, at ease. They got on all right, but it was not an easy or friendly relationship, such as Ted had with Willie Whitelaw, Jim Prior and others. That might have blown up. There might have been a huge row, and Iain Macleod might have stomped out of the Heath Cabinet as another, Michael Heseltine, stomped out of the Thatcher Cabinet.

Or – this, I think, is more likely – there would have been a level-ling effect. Macleod was interested in quite different things from Ted Heath, and would have acted – not exactly as a brake, because he would often have been a stimulus or accelerator – in one way or another to create a rather different and more intellectual type of Toryism than Ted did. When they got to the miners' strike at the beginning of 1974 and the end of 1973, maybe he would have been put in charge of that. He had been Minister of Labour.

He was definitely a peacemaker. He was in the Walter Monckton tradition of Tory Ministers of Labour, whose main anxiety is not to let anybody rock the boat: 'Doucement, douce-ment, and we'll solve the dispute.' He did that, and he was rather good at it. There was a bus strike which Macleod helped solve. He was gaining quite a reputation for that. Maybe, when we got to all the horrors of the incomes policy and when we got into the business of deciding by law what certain things should cost, Macleod would have prevented that and said, 'No, we can't. We're a Tory government. We can't behave in that kind of way.'

I do not know. I did not know Macleod well. I knew Ted well, and I knew how stubborn he was, but also how very anxious he was to follow Macleod. He was a One-Nation man. He really believed it quite wrong that the Tory party should be associated with unemployment. That is one reason why he was very hostile to a good deal of what Margaret Thatcher said and did, particularly what she said. He might well have been won round by Macleod, had Macleod gone hammer and tongs for the pure One-Nation approach or anything like that. There would have been, at the heart of the Cabinet, a remarkable man – a man of great ability, of great powers of communication and of great clarity of thought. The effect on the Tory government of 1970, whatever that effect might have been, would have been very substantial. Macleod was not, and could not have been treated as, a negligible figure.

I did not know Macleod well, but I was a great admirer. I remember sitting in the civil service box in the House of Commons and listening to him. Of the people I remember as orators – Foot was an orator; Enoch was an orator – they were all, in the end, on the wrong side. Ted was not an orator, although he sometimes made good speeches. Here you would have had Macleod as a formidable performer in his own right, loyal to the Prime Minister – I think he would have probably stayed loyal – but emphatic about a view of his own and the way in which the Tory party, in which he passionately believed, should progress and succeed.

1   Lennox-Boyd was Colonial Secretary from 1954 to 1959, holding the only post he ever wanted. See Julian Amery, 'Alan Tindal Lennox-Boyd', in Hugo Young (ed.), *Political Lives* (Oxford: Oxford University Press, 2001), pp.426–9.
2   Speech at the Conservative Party Conference, Brighton, 11 October 1961.
3   Robert Shepherd, *Iain Macleod* (London: Hutchinson, 1994).
4   House of Lords: Official Report (Hansard): 7 March 1961, cols 306–7.
5   For a succinct overview, see Nigel Fisher, *The Tory Leaders* (London: Weidenfeld & Nicolson, 1977), pp.101–12.
6   See Shepherd, *Iain Macleod*, pp.313–16.
7   See Nigel Fisher, *Iain Macleod* (London: Andre Deutsch, 1973), pp.76–9. There were nine original members. The name 'One Nation' was proposed by Angus Maude and agreed with Macleod.
8   *Oxford Dictionary of Quotations*, 3rd edn (Oxford: Oxford University Press, 1979).

Roy Jenkins

Andrew Adonis
Delivered on 25 October 2011

Biographical note

Roy Jenkins

Roy Harris Jenkins, born 11 November 1920, son of Arthur Jenkins (MP for Pontypool, 1935–46). Educated at Abersychan Grammar School, Balliol College, Oxford (Secretary and Librarian, Oxford Union Society). Married 1945 Mary Jennifer, daughter of Sir Parker Morris. Army service 1942–46. Staff of Industrial and Commercial Finance Corporation 1946–48. Labour MP for Southwark Central 1948–50, Birmingham Stechford 1950–76; SDP/Alliance MP for Glasgow Hillhead 1982–87. Minister of Aviation 1964–65, Home Secretary 1965–67, Chancellor of the Exchequer 1967–70. President, European Commission 1977–81.

Chairman, Fabian Society 1957–58. Director of Financial Operations, John Lewis Partnership 1962–64. Director, Morgan Grenfell Holdings, 1981–82. Member, Labour Party National Executive Committee 1970–72; Deputy Leader, Labour Party 1970–72. A founder of Social Democratic Party 1981, Joint Leader 1981–82 and Leader 1982–83. Created Lord Jenkins of Hillhead 1987; Leader, Liberal Democrat Peers 1988–97.

Privy Counsellor 1964. Order of Merit 1993. Chancellor of Oxford University 1987–2003. President, Royal Society of Literature 1988–2003. Charlemagne Prize 1972, Robert Schuman Prize 1972, Prix Bentinck 1980. Author. Died 5 January 2003.

Jenkins established a reputation as a leading thinker on the Labour right. A noted Europhile, he left Parliament to serve as President of the European Commission, before returning to British politics and helping found the Social Democratic Party.

As a biographer, Roy Jenkins had something to say about several of Mr Speaker's predecessors. He didn't have a great deal of time for Mr Speaker Thomas, but then George Thomas suffered the severe defect in Roy's eyes of being both Welsh and proud of it, a condition which Roy never experienced even as a boy in Pontypool.

Nor was Roy much enamoured by Mr Speaker Clifton Brown. They were together on a parliamentary delegation to Rome in 1949, but Roy wasn't quite sure why Mr Speaker was there. 'He was a rather surprising participant, particularly as he appeared not much to like abroad,' he comments.[1] Even at the age of twenty-eight, the Jenkins world divided into pro- and anti-Europeans.

Then there was Mr Speaker Hylton-Foster, Solicitor-General under Macmillan, with whom Roy crossed swords when he was striving to reform the law on print censorship. At a crucial meeting of the Bill committee, most of the Tories failed to turn up, exposing Hylton-Foster to a string of embarrassing defeats. Roy writes: 'He was, however, compensated for his punishment by his being made Speaker six months later.'[2] In those days, if you failed as censor you became Speaker. Nowadays I think Mr Speaker rather wishes the two offices went hand-in-hand.

These lectures commemorate the centenary of the Parliament Act of 1911, the culmination of the struggle between Asquith's Liberal government and the Tory-dominated House of Lords. The Parliament Act was the subject of one of Roy's first books

– entitled *Mr Balfour's Poodle*, after Lloyd George's famous quip: 'The House of Lords is not the watchdog of the constitution: it is Mr Balfour's poodle.'

Re-reading *Mr Balfour's Poodle*, published when Roy was thirty-three, I am struck by the already powerful admiration of the urbane and worldly-wise Mr Asquith.[3] This admiration flowered in Roy's later biography of Asquith,[4] and perhaps more profoundly still in his own political career, which was Asquithian throughout: the steady, moderate liberal reformer, the delight in the good things of life, the intellectual self-confidence and fastidiousness, the passion behind the urbanity, the courage in the face of age and defeat.

Roy told me he was thinking of Paisley, Asquith's triumphal by-election return to the Commons in 1920, as he sought and won his own by-election return at Glasgow Hillhead in 1982. Both triumphs were short-lived and forlorn. But the courage is undeniable, not just at Hillhead but at the very end of his life when, at the age of eighty and seriously ill, he struggled to complete his magisterial biography of Churchill, the longest and to my mind the best of his books. Aficionados will also be glad to note that *Mr Balfour's Poodle* already displays the orotundity which was to captivate Roy's admirers and critics alike.

Asquith is introduced to us as 'in the fullness of his great powers of physical resilience ... his constructive intellectual equipment ... certainly more massive than that of any Prime Minister since Gladstone'. In plain English, he wasn't often ill and he got a first at Balliol, which in Roy's estimation was the highest and purest of intellectual achievements.

Better still is this description of Asquith's political make-up:

> He was circumscribed by the limitations which had beset his predecessor [Campbell-Bannerman] and was prevented, partly by these and partly, perhaps, by his own temperament, from that feeling of impatience to put his hand to the plough and to strike out in new directions which was to be experienced most strongly

by Lloyd George and by Churchill when they, in turn, ascended
to the central control of affairs.

In other words, Asquith was calm and collected, unlike that
rash and impetuous Welsh upstart. Of Churchill, Roy was more
tolerant. After all, Churchill saved Britain from Hitler, whereas
Lloyd George merely wrenched Downing Street from Asquith.

The question I want to address in this lecture is this: in what
respect was Roy Jenkins great? Put differently, what is his enduring inspirational quality?

Roy, of course, never ascended to the central control of affairs.
Nor was he in the very front rank of twentieth-century orators,
in Parliament or outside, although he was a sharp debater and
he coined good and telling passages. This was true right down to
his last speech in the House of Lords, in the recall of Parliament
to debate the Iraq crisis in September 2002, three months before
his death. His speech contains this insightful and prescient
passage about his friend Tony Blair:

> I have been repelled by attempts to portray [Tony Blair] as a vacu-
> ous man with an artificial smile and no convictions. I am reminded
> of similar attempts by a frustrated right to suggest that Gladstone
> was mad, Asquith was corrupt and Attlee was negligible. My view
> is that the Prime Minister, far from lacking conviction, has almost
> too much, particularly when dealing with the world beyond Britain.
> He is a little too Manichaean for my perhaps now jaded taste,
> seeing matters in stark terms of good and evil, black and white,
> contending with each other, and with a consequent belief that if
> evil is cast down good will inevitably follow. I am more inclined to
> see the world and the regimes within it in varying shades of grey.[5]

That was six months before the invasion of Iraq. It was also
fifty-four years after his first speech in the House of Commons.
But as I say, it is not for his speeches that I believe Roy will be
remembered above all.

What of Roy's large and fertile hinterland? Apart from Churchill, he was the most prolific and successful author to hold high office in the twentieth century, and his books continue to be read. But I find little evidence for the view that hinterlands – literary, social, sporting or collecting – tend to make politicians more effective, although sometimes they make them more agreeable. Politics is a profession, and in my experience and observation those who do best at it are generally those who work hardest and most skilfully at it.

Anyway, it is quite wrong to see Roy as a part-time or dilettante politician. He fought every general election from 1945 until 1987 apart from 1979 when he was President of the European Commission, as well as three by-elections, two of which he won, and the 1975 Europe referendum, as a leader of the yes camp. In all, he was a parliamentary candidate fifteen times, spent twenty-eight years in the Commons, was a minister or Commission President for twelve years, and topped it off by founding and leading a new political party, then leading the Liberal Democrats in the House of Lords. If that isn't a professional politician, then I don't know what is. As for Roy's literary pursuits, his books were almost exclusively on British politics and politicians, and all were written while he was in opposition or retired. For Roy, writing was politics by other means; it wasn't a life apart from politics.

However, being professional at politics isn't the same as being ruthless in the pursuit of power. Here, Roy hesitated, fatally for his prospects of ascending to the central control of affairs. He hesitated to move against Wilson when he might have done successfully in 1968 and 1969; then, by resigning the deputy leadership of the Labour Party three years later, he in effect threw up any prospect of leading the Labour Party. Harold Wilson made a telling remark to Mr Speaker Selwyn Lloyd on the evening of Roy's resignation of the deputy leadership. 'It has worked out for the best,' said Wilson. 'Roy will go off and write books, which is what he most likes doing, and we will all have a more comfortable life.'[6]

If Roy's enduring legacy doesn't in my view lie in oratory, hinterland or supreme leadership, nor is it ultimately in broad ideas and programmes. There were Jenkinsites, fiercely loyal to Roy personally; there were also Jenkins causes, of which more anon; but there was no Jenkins-ism.

Roy did of course found a new political party. As a personal quest this was brave and courageous. Jim Callaghan told me it was one of the most courageous things he had seen in politics, by someone who wasn't mad or bad or both, and some of us here were proud to belong to the SDP. Perhaps the SDP helped rebuild the Labour Party, perhaps it delayed the process; you can argue both ways. But in terms of its social democratic programme, it essentially followed in the well-trodden path of Roy's friend and rival Tony Crosland, except on Europe, where Crosland was equivocal while Roy was unflinching.

I say 'except on Europe'. That is a pretty big caveat. Without the Jenkinsites, Britain's entry into the European Community would have been still more difficult in the 1970s. But except on Europe, the label 'Jenkinsite' didn't go with a bold forward agenda on a par with being a 'Thatcherite' in the 1980s or a 'Blairite' after 1997. I remember even at the time, as a student Jenkinsite, being a bit depressed in the 1983 election when the best that Roy could say about the future of British industry was that he did not favour more frontier wars between the public and private sectors. It was a good phrase but grist to Ralf Dahrendorf's jibe that the SDP stood for a better yesterday.

This goes to the heart of Roy's most intriguing remark about his own career. He said that he would like to have been Prime Minister, but didn't think he would have enjoyed being Prime Minister. In truth, faced with the violent industrial and social conflicts of the 1970s and 1980s, Roy did not have enough self-belief that his own leadership and vision were the answer. To make a Jenkins-style analogy, he was Adlai Stevenson rather than J. F. K.

I am aware that I'm beginning to sound a bit like Roy himself, awarding alphas, betas and gammas – as he was wont to do, in great

Oxford style – for different categories of achievement. So far we have been in the realm of what Roy I guess would have judged beta triple plus, with touches of beta alpha, in the twentieth-century parliamentarian stakes, a rating I recall him giving to Stanley Baldwin when we played this parlour game one day over lunch at Brooks's. He gave Attlee alpha beta, Macmillan beta alpha, Eden straight gamma. Asquith, of course, was straight alpha, until 1915 at least.

In Roy's case, I would apply alpha to his record as a minister. It is as a minister, not as a parliamentarian or political leader per se, that Roy Jenkins is an enduring inspiration.

Roy was good or outstanding in all his positions of executive leadership – as Home Secretary twice, as Chancellor of the Exchequer, and as President of the European Commission.

I shall argue in a moment that as Home Secretary in the 1960s, he wasn't simply outstanding; he was the model of the transformational minister.

But in all his executive posts, he demonstrated remarkable qualities of clarity, decisiveness, confidence, administrative competence and the ability to mobilise middle as well as radical opinion.

Roy became Chancellor in 1967 in the wake of devaluation, a catastrophic collapse in the central plank of a government's economic policy matched in recent times only by Black Wednesday in 1992. Within two years, acting decisively on public spending and on what we would today call the 'growth agenda', and exuding confidence and measured optimism, he had largely restored the government's economic credibility.

Roy liked to quip that most Labour governments require two Chancellors – one to get into an economic mess, the other to try to get out of it; except for Denis Healey, who as he put it, 'had that India rubber quality to get himself into the crisis, and then out of it, as if he were two entirely different people'. In this view Roy was to Callaghan as Cripps was to Dalton. Labour still lost in 1970. Whether Roy's 1970 Budget helped or hindered

Labour's prospects is much debated; but compared to the situation when he took over the Treasury, the remarkable fact is that Wilson was in with a shout at all.

Roy was similarly solid in adversity as President of the European Commission for four years from January 1977. He took and initially treated the job as a consolation prize for not getting the Foreign Office when Callaghan succeeded Wilson and gave it to Crosland. The condition of the European Community was similarly depressed in the wake of the mid-1970s oil and inflation crises.

Arriving in Brussels, Roy's morale was poor and his agenda thin. He even had to fight, semi-farcically, to be allowed to attend European summits alongside heads of government.

But once he got into his stride, he set and largely achieved a bold agenda. Greece joined the EU – Europe rejoices still – and Spain and Portugal were put on the path to membership. His greatest impact was on monetary integration. Once Roy set about promoting a European Monetary System in his Florence speech of July 1977, momentum for the idea grew. The European Monetary System was set up less than two years after the Florence speech, in March 1979. Without Schmidt and Giscard it would not have happened; but without Roy, they may not have wanted it to happen in the first place. And, of course, the EMS led on to other things, which I won't get into here.

Roy was a one-term President of the Commission. In that one term he reinvented the office. He turned it into an essentially ministerial and political office, an achievement not lost on Jacques Delors in particular. The general view in mid-1970s Brussels was that Walter Hallstein had been a founding one-off, and that the weak and almost immediately forgotten bureaucratic tenures of Rey, Malfatti, Mansholt and Ortoli were par for the course – and I had to Google those four even to recall their names. After Roy, the presidency of the European Commission was a post for Prime Ministers and dominant ministers. All of Roy's successors have been Prime Ministers apart from Delors himself.

So as Chancellor and as Commission President, Roy was a highly effective executive leader. But it was as Home Secretary in the first Wilson government that he was transformational.

It is an astonishing fact that Roy was Home Secretary for only one year and eleven months, from 23 December 1965 to 30 November 1967, and those twenty-three months included the 1966 general election. But it is not too much to say that in those twenty-three months he and his allies changed the face of society.

The legalisation of abortion. The legalisation of homosexuality. 'No fault' divorce. The prohibition of racial discrimination. The abolition of stage censorship. The abolition of flogging in prisons. Radical reform of the police. Majority verdicts in criminal trials. Individually these reforms were important, some of them seismic. Taken together – and together with subsequent reforms extending their principles, including, equally radically, the Sex Discrimination Act of 1975, a fruit of Roy's second Home Secretaryship – taken together, as I say, they changed the face of society.

Several of these reforms took the form of Private Members' Bills, and some were not finally enacted until after Roy left the Home Office.[7] But few if any of them would have passed in the mid-1960s without Roy as Home Secretary. It was Roy's bold and skilful ministerial leadership, including the way he supported Private Members' Bills, which got them seriously going.

Roy always intended these reforms to be taken together and to be seen as a whole. He didn't see himself as a Home Secretary enacting a few liberal reforms, he saw himself – unashamedly – as a liberal Home Secretary. The Home Secretary chapter in his memoirs is entitled 'The Liberal Hour'.[8] He intended his reforms to foster, across society, a liberal spirit to challenge rigid social control of the individual by, as he put it to me, the bishops and the bigots. (He didn't, I hasten to add, see these two groups as entirely congruous: he liked some bishops, particularly those who didn't go on about God, in the way that Trollope was fascinated by Barchester.)

Long before becoming Home Secretary, in his 1959 book *The Labour Case*, Roy set out a whole unauthorised programme of proposed liberal reforms.[9] 'There is the need for the State to do less to restrict personal freedom' was his theme, and he sought, systematically, to promote and enact as much as he could of this programme as Home Secretary.

In the rest of this lecture I dissect Roy's first stint as Home Secretary, to present the anatomy of the transformational minister. Before doing so, what of the obvious point – wouldn't it all have happened anyway?

The answer, in respect of the major liberal reforms, must of course be: 'yes, over time'. It was a matter of time, in Britain as across secularising Europe, before abortion and homosexuality were legalised, divorce made easier and censorship on grounds of morals abolished. You could make the same long-term inevitability point about, for example, the privatisation of industry in the 1980s, devolution to Scotland in the 1990s – or indeed, the limitation of the powers of the House of Lords by the Parliament Act of 1911: they had all become more or less inevitable, given the spirit of the age.

But because something beneficial is in the long-run inevitable doesn't reduce the benefit of doing it sooner rather than later, doing it boldly rather than grudgingly and doing it well rather than badly. The purpose of the politician as reformer is to do precisely this, and this is what Roy did.

One only has to look, for example, at the vexed history of abortion across western democracies to see what this means in the specific context of the Jenkins reforms. In Britain, illegal abortions were running at between 40,000 and 200,000 a year, with dozens of women dying each year from criminal abortions, before the change of the law in 1967. In France the equivalent reform did not happen until 1975, in Italy 1978 and in the Netherlands 1980. In Belgium it was 1990. In West Germany and later the united Germany, the right of women to abortion was fought in the courts throughout the 1960s, 1970s, 1980s and

1990s until a general legal right was finally established in 1995, a whole generation after Britain. For years, women from all these countries came to Britain for abortions because they weren't legal at home. And I haven't time even to start on the Republic of Ireland or the United States.

It can be said with reasonable confidence that some if not all of the major Jenkins reforms would have been delayed several years without him, and even then they might have been implemented more tentatively and piecemeal.

In the case of abortion, Bill after Bill had failed in the previous twenty years, while on homosexuality there had been no progress whatever since the Wolfenden Report nine years earlier. Rab Butler, Home Secretary after Wolfenden, did a hand-wringing response, saying it was all too difficult, and although he wasn't necessarily against legalisation in principle, more time was needed for research and the education of public opinion.

However, for a 1960s counterfactual of the Home Office without Jenkins there is no need for a crystal ball; just consider the other two Home Secretaries in the Wilson government – Roy's predecessor Sir Frank Soskice, and his successor Jim Callaghan.

Frank Soskice has the distinction of being the first Home Secretary not to hang anyone. In other respects he was weak, indecisive and behaved almost apolitically as a lawyer. Only months before Roy became Home Secretary, a Private Member's Bill to legalise homosexuality was defeated outright on a free vote in the Commons, with Labour whips organising against because, as Richard Crossman recorded, they 'objected fiercely that it was turning our working-class support against us'. Soskice wouldn't even countenance a law against racial discrimination, arguing that this might stir up racial prejudice. At a loss for a policy on immigration and racial tension, in late 1965 he proposed a Royal Commission. Crossman records the Cabinet discussion thus: 'It is difficult to conceive of a sillier proposal. By setting up a Royal Commission we should simply announce our determination to postpone any action at all for years. ... Fortunately Gerald

Gardiner [Lord Chancellor] and Bert Bowden [Leader of the House] bashed poor Frank Soskice right away.'[10]

No one could accuse Jim Callaghan, Roy's successor, of being apolitical or weak. In opposition, Callaghan had been parliamentary spokesman for the Police Federation; he was the archetypal bluff and tough Home Secretary. Callaghan wasn't hostile to all liberal reform. He saw through three Jenkins reforms which were in train but not yet enacted by the end of 1967 – the Bills on race discrimination, divorce and censorship.

But a mid-1960s Callaghan Home Secretaryship would clearly not have been in the Jenkins mould. One need only look at the positions he took at the time. When in late 1966 Roy asked the Cabinet for government time to enable the Private Member's Bill to legalise homosexuality to make progress, and to be allowed to speak and vote in support of it, Crossman records the discussion as follows: 'Callaghan, Wilson, George Brown and others asked why any time should be given at all to such a Bill and why we should abandon the neutrality which the Labour Cabinet had always shown to such controversial issues as homosexuality, abortion, divorce and Sunday opening of cinemas.'[11] Roy prevailed, but when the Bills on abortion and homosexuality came before the Commons, Callaghan did not vote for either of them, either on second reading or at any subsequent stage.

As for the forces strongly opposed to change, on both Bills they included Willie Ross, Wilson's old school Secretary of State for Scotland, who even after the legalisation of homosexuality in England and Wales refused to support legalisation north of the border – and so it remained in Scotland, illegal, until 1980, thirteen years after the change of the law in England and Wales. In Northern Ireland, homosexuality wasn't legalised until 1982.

Let me make another general remark about the Jenkins reforms. A moment ago I included police reform and majority verdicts in the summary of his greatest hits. To be precise, Roy culled the number of police authorities in England and Wales from 117 to forty-nine, where – plus a few further amalgamations taking the number to forty-three in the early 1970s – it has remained ever since, impervious to further rationalisation.

On juries, Roy carried legislation abolishing the rule that jury verdicts in England and Wales had to be unanimous. Instead they could be 11–1 or 10–2. This now seems plain common sense, but the unanimity rule dated back to the fourteenth century and was still in the 1960s regarded as sacrosanct by traditionalists on the right – including Margaret Thatcher – as well as most of the legal and civil rights community on the left, despite evidence of jury-nobbling undermining trials in serious criminal cases.

These police and jury reforms were essentially about modernisation. They weren't inherently liberal. But Roy presented them as integral to his liberal programme, arguing that by improving the efficiency of the police and the courts, and thereby tackling crime more effectively, the public was better protected and populist demands for drastic punishments would reduce. Fewer police authorities improved the capacity of the police in respect of serious organised crime, while majority verdicts increased the conviction rate which, as Roy put it, 'fitted in well with my general approach to deterrence, which was to regard the likelihood of detection and conviction as more powerful factors than an enormity of punishment'.

As an aside, there is an article in *The Economist* on the fiscal crisis in California, where on the back of three-strikes-and-you-are-out and draconian prison sentences, spending on prisons has risen from 4 per cent of the state budget thirty years ago to more than 10 per cent today, which is more than the state spends on universities. California's governor is seeking to reverse this trend by more efficient courts and better non-custodial sentences. *The Economist* says: 'The idea, based on research and recent experience in states such as Texas and Hawaii, is that people change behaviour in response to swift and certain consequences, not necessarily severe ones.' That is word for word the Jenkins view of fifty years ago, although territory less agreeable to Roy than Texas and Hawaii it is hard to conceive. As his son Charles said at his funeral, 'I suspect he always wished that Boston was on the mouth of the Gironde.'

My point is this. Roy understood that to carry middle opinion behind progressive reform, you have to be big on modernisation and efficiency as well as big on reform; and you have constantly to make the connection between the two. Then you are in a good position to build consensus across party lines, and you should seek to do so. On majority verdicts, Roy cultivated both Quintin Hogg, his Tory shadow, and Michael Foot, leader of the back-bench left. Neither were natural bedfellows, yet both supported the reform on free votes.

Part of Roy's skill at the Home Office was to counter the notion that liberals are soft on crime, and to create a powerful sense that being modern and liberal are two sides of the same coin.

This is the first point in my anatomy of Roy Jenkins as transformational minister. The successful reformer is also the successful moderniser.

My second point is implicit in noting that Roy was Home Secretary for only twenty-three months. It is not length of tenure that makes a transformational minister, but having a credible agenda and being able to implement it. As it happens, twenty-three months is only marginally shorter than the average tenure of Cabinet ministers in Britain since the war, which is twenty-eight months according to a recent Institute for Government study. So although Roy's tenure was brief, it was typically brief. By contrast, none of the longest-serving Home Secretaries since the war have much by way of reform to show for it. To be fair to Michael Howard, who held the post for four years, I don't think he ever wanted the word 'reformer' on his tombstone. But Chuter Ede, Home Secretary for the entire Attlee government, might have been expected to strike out more radically, yet didn't. Rab Butler, much respected by Roy, not least as a fellow President of the Royal Society of Literature, was Home Secretary for five-and-a-half years and had little to show for it either.

Clearly if you have only got twenty-three months and you

want to be a reformer, it is not enough to work up an agenda over time. You generally need to arrive in the job with a broad plan pretty well worked out.

This isn't just about length of tenure; it is also about the nature of power. As a minister, you are rarely more powerful than in your opening months in post, when you set the pace and expectations of your ministerial life and people expect you to be there for at least a while.

Roy arrived as Home Secretary with his reform plan pretty well fully worked out. He was receptive to technical advice, but he had made up his mind on the big issues and he wasn't put off by civil service or media conservatism. For more than a decade he had been forming his views on how to liberalise the state and free the individual, and from day one he simply got on with it.

But it's not just that Roy knew what he wanted to do. He was passionate about it, and his passion was infectious. I am taken by a remark of Jonathan Freedland's in a recent article. It's quite untrue, he writes, that people believe in ideas. Rather they believe in people who believe in ideas. The two go together and that was certainly true of Roy Jenkins. As David Marquand, one of the 1966 Jenkinsite intake of Labour MPs, puts it: 'It is hard to recapture in retrospect the excitement Roy generated as Home Secretary.'

This leads to my third point. In order to be a transformational minister, it helps if you want to do the job. This may seem stark staring obvious; but it is remarkable how often Cabinet ministers occupy posts in which they evince little interest, let alone passion, simply because it's what they were offered. Conversely, it is all too rare for a Prime Minister to choose someone for a post who knows what they want to do with it and could set out a semi-coherent plan at the time of their appointment.

In Roy's case, not only did he badly want to be Home Secretary, but as a minister outside the Cabinet he adopted the exception-ally high-risk strategy of turning down Harold Wilson's first offer of the Cabinet.

It was January 1965, the first reshuffle after the 1964 election. Wilson offered him Education Secretary, a significant promotion and in the Cabinet. Roy asked for a few hours to think it over, and decided he would chance it and hold out for the Home Office, or another post in which he was more interested, at a later stage. And so he told Wilson. When I read the account of this in Roy's memoirs twenty years ago, I took it at face value. Re-reading it, with my experience since, I am awestruck. In all my time in No. 10 and as a minister, I cannot think of a single case of an ambitious up-and-coming minister refusing a significant promotion, let alone a first job in the Cabinet, for any reason, let alone because they weren't particularly interested in the subject matter of the job on offer and preferred to hold out for another. It wasn't even the case that the Home Office was imminently vacant. Frank Soskice had been there for only three months; it took nearly a further year, and plenty of ups and downs, before it came Roy's way.

All in all, it testifies to an extraordinary political nerve and strategic sense.

I particularly treasure Roy's exchange with Wilson when turning down the Education Secretaryship – which Tony Crosland promptly accepted. In his memoirs he puts it thus:

> Looking for an excuse, I said that all three of our children were at fee-paying schools and that this surely was an obstacle to being Minister of Education in a Labour government. Wilson brushed this aside as being of no importance. 'So were mine', he said.[12]

Just to add, it is certainly true that Roy wasn't much interested in education – or rather in schools, since he became interested in universities as Chancellor of Oxford. Schools are a particular concern of Jennifer [Roy's wife] and mine, but the only conversation I remember with him on the subject was when, on one occasion, his trainspotter and high-society sympathies came together and he rattled off all the headmasters of Eton since Robert Birley.

To recap: three features so far of the successful reforming
minister, exemplified by Roy Jenkins as Home Secretary. You
have got to want the job. You have got to have a plan at the
outset. And the plan needs to combine reform with modernisation. But all this is to no avail unless you can get the machine to
work and do your bidding.

The machine, for a minister, is Whitehall, your party, the
media and Parliament; without reasonable competence in all
four arenas, the most passionate and well-prepared minister
comes to little. Roy mastered all four as Home Secretary – and,
again, he is a case study in how to do it. Let me take them
in turn.

Whitehall, for a minister, is two overlapping but distinct enti-
ties: your ministerial colleagues and the civil service. The most
important relationship for a Home Secretary is of course with
the Prime Minister. Harold Wilson had a high opinion of Roy,
even when they fell out, not least for his writing. The story goes
that Wilson read Asquith on the plane to Washington for his first
meeting with L. B. J. [Lyndon B. Johnson] after the 1964 election, and muttered to his private secretary something like: 'That
man should be in my Cabinet.' He appointed Roy as Home
Secretary largely on merit, telling him the Cabinet Secretary
said he was the best minister in the government. As ever, there
were personal and factional factors; but competence, dynamic
energy and strong media reputations were at a premium by the
end of 1965, and Roy supplied all three.

For his part, Roy cultivated Wilson carefully. The relationship
became strained when he was Chancellor as Wilson came to see
plots all around him, most of them real. It broke down completely
in opposition after 1970, for which they were about equally responsible. It recovered a bit, but was frosty at best during the second
Home Secretaryship. But during the first Home Secretaryship it
was generally good, with mutual respect and tolerance.

Tolerance was essential, because Wilson – MP for Huyton in
Liverpool – was, politically and personally, no fan of the Jenkins

reforms. Like Callaghan, he voted for neither the legalisation of abortion nor homosexuality in the Commons. He wasn't even keen on abolishing theatre censorship. The stage adaptation of *Mrs Wilson's Diary* was threatening to erupt on the West End in the summer of 1967. Wilson had been warned that the script 'made him out to be a complete mugwump', as he told Crossman, and he tried to get Roy to drop the measure, on the excuse that Buckingham Palace feared it might lead to the Royal Family being satirised. Roy didn't budge, *Mrs Wilson's Diary*, uncensored, was a success, and that was that. Wilson needed Roy's cachet as a strong and popular minister – he didn't have many others – and at every crucial juncture, he backed him.

Roy's relations with other colleagues were serviceable. He allowed Callaghan to patronise him, Crossman to lecture him, and George Brown to rant at him, periodically at least.

As for the civil service, Roy was the mandarin's minister. Among top civil servants I have spoken to over the last twenty-five years, only Michael Heseltine receives as many plaudits. This isn't because he was conventional, let alone supine. His first act on becoming Home Secretary was to sack his permanent secretary, after bitter exchanges about working practices and Roy's desire to widen the net of official advice. He also relied heavily on special advisers, then a new and distrusted breed – now they are just old and distrusted. His long-serving special adviser and friend John Harris was at his right hand throughout his ministerial life. They became so close, in manner as much as opinion, that John came to speak like Roy, act like Roy, think like Roy, drink like Roy, even look like Roy – indeed, when they sat side by side in the House of Lords in their last years, John the Lib Dem Chief Whip to Roy as Leader of the Lib Dem peers, the one was easily mistaken for the other.

Being unconventional in such ways – indeed in any ways – can easily set the Whitehall machine against you. But Roy's strategy wasn't to circumvent the machine but rather, by decisive moves early on, to establish working practices which suited him, to surround himself with officials he rated and trusted, then to depend on them totally and deploy them as his agents with the machine beyond. This generally worked well. His key private secretaries were so close, they moved from department to department with him – or in the case of Hayden Phillips, to Brussels from the Home Office. Apart from the one he sacked, his permanent secretaries and top officials in Brussels became confidants as well as advisers, and were proactive and protective on his behalf. For his part, Roy was solicitous not only for their careers, but also for their honours – a cause dear to the heart of Sir Humphrey, which Roy took immensely seriously. When I worked at No. 10 for Tony Blair, there was almost no subject on which Roy had a stronger opinion than the composition of honours lists, particularly the deserving nature of those who had worked for him in the past or – in the case of vice-chancellors of Oxford – in the present.

So much for Whitehall. As Home Secretary, Roy was equally effective at mobilising his party. Again, this wasn't by means conventional, let alone supine. Roy arrived at Westminster, the baby of the House at the age of twenty-seven in 1948, with the purest of Labour pedigrees. His father, Arthur, had been Labour MP for Pontypool after a long and distinguished service in the South Wales Miners' Federation. Arthur was PPS and friend to Attlee, who spoke at Roy and Jennifer's wedding, and who gave Roy the run of No. 10 to write his biography, which was Roy's first book, published in the same year he became an MP.[13] If there was a post-war Labour aristocracy, Roy was born into it with almost ducal pretensions.

It didn't turn out quite that way. Oxford and Brooks's shaped Roy more than Pontypool and the miners. Even in the 1950s he rarely described himself as a socialist. He took, uncompromisingly, the 'radical moderate' course in almost every internal Labour battle from Gaitskell v. Bevan in the 1950s, to the conflicts over Europe in the 1970s, to the decision to split the party in 1980 rather than launch an internal fightback against Bennism.

Put like that, it sounds like a steady linear progress from the Welsh valleys to the bosom of the Liberal establishment, whose historic leaders Roy admired so much.

But that is quite unhistorical. After the deaths of Bevan and then Gaitskell, and three election defeats in a row, Labour under Harold Wilson went through a short but successful period determined to win, with factions at bay. Wilson and his white-hot heat of the technological revolution was the New Britain; the 14th Earl of Home was Old Britain; and it was as a broad church of the centre and left that Labour won in 1964 and 1966.

Roy was well within this broad church. As Home Secretary and Chancellor, he came to symbolise it more than the Prime Minister himself. But although he was in some ways a liberal right marker of the Labour coalition, he wasn't at this stage a notably divisive figure, and he cultivated support among the unions and across the party.

This included the left. When conducting interviews about Roy in the late 1990s, I was struck by how near-universal, on the left, was praise for Roy as Home Secretary. Barbara Castle was effusive. Michael Foot told me, in his pokey *Tribune* office on Gray's Inn Road, that Roy was 'a damn good Home Secretary' although he was quick to add 'it went downhill after that'. This wasn't just because he supported the liberal reforms. Roy took care to court Foot for the modernising reforms as well, as I noted earlier.

Roy was especially popular among the large and young 1966 Labour intake, where – left and right – he was seen as a dynamic force and perhaps the face of Labour's future as Wilson became increasingly embattled and jaded. It wasn't to be. But these were the MPs who rallied to Roy as Home Secretary, sticking it out across the all-night sittings needed to get the liberal reforms through the House of Commons – which being Private Members' Bills, were not subject to government whips.

If Roy's position was strong in the late 1960s Labour Party, it was stronger still in the media. In the 1960s he was a highly adept media operator. The liberal left media loved him, and he cultivated them assiduously. *The Observer* was a particular fan. David Astor, *The Observer's* proprietor-editor throughout the 1950s and 1960s, wasn't just an admirer of Roy's: he put Roy on his payroll before the 1964 election as a feature writer, giving him far greater prominence than he would have got as a mid-ranking opposition spokesman.

But Roy wasn't just the darling of the liberal press. He had a strong following on Hugh Cudlipp's *Mirror*, as well as, in the centre and centre-right, *The Times* under William Rees-Mogg, *The Economist* under Alastair Burnett, and much of the BBC. Here it was Roy the Balliol moderniser and capable administrator which appealed, rather than the liberal reformer. Rees-Mogg, ex-Balliol but a Catholic, wasn't remotely in the liberal space, yet *The Times* strongly supported Roy to succeed as Chancellor. As for *The Economist*, Roy nearly became its editor in the early 1960s, so much did they admire him, and the paper gave John Harris a job after the 1970 defeat, whereupon he continued to assist Roy much as before, not least over lunch with journalists at the Reform Club.

Roy's media popularity continued into the 1970s and 1980s. By the mid-1970s it far exceeded his popularity inside the Labour Party. By the late 1970s the mainstream liberal and right-wing media alike were urging him to break with Labour, and they were keen supporters of the formation of the SDP. Indeed, the whole SDP project was in effect launched by Roy in a prime-time lecture on the BBC – the Dimbleby lecture of November 1979.

If the media could collectively have chosen a Prime Minister, at almost any time from 1967 to 1983 it would probably have been Roy Jenkins – at any rate, if the election had been by AV.

This brings me finally to Roy Jenkins the parliamentarian. I put this – the seventh attribute of the transformational minister – last not because it is least. Rather I come to it last for this reason: for a reform-minded minister there are parliamentary skills which are essential but ephemeral, and those which are essential and critical, and the two need to be distinguished.

By starting this analysis of Roy as Home Secretary with policy and ending with Parliament, the classic trophies of parliamentary fame – the set-piece dispatch box triumphs – can be seen for what they are to the reforming minister: essential but ephemeral. They are essential, in that a minister who can't survive in Parliament can't survive at all. Roy had no difficulty in this respect. His greatest parliamentary test as Home Secretary was the escape of the Russian spy George Blake from Wormwood Scrubs in October 1966. Ted Heath tabled a censure motion after Roy mishandled the initial response. In a debate of high drama, Roy trounced Heath and Quintin Hogg by demonstrating that everything he had done and not done as Home Secretary in dealing with prison security, his Tory predecessors had done and not done worse. Crossman described it as 'a tremendous annihilating attack which completely destroyed the opposition'. There was much cheering, waving of order papers, and all that.

Yet as Roy put it in his memoirs:

> It was all rather ludicrous and showed that debating ... really is the harlot of the arts ... [For] nothing of substance had happened ... It was as foolish to pretend before the debate that I had any real responsibility for who got over a wall in W12 as it was to suggest that I had suddenly become a superman whose ability to deflate leaders of the opposition more than compensated for my inability to find absconding spies.[14]

The parliamentary triumphs which mattered to Roy weren't the set-piece parliamentary dramas, but the subtle and collaborative work needed to facilitate the passage of his contentious reforms.

His key challenge was to get through Parliament the two highly sensitive liberal reforms on which he immediately fixed his sights – the legalisation of abortion and homosexuality – but which, as I explained earlier, he couldn't conceivably get Wilson and the Cabinet to endorse as government measures.

It had to be done by the way of Private Members' Bills. This was hazardous at best, but here Roy's parliamentary experience was invaluable. He knew the Private Member's Bill world back to front from his 1950s campaign to abolish print censorship on grounds of morals. After years of literary and parliamentary agitation, Roy succeeded in piloting a Private Member's Bill through in 1959 allowing for a defence of literary merit. It was a half measure, although it turned out to be a sufficient half measure when Penguin Books was acquitted in the Lady Chatterley trial which followed. But it was the best he could get past the sphinx-like Rab Butler, who as Home Secretary was prepared to open the shutters a bit, provided the Tory colonels and matrons weren't too scandalised.

The lesson Roy drew from this, and from the abolition of hanging after the 1964 election, was that the Private Member's Bill route was serviceable, so long as you had the right back-bench promoter and so long as the Home Secretary came in behind a Private Member's Bill with total support, even while the government was officially neutral and the issue a matter of individual conscience. This had to include vocal and organisational support, and providing however much government time was needed on the floor of the Commons to break filibusters, so making the Private Member's Bill a quasi-government bill but without collective ministerial responsibility.

This was a significant parliamentary innovation. As we have seen, it was also controversial within the government, once colleagues realised what Roy was up to. But Roy did more than this. With an instinct for seizing the initiative and building momentum, he decided immediately after the 1966 election to move in this way not just on one of the two legalisations, but on both abortion and homosexuality at the same time. This was another high-risk strategy. Not only did it double the controversy; it also divided the support. Some of the leading supporters of legalising homosexuality – including Leo Abse and Norman St John-Stevas – were strongly opposed to legalising abortion, which involved, as Roy put it, treating the same MPs as 'heroes' and 'hobgoblins' on different days while retaining their goodwill throughout.

But Roy's calculation was that this risk was outweighed by the narrow window of opportunity to mobilise, on the run, the 1966 influx of new and progressive Labour MPs, while they were still enthusiastic and while he was still Home Secretary. This judgement was vindicated, in that both Bills passed in the first session after the election. By the second session Roy was no longer Home Secretary, Jim Callaghan was in his place, and glad confident morning was receding fast on the Labour back benches.

As for the tactics needed to get the Bills through, the Private Member's Bill route required a high degree of collaboration. David Steel, who promoted the Abortion Bill, and Leo Abse, the Sexual Offences Bill, were effective parliamentarians of great energy and persuasion. Without them there would have been no Bills. But without the Home Secretary behind them, their Bills wouldn't have stood a chance. It was a remarkable team effort. The Home Office not only drafted the Bills but also provided back-up support. Roy orchestrated Whitehall and the parliamentary machine in the ways I have described, including repeated allocations of extra government time on the floor of the House to enable the passage of the Bills. Roy's junior ministers also played an important part in facilitating the passage of the Bills.

I said a moment ago that Roy got the Cabinet to agree he could speak and vote for the two Bills. This wasn't just a symbolic gesture. He spoke strongly in support of both Bills at every stage on the floor of the House. On the Second Reading of the Abortion Bill he described the status quo as 'harsh and archaic' and 'in urgent need of reform'.[15] On the Sexual Offences Bill he didn't hide behind arguments about enforcement and police corruption; he stated boldly that homosexuality was a fact of life, and not 'a matter of choice', for a sizeable minority; 'it is not concentrated in any particular social classes or occupational groups ... the majority of homosexuals ... [are] ordinary citizens who do normal jobs', and

deserved legal protection not legal oppression. Taking head-on
Rab Butler's argument that public opinion was unprepared, Roy
simply asserted that more time had passed and 'to a substantial
extent public opinion has now been educated'.[16]

It took three all-night sittings to get the two Bills through
their final stages on the floor of the Commons, after months in
committee. Roy was on the front bench throughout, voting in all
forty-five divisions on the two Bills, and both speaking and voting
against every significant proposed amendment to water down
the Bills.

The third all-nighter, on the Abortion Bill, started at 10.15 p.m
on a Thursday and finished at noon on the Friday. A mammoth
filibuster ended only when it was clear to the opponents that
Roy and David Steel had rallied enough supporters to keep the
House sitting through a second night and into Saturday if necessary to get the Bill through. So it was that the Sexual Offences
Bill became law at the end of July 1967, and the Abortion Bill
at the end of October, a month before Roy ceased to be
Home Secretary.

In his life of Wilson, Ben Pimlott states boldly: 'Most Home
Secretaries are unpopular and fail; Jenkins was popular and
succeeded.'[17] I have tried to explain why Roy succeeded: the
interaction between the skilful parliamentarian, the effective
policy-maker, the energetic moderniser, and the bold and inspirational minister.

But to me – and now I speak personally and not analytically –
Roy's achievement isn't that he was so technically accomplished,
but that he was so accomplished in a cause which was so great.
For millions of men and women, then and since, the Jenkins
reforms helped bring liberation, dignity, freedom. They built a
stronger, more open society. They demonstrated the nobility of
politics at its best.

For years after, debate raged on the pros and cons of the
so-called permissive society. Roy always called it the civilised
society; and as he pointed out, not one of his reforms was

reversed, even under Margaret Thatcher; indeed almost all of them have been extended. David Cameron told the Conservative Party conference that the government intends to legislate for gay marriage. The Prime Minister claimed this as a great Tory cause to strengthen social bonds. He was speaking forty-five years almost to the day after the introduction of the Sexual Offences Bill.

A final recollection. Roy's memorial service, in Westminster Abbey, was for me somewhat fraught. Tony Blair had been due to give the address – I still have the draft – but he had to pull out at the last moment to fly to Washington to commune with George Bush about Iraq. Quite some irony. Shirley Williams stepped in and, of course, was brilliant. I undertook to get her a message to read from the Prime Minister. Until she started speaking I wasn't sure she had received it by email, but all was well.

As Shirley spoke I glanced up, to see I was sitting next to the simple memorial tablet to Asquith. On it are the words of Milton:

Unshaken, unseduced, unterrified
His loyalty he kept, his love, his zeal.
Nor number, nor example with him wrought
To swerve from truth, or change his constant mind.

It is what Roy admired in Asquith. It is what so many of us admire in Roy.

1   Roy Jenkins, *Life at the Centre* (London: Macmillan, 1991), p.75.
2   Jenkins, *Life at the Centre*, p.123.
3   Roy Jenkins, *Mr Balfour's Poodle* (London: Heinemann, 1954).
4   Roy Jenkins, *Asquith* (London: Collins, 1964).
5   House of Commons: Official Report (Hansard): 24 September 2002, Vol. 638, col. 893.
6   Jenkins, *Life at the Centre*, p.349.
7   See Peter Richards, *Parliament and Conscience* (London: George Allen & Unwin, 1970).
8   Jenkins, *Life at the Centre*, Ch. 10.
9   Roy Jenkins, *The Labour Case* (Harmondsworth: Penguin Books, 1964).

10 Richard Crossman, *The Diaries of a Cabinet Minister*, Vol. 1 (London: Hamish Hamilton and Jonathan Cape, 1975), p.366.

11 Richard Crossman, *The Diaries of a Cabinet Minister*, Vol. 2 (London: Hamish Hamilton and Jonathan Cape, 1976), p.97.

12 Jenkins, *Life at the Centre*, p.170.

13 Roy Jenkins, *Mr Attlee* (London: Heinemann, 1948).

14 Jenkins, *Life at the Centre*, p.203.

15 House of Commons: Official Report (Hansard): 22 July 1966, Vol. 732, col. 1141.

16 House of Commons: Official Report (Hansard): 11 February 1966, Vol. 724, cols 849–50.

17 Ben Pimlott, *Harold Wilson* (London: HarperCollins, 1992), p.487.

Margaret Thatcher

John Whittingdale
Delivered on 15 November 2011

Biographical note

Margaret Thatcher

Margaret Hilda Roberts, born 13 October 1925, Grantham, daughter of Alfred Roberts. Educated Kesteven and Grantham High School, Somerville College, Oxford (BSc). Married 1951, Denis Thatcher MBE TD. Research Chemist 1947–51, Barrister. Conservative MP for Finchley 1959–92. Joint Parliamentary Secretary, Ministry of Pensions and National Insurance 1961–64; Secretary of State for Education and Science 1970–74; Leader of the Opposition 1975–79; Prime Minister 1979–90.

Privy Counsellor 1970, Fellow of the Royal Society 1983, Order of Merit 1990, Lady of the Garter 1995. Presidential Medal of Freedom (USA) 1991. Created Baroness Thatcher 1992. Chancellor, Buckingham University 1992–98.

Margaret Thatcher was an unexpected victor over Edward Heath for the Conservative Party leadership in 1975. Her time as Leader of the Opposition was not notably successful, but after leading her party to victory in 1979 – becoming Britain's first female Prime Minister – she came to dominate both her party and the House of Commons. She also generated an eponymous philosophy – Thatcherism – and was a controversial figure both at home and abroad, dubbed 'The Iron Lady' for her resolute pursuit of policies. She built a notable alliance with US President Ronald Reagan.

She led her party to three successive election victories and had the longest continuous service in No. 10 in modern British history. She resigned in November 1990 after failing to gain enough votes to win outright in the first ballot of a leadership contest.

It was twenty-one years ago yesterday that Michael Heseltine formally notified Cranley Onslow, the Chairman of the 1922 Committee, that he wished to be a candidate for the leadership of the Conservative Party. In some ways the reverberations of that event are still felt in the party, even now. It certainly caused huge trauma to the party. The period of office of Margaret Thatcher still generates intense controversy and is remembered for good or ill by the vast majority of people who were alive at that time. The recent biopic, *The Iron Lady*, with Meryl Streep as the lead, is an indication of the interest that still exists. In my own constituency and, I suspect, in many Conservative constituencies, we are familiar with the cry on the doorstep, 'Oh, bring back Maggie!' If you go into the mining communities of the north there are equally strong feelings about her – perhaps not quite as warm.

It seems to me that Thatcher's period in office and the major events that occurred – the Falklands war and the 1981 Budget, and all the things that were achieved during that time – are as familiar to most as they are to me, and simply to reprise them would not help. So, to some extent, this is a personal, anecdotal take on the Iron Lady, while also describing the importance to her of Parliament.

Early years

To understand her, it is necessary to look at her background, the locality from which she came – Grantham, in Lincolnshire – and the influence of her parents, particularly her father, so readily expressed in her memoirs.[1] She recalls her father's sense of duty and the enormous importance that he attached to his principles. She talks about his devotion to family and to civic duty, and about how he taught her that the most important thing was to stand by one's convictions.

He was, of course, a strongly religious man – a Methodist – though interestingly he supported Sunday opening in order to give the servicemen who had previously served their country in the war somewhere to go. Obviously, Sunday opening was one of the issues that proved so controversial during Thatcher's period in office; I think it was the only occasion on which the government lost a Second Reading division in the House.[2] Perhaps one gets a greater understanding if one sees it was something her father believed in.

He was also a Rotarian and regarded his political involvement as a civic duty – Thatcher quotes the motto 'Service Above Self'. It is with anger and sadness that Thatcher recalls her father being voted out as an alderman after the Labour Party won the local council elections in 1952 – and the parallels between this and the treatment she later received are not hard to draw. She gained strength from the way her father dealt with the situation – he did not resent what had happened, but behaved with dignity throughout.[3]

She does talk about her mother as well; she learned the value of thrift and the importance of hard work. She also learned how to iron a man's shirt, which may not have been quite as important to her fundamental principles.

I think her father is the most important character. It is said that he treated her as a man and he was determined that she should have the maximum opportunities in education. Again, some of the things that we now associate with her – her strength as a debater, her love of argument (she used to have arguments in the queue at the fish-and-chip shop!) – sprang from that. He ensured that she was taken to what were called extension lectures, mounted by Nottingham University, where she was able to hear some of the great speakers and debate with them. It was that opportunity which, I think, made her slightly different from many of her female contemporaries.

It was unusual for a woman to have the chance to enter political argument or to debate. Certainly, when she went to Oxford she did not have the background of many others there who had come through the public school system and who were used to debating societies – she had never experienced that. Equally, the other formative place for many future statesmen – the Oxford Union – was denied to her, because women were not allowed in. Instead she became involved in OUCA – the Oxford Union Conservative Association – and went on to become its president. She undoubtedly did hone a lot of her skills as a political debater in OUCA; it used to mount annual debates against the Labour club and invite many speakers. Interestingly, in some ways, she found the OUCA more valuable than the Oxford Union; she had a view that to do well at the Oxford Union you had to have a quick wit and repartee. She always felt that was not, perhaps, her strongest suit.

She became intensely political and it never crossed her mind to be anything other than a Conservative. She became a warm-up speaker in the general election in Grantham in 1945. I think she learned that her strength at argument and her love of debate – which I certainly recall, being on the end of it sometimes – were among her greatest attributes. It was that which caused her to have such a great love of Parliament and in particular the chamber of the House of Commons.

Into Parliament

When I was first elected to Parliament in 1992, I can remember her advice to me. She said, 'Take your time. There's no rush. Go and sit in the chamber. Spend a lot of time there. Just absorb the atmosphere. Become familiar with the way in which the chamber works. Certainly don't feel in any need to rush into making a maiden speech.' In her case, that was not what happened at all. Though she had different intentions, remarkably, in her first session as an MP, she came second in the ballot for Private Members' Bills and so, instead of having quite a few months to get the feel of the place before making her maiden speech, she suddenly found she was introducing her own Bill.

Before this good fortune, she had planned to make her maiden speech, once the time came round, on Lord Radcliffe's report on the working of the monetary system. I am sure it would have offered a fascinating insight and been of great use, but perhaps would not have got her the press attention that she received when she decided to adopt a Bill to give the press – and indeed others – a statutory right of admission to council committee meetings.

As is common even today, the Whips' Office encouraged her to adopt one of the favoured measures that it had ready and waiting – I understand it was to do with rights of appeal in cases of contempt of court. She did indeed think about that, however, she felt it was rather dry and rejected it. She also contemplated a Bill on the closed shop but was informed the Conservative government would not support it and so took it no further.

She worked very hard to get her Bill through; she wrote 250 letters by hand to government backbenchers. Indeed, she will still write, at great length sometimes, letters by hand to people and she believes that it has an effect like nothing else. I have to say that I think she is right. Certainly in this case it was successful, as she managed to persuade over 200 backbenchers to attend the chamber on a Friday morning. As a result, she obtained the Second Reading of her Bill.[4] As a new MP, that was quite an achievement and the press subsequently claimed that a new star was born.

Into Government

She went on to follow her own advice and spent quite a lot of time understanding the House of Commons. She attended back-bench committees; she attended the dining club for Members first elected in 1959. Then, perhaps in part because of her success with her initial speech and in getting a Bill on to the statute book, she was made a minister, becoming Parliamentary Secretary in the Ministry of Pensions and National Insurance. It was there that she acquired the qualities anyone who has worked with her will be familiar with: an extraordinary mastery of detail, a wish to understand every aspect of any issue and a reluctance just to accept the advice given to her. She always wanted to question it.

It is said, as anyone who has worked in what is now the Department for Work and Pensions will know, that she received a huge volume of letters from colleagues in Parliament raising constituency issues, and that she was unwilling to sign any reply unless she knew precisely why that reply was correct and the issues behind it. She used to send the letters back and demand an explanation from officials if she was not satisfied. This, I have to say, was something that she continued to do throughout her time in government.

She then became shadow Minister for Housing and Land, having voted in the 1965 party leadership contest for Ted Heath. He famously made her a Treasury spokesman, and then shadow Secretary of State for Fuel and Power, and then for Transport, and finally Education, so she had a very broad experience in shadowing different departments. This was an important grounding and an education in the process of government. The one area in which she never worked – indeed, in which no woman had ever worked – was the Whips' Office. This omission did not always play to her advantage later in her career.

It is well known that in the 1970s her guru was Sir Keith Joseph.[5] Sir Keith had set up the Centre for Policy Studies, where he had developed the monetarist philosophy – a different approach to Conservative politics – and he invited her to become vice-chairman of it. She was clear in her own mind that he was the man who should succeed as the next leader of the Conservative Party. She wanted him to stand but, of course, he delivered that famous speech in Edgbaston in 1974 which received a lot of adverse criticism and was felt to have destroyed his chances.[6] Reaching the conclusion that he should not stand, she famously quipped, 'Well, Keith, if you aren't going to then I shall have to.'

She was lucky in a way. Although she was extremely well regarded – she had a very strong press write-up for her performance in all her shadow roles and was regarded as a formidable debater – she was not particularly well known in Parliament among her colleagues. She did not, perhaps because she was a woman, go to the bar much or indeed to the tea room. She did have two very important allies, however, without whom she undoubtedly would not have succeeded. The first was her rival for the job, Edward du Cann, MP for Taunton and the then Chairman of the 1922 Committee. He already had a campaign in place and a number of people committed to supporting him, but he eventually decided that he did not want to run. Du Cann's campaign manager, learning Thatcher had no campaign team, duly became her campaign manager, bringing with him the du Cann troops. That manager, of course, was Airey Neave.[7]

Interestingly, this is an example, and I say this not just because I happen to be its vice-chairman, of the fact that the 1922 Committee can, at pivotal moments in the history of the Conservative Party, play an extremely important role. The 1922 Committee can, for long periods, seem rather lacking in influence and rather unimportant, but then something happens – we have seen that in recent years as well – and it suddenly becomes very important.[8] Certainly Edward du Cann helped to deliver the leadership, since it was he who had decided after the 1974 election that Ted Heath ought to go. He made that very plain. Ted Heath had hoped that when the '22 elections came around in November, du Cann and his allies would be voted out but, instead, they were re-elected. I think that sent the signal to Ted that almost certainly he was in a degree of trouble.

Heath conceded the case for a new leadership election and the contest took place early in 1975. Thatcher triumphed, out-polling Heath in the first ballot by 130 votes to 119. Heath withdrew from the contest and in the second ballot a week later with new challengers – Willie Whitelaw was seen as the main contender

– Thatcher increased her vote to 146: Whitelaw received only seventy-nine.[9] The party acquired its first female leader.

Prime Minister

It is said that Thatcher thought she was not a great Leader of the Opposition and certainly in some exchanges during Prime Minister's Questions, Jim Callaghan came off better.[10] There was a lot of anxiety as to whether or not she could win an election. Had Callaghan had the courage to go to the country the previous October, he might have won but, there was he, waiting at the church. There was still – I remember well, although I was still at university at the time – a large part of the Conservative Party that thought the party was in the grip of insanity. They thought it was a huge mistake to have chosen Thatcher. They thought it impossible that she could ever become Prime Minister. That feeling continued even after the 1979 general election, including among one or two people in her Cabinet. People such as Ian Gilmour and Jim Prior made little secret of the fact they had little time for her.[11] They thought this period of madness would soon be set aside and the party would return to the familiar Tory leader.

Thatcher fended off her critics. She relied heavily on her own instincts, but she also drew on a small team of close supporters. As well as the Chairman of the 1922 Committee, a crucial position is that of Parliamentary Private Secretary to the Prime Minister. Of course, Thatcher had Ian Gow as her PPS for her first Parliament, an extraordinary man who was perhaps literally in love with her, worshipped her and was prepared to do anything for her.[12] He was also immensely popular in the House of Commons and acted to ensure that she was always kept aware of what was happening on her back benches and what the feeling was. He was her greatest champion and his loss was one of the huge blows to her, personally and politically.

He was followed by a number of PPSs: Michael Alison, who many felt was not necessarily an obvious choice and who certainly did not have the same affinity as Gow with his parliamentary colleagues. Then there were the three that I sat opposite in No. 10: Archie Hamilton, Mark Lennox-Boyd and Peter Morrison. Archie, I remember, used to rather dismiss any concerns on the back benches. 'Oh, they're all just panicking. Don't worry about that, Prime Minister.' Mark, on the other hand, would go to the opposite extreme and say, 'Prime Minister, it is absolutely dreadful. There's mutiny in the ranks.' I'll come back to Peter later. It was a critical role in maintaining relations, because Thatcher was not necessarily terribly good at doing so. She is not the greatest listener. She loves arguing but she does not always appreciate the other point of view.

Those around her sought to protect her, but she was never free of critics within the party. Jumping forward to 1989, when I was working for her, the first real sign of trouble was the challenge to her leadership from Anthony Meyer, a little-known backbencher who challenged her for the leadership when no senior figure was prepared to do so.[13] She saw him off quite comfortably. She obtained 314 votes against only thirty-three for Meyer, and another twenty-two spoilt ballot papers or abstentions. But it was her campaign manager of the time, George Younger, who came to her afterwards and said, 'Don't be deceived by this. Yes, you have won easily, but I can tell you, as the person who was out talking to MPs about whether or not they would support you, many have said that they will do so on this occasion, but that you have got to understand the depth of concern and you have got to change in some areas.'

As a result of that, she agreed that she would have regular meetings with groups of backbenchers so they would have greater access to her and she could listen to their concerns. One of my jobs was to arrange those meetings alongside the PPS, and the two of us also attended. I have to say they were largely counter-productive. She would invite every person present, going around the table, to put their point. She would studiously listen and take notes. Then, when each person had had their turn, she proceeded to demolish them, one by one. The idea was that she was listening and absorbing and perhaps taking account of their concerns but I do not think many went away feeling they had necessarily had much impact. But that, to some extent, was so much her. She used to love the power of argument and combating other people's positions. She could never quite understand why other people couldn't grasp her argument. She found it very difficult to see how people, particularly in the Conservative Party, could not share her view on most issues and, I am afraid, the exercise we initiated was not terribly helpful – perhaps particularly so when it came to the vote a year later.

Nevertheless, and as I have said, Thatcher attached great importance to Parliament. Even though, certainly after the 1983 election and indeed after the 1987 election, she had a very sizeable majority, she made a point of being in the lobbies. She had a very strong voting record not because the government needed it or because necessarily she felt it was an opportunity to talk to people, but just because she felt she should. She felt that she was elected as a Member of Parliament and that it was her duty to exercise her vote on behalf of her constituents.

She had – does have – an immense respect for the institution of Parliament. Colleagues from the House of Lords will know that even though she does not speak in the House of Lords, she gets pleasure from attending. She certainly had a very good relationship with the Speaker when she was first elected. She and George Thomas had quite a close relationship and had great respect for each other. Of course, he was a Methodist and, later, he shared her views about Europe.[14] She perhaps didn't have quite the same close relationship with his successor, Bernard Weatherill.[15] He was not her first choice to be Speaker and she was somewhat suspicious about the way in which he gave favour to backbenchers, particularly those who might be critical of the government. Although that is an important role for the Speaker, it is not always necessarily appreciated by the Prime Minister.

I'm told she was intensely suspicious of select committees, even though they were born in their modern form at the beginning of her administration. Obviously, Norman St John-Stevas created the departmental select committees.[16] She thought it was a bit of a dangerous innovation and that it might also provide an opportunity for backbenchers to cause difficulty for her government. I remember she was also very hostile to the idea of televising Parliament.

A huge event that occurred twice a week was Prime Minister's Questions, to which she attached enormous importance. Occurring on Tuesdays and Thursdays, they lasted just fifteen minutes in those days. I calculated that she would spend something like six or eight hours preparing for those fifteen-minute slots. She would have all the details from every department in Whitehall, about all the major areas of controversy that might be raised. She would go through them either very late at night or at six o'clock in the morning, and we would have a meeting at nine o'clock to go through the papers. Well, we didn't actually go through the papers because she never read a paper. She had a very strong view that almost anything in the papers was bound to be critical of her and therefore it was far better not to read it. So we relied very much on a press summary prepared by Bernard Ingham. It occasionally gave a certain colour to the news and Bernard sometimes toned down one or two things or exaggerated others. Essentially, he gave her what were the major stories of the day. We would discuss outlines of the kinds of responses we would make if particular stories were raised and then the officials would be dispatched to go and summon yet more voluminous briefing from around Whitehall to deal with these issues.

I, alongside the PPS, used to spend the next two hours ringing up Conservative Members on the Order Paper and asking whether they had any particular idea of what they would like to put to the Prime Minister, because it would obviously ensure that they got a much more helpful reply if she had some advance warning. On some very rare occasions, I would say to them, 'Well, if you don't have a particular strong view, I know that the Prime Minister would greatly appreciate it if you could ask a question along these lines.' Most of the time, they were very co-operative.

Now, of course that did not help in terms of the amount of preparation she had to undertake to deal with questions from the Opposition – particularly the questions from the Leader of the Opposition. She was fortunate, however, that the leader, in my time, was Neil Kinnock.[17] Some might say so much preparation for these fifteen-minute sessions was an enormous waste of the Prime Minister's time but it was absolutely critical to the way in which she ran the government. She had to have total command of every policy pursued by her government, and she had to be satisfied with it.

Indeed, while in the Ministry of Pensions and National Insurance, she was never prepared just to take a line. She would always want to know why that was the case, what the counter-argument was and how she should deal with it. I can remember, quite frequently, she would receive the line to take with a background note from the department, and she would look at it and say, 'This is hopeless.' I would then be dispatched to the corner of the study to pick up the telephone and call the poor private secretary of the minister responsible for the policy and inform him of her view. Sometimes, she would be so agitated about the utter incompetence of the minister that she would stride across and grab the telephone from me, and proceed to harangue the private secretary about the inadequacy of both the brief and, quite often, the policy as well. I used to have a vision that all over Whitehall, between the hours of about one o'clock and half-past two, private secretaries would be looking at their telephone in absolute terror in case it actually rang.

But it was a very effective way of ensuring that she was able to deal with every potential criticism of her government. Of course, it meant not only that she was equipped for interviews, speeches and every other aspect, but also that quite often government policy changed if she really did not feel convinced by the answer.

We would spend some time rehearsing exchanges and anticipating questions. I occasionally had the role of Neil Kinnock, which was fairly terrifying because she took it all very seriously and had great pleasure in destroying whatever argument I advanced.

Sometimes it was more difficult because I had the task, alongside one or two of my colleagues, of persuading her to say something that she did not want to. The best example that I can recall is when it was becoming fairly widely known that the Chancellor of the Exchequer, Nigel Lawson, had, to some extent, lost her confidence. There were considerable arguments between them over the issue of shadowing the Deutschmark and there was a great deal of speculation that his position was in danger.

We anticipated correctly that the first question of the Leader of the Opposition would be whether she had confidence in her Chancellor of the Exchequer. She insisted that the answer ought to be, 'The economy is doing extremely well. We are performing admirably,' and anything but, 'Yes.' I think it took four of us about half an hour of saying, 'Prime Minister, you have got to say "Yes". If you say any other answer than "Yes", I promise you that the next day's headlines will be that you have no confidence in your Chancellor.' Right up until she went into the House of Commons, she absolutely gave no quarter at all. There was no inkling that she would accept this argument. She was determined that she would answer in her own way. As it was, when she did have the question put to her she said 'Yes' – but I think it was through gritted teeth.

By the time I was helping her prepare for Prime Minister's Questions, she had been Prime Minister, I suppose, for eight years, and the surprising thing is that she was still always remarkably nervous. It was visible. You could see her leg shaking as she stood at the dispatch box, and afterwards we used to have to spend quite some time in a sort of post-mortem session reassuring her. We used to go through each answer and tell her that it was absolutely right, that she had undoubtedly won the exchange and that it had been a great occasion, and that continued right until the end of her time as PM. I hope I never have to answer Prime Minister's Questions – I am sure I won't – but

I have no doubt that anybody who is in that position, no matter how experienced, will find it an immensely intimidating experience. That is reflected, I think, in the comments of almost every person who has ever had to do it.

Making speeches

If Question Time took up an immense amount of time and preparation, the activity that took up even more time was speech-making. We had an unending list of set-piece speeches coming one after another, a lot of which were political – the women's conference, the spring conference, the Scottish conference, the Welsh conference and then the annual conference, each one of which required a major speech – plus the more governmental ones, such as the Lord Mayor's banquet and one or two special invitations.

It was an extraordinary ordeal to prepare those speeches. Hours and hours were spent in preparation and there were weekends at Chequers for months ahead. I worked out that for the biggest speech of the year, the Conservative Party conference speech, which lasted roughly forty minutes, she spent around eighty hours in preparation. We would commission contributions from a huge range of people. She had favourites who would be asked to submit: George Walden was always invited to submit something on education;[18] John Gummer was always invited to submit something on the environment;[19] and Chris Patten was another regular.[20] Then we had the home team: John Redwood I know contributed,[21] journalist John O'Sullivan was one of the architects of the jokes and the former playwright Ronnie Millar, as well.

She believed there were certain people who had an extraordinary ability to put forward arguments that were pure gold and that we should immediately get hold of their latest thoughts and incorporate them into the speech. She felt most strongly about Woodrow Wyatt's column in the *News of the World*, which, I have to say, did not seem to me to be full of great political wisdom – it was, after all, written for readers of the *News of the World* – but every time we had a major speech and reached a patch where we were struggling somewhat, she would say, 'How does Woodrow put it?' I would be dispatched to get Woodrow Wyatt's column, which would be read in reverential terms like tablets from a mountain.[22] Putting together the speeches was an extraordinary exercise and one that could go on and on.

The speeches actually had quite a major effect. In 1988 there were two speeches, in both of which I was only peripherally involved, that changed the whole political debate. One, the Bruges speech, is very famous, and was the first time she really set out her views on how Europe was going in the wrong direction. Her views about Europe obviously became stronger and more hard-line over time.

She did, of course, campaign for a 'yes' vote in the original 1975 referendum on continued membership of the European Community.[23] She was a very strong supporter of the single market. Many people subsequently said to her, 'How can you be so hostile when it was your government that passed the Single European Act?' She always said that she had been advised by lawyers in the Foreign Office that the provisions to create a single market could be used only for a narrow range of issues. Once the single market was in place, qualified majority voting would, on its own account, no longer be necessary and so would disappear; once you had the single market, there was no longer any need for qualified majority voting. Unfortunately, the definition of a single market in her mind was much narrower than that of the rest of Europe. She suddenly found, therefore, that qualified majority voting was being used for things she had never intended. Famously, when somebody said, 'You voted for the Single European Act and you enacted the Single European Act', she said, 'Yes, if you have had your hand burned once, you don't put your hand back into the fire.'

She had an immense suspicion of Germany and was quite openly trying to win support among other western nations against reunification. The Bruges speech in 1988 was a landmark.[24] It changed the course of the political debate about Europe. It made it plain that she was determined to go in a different direction and, of course, it then led to the tensions that arose within the Conservative Party with those who took a different view.

The other major speech, delivered just a week later, was equally an extremely important one. As a Fellow, she had been invited to address the Royal Society, something she regarded as a great honour. She wanted to have a theme to her speech: Crispin Tickell[25] had been to see her and had convinced her that there was a real environmental danger from climate change. So she discussed the threat to our planet as a result of the actions taken by man, both in terms of potential climate change – although these were very early days – and also, at that time, of the ozone layer. Some of these things turned out not to be so significant a problem, but I think it was the first time that a British Prime Minister had devoted an entire speech to global environmental challenges. That, too, was quite a landmark.

I was mainly involved with writing the political speeches. The hardest element of writing a speech for Thatcher was the jokes. She always knew that humour was not her strong point and found making jokes very difficult. But she knew they were very important and so we would spend hours trying to incorporate jokes into her speeches. This is not to say that she does not have a sense of humour; Thatcher has a very dry wit. My favourite Thatcher comment came when we lost the European Cup semi-final against Germany, and somebody said to her, 'Prime Minister, appalling – the Germans have beaten us at our own national game,' to which she replied, 'Yes, dear, but we beat them twice at theirs.'

I recall two successful occasions at incorporating jokes into her speeches – and both were hard work. The first saw her addressing a European election rally and we had a well-known actor – and Conservative – introducing her: John Barron, who played the part of C. J. in *The Fall and Rise of Reginald Perrin*. We included in her speech a section in which she said, 'I didn't get where I am today by not fighting for what I believe and standing up against socialism', and she said, 'No, no, no. You can't. You've got to be positive: "I got where I am today by fighting for what I believe."' We said,

'That's not the point, Prime Minister. This man has one of the most famous catchphrases in British comedy, which is "I didn't get where I am today by doing this."' She still did not quite understand why it was so important, but we did eventually persuade her.

That was a starter for what was most certainly the more difficult one. I apologise to the people who have heard me tell this story – I have told it on a number of occasions – but it is one of my favourite Thatcher stories: the saga of the dead parrot sketch. John O'Sullivan had the bright idea that the Prime Minister could compare the newly adopted logo of the Liberal Democrats – the bird, which they still use – with Monty Python's dead parrot, so he included in the text of the speech almost the entire dead parrot sketch. While going through the speech with Thatcher, we got to the section that began 'Shuffled off this mortal coil, ceased to be' and all the rest of it. She sort of looked at him and she had plainly decided that he had gone completely mad. 'What is this?' she asked. We all knew that this was going to happen, so we had agreed that we would all pitch in. 'Prime Minister, this is the most famous joke in British comedy. The entire audience will recognise it instantly. You will be a national hero. They will be falling about in the aisles.' She looked hugely unconvinced by this and said, 'Oh well, all right.' It survived the first couple of drafts, but you could see that she was uncomfortable.

Later she said, 'If I'm going to do this joke, I'm going to have to see it.' I got hold of the tape, which I think was called *And Now for Something Completely Different,* and we sat – Peter Morrison, who was her PPS, me, Robin Harris, John O'Sullivan and the Prime Minister – in my office in Downing Street, watching the dead parrot sketch on the television. The rather surreal nature of the occasion caused it to seem even funnier than usual. We all had tears rolling down our cheeks and were barely capable of controlling ourselves. Thatcher sat impassive, watching this performance. She could see that it had great effect, so she agreed, reluctantly, to include it. As was ever the case with Conservative Party conference speeches, we went through the text a few times and each time she asked, 'Are you sure this is funny?' We would say, 'Yes, Prime Minister – absolutely hilarious. Just wait – you will have them crying with laughter throughout the entire hall.' She plainly was not completely convinced by this, but through force of numbers we persuaded her to keep it in.

Just before she was ready to go on stage, you could see her still trying to think of a reason why she should not deliver this particular joke. She was clearly not persuaded that it was going to work and she suddenly had a brainwave. She turned to me and said, 'John, Monty Python – are you sure he's one of us?' I was not even going to try to explain to her that Monty Python did not really exist, so I just said, 'Absolutely, Prime Minister', and she went on and delivered the speech. I have to say it was a great success.

The last years

In many ways, I think perhaps the greatest speech she gave was the last one in Parliament.[26] Given the circumstances in which it was delivered, it was a complete *tour de force*. I worked in No. 10 for Thatcher's last three years as Prime Minister and it is fair to say that the storm clouds gathered during this period. She lost a number of very close friends and allies whom she had relied on: Norman Tebbit,[27] who after the Brighton bomb was very badly hurt and subsequently retired from government;[28] Ian Gow, who was killed by the IRA in July 1990; and Nick Ridley, who had to resign from government.[29] These were people who were absolutely her closest allies, and the people who replaced them were perhaps less loyal and devoted than they were. Actually, one of her problems is that, because she is so certain her argument will win, she is convinced that everybody must see the force of it. Therefore she expected that her Cabinet would share her views.

Some of the people who were appointed to the government were not actually her allies at all. I remember a famous 'No Turning Back' group dinner. She asked her praetorian guard – her greatest supporters in Parliament, mainly fairly new young MPs –'What should I be doing? Give me some advice.' Eric

Forth[30] – bless him – said, 'Well, you can start by giving some of us jobs.' Actually, he had a point, because it was strongly felt that she was not good at recognising her true supporters and believers. She had a habit of advancing people who were not necessarily of her opinion.[31]

This was not particularly helped by the fact she got through several Chief Whips. Her last Chief Whip, Tim Renton, was appointed because he was close to Geoffrey Howe, and it was felt that he might do something to bring the two together. I don't think Renton served her very well and was perhaps why, when we got to the final debacle of the famous meeting with each successive member of the Cabinet, the majority came out against her.[32]

While losing friends, her relations also soured with some of her previous supporters, principally Nigel Lawson, who resigned in 1989, and indeed Geoffrey Howe, who resigned rather spectacularly the following year. I have to say that she did not treat Geoffrey terribly well when she repositioned him in 1989. (He was moved, much to his surprise, from the Foreign Secretaryship to the post of Leader of the House of Commons.) She could be very dismissive. I think he was wounded by the move and this was certainly reflected in his resignation speech to the House of Commons in November 1990. I have always thought that, if Ian Gow had lived, her relationship with Howe would never have gone as sour as it did because Ian was very close to both of them. I don't think he would have allowed it to happen.

The problem towards the end of her premiership stemmed from criticisms that she had become out of touch and that she hadn't spent enough time with her supporters. But, to some extent, it was also about policy. There were two issues: Europe, on which she had differences with the senior members of her government but a lot of support on the back benches (which is slightly familiar), but most of all, the community charge. She was convinced of the wisdom of the community charge but it was to some extent sabotaged by the Treasury, which ensured that the level at which it came in was far higher than was intended. It was also the polls and the concern of the backbenchers that unless changes were made they would lose their seats at the subsequent election. It came down to the fact that, if she were not prepared to change the community charge, a large number had decided the only alternative was to change her.

She had a disastrous campaign. There is no question about that. She didn't really have a campaign at all, actually. There was an expectation, particularly on the part of her PPS Peter Morrison, that everybody would support the Prime Minister and that matters did not really need checking. If they hadn't said that they would not support the Prime Minister, it could be assumed that they would do so. There are famous stories of Alan Clark finding Peter Morrison asleep at No. 10. I remember a phone call from the 'No Turning Back' group, saying, 'It is really bad news. Lots of people who you expect should support her are not doing so.' But those concerns were dismissed, famously resulting in 204 voting for her, 152 against and sixteen abstentions – just four votes short of what she needed.[33] Had two MPs switched their votes, she would have won.

I discussed with her subsequently whether, if she had come back and had really thrown herself into a campaign, and if she had started having meetings and going into the Tea Room, she could have won the second ballot, particularly since she would no longer need the super-majority requirement in the first ballot. She would have just needed one more vote. (Only a simple majority was required.) She always said to me, 'It doesn't matter.' She said that she had lost the confidence of a large section of the party and of the Cabinet, and it was in the interests of the party that she should go.

I have to accept that was probably the right decision. But it was an extraordinary forty-eight hours. We had been preparing for different outcomes when she went off to Paris for an international conference. The outcome that actually proved to be correct was one we had not spent a great deal of time on. Nevertheless, she did deliver it, came back to Downing Street and, of course, had the famous meetings with the Cabinet, seeing each member individually, leading to her decision to resign.

Having taken that decision, typically, she started preparing her speech for the following day. Not only did she have to prepare for the no-confidence motion that had already been tabled by the Labour Party, she also had Prime Minister's Questions. Being the Prime Minister that she was, she spent an enormous amount of time preparing her speech, and we had the home team sitting around the table, plus one or two others. She didn't tell us that she was going to resign the next morning but everybody in the room knew that was the case. It was, again, a somewhat surreal experience.

That night was punctuated by calls from people trying to persuade her to stay on, particularly Labour MP Frank Field, who came to say that Michael Heseltine was hoovering up votes in the lobby and that she needed to counter him. There was also a delegation composed of Tory MPs Michael Portillo, Michael Forsyth and Michael Fallon – the three Michaels – and I sent them away on the basis that she was busy speechwriting and could not be disturbed. But she said to me, 'No, no, of course I would have seen them.' I called at midnight and happened to catch Michael Portillo, who came back. He saw her and, again, failed to persuade her.

It was an extraordinary night. I left Downing Street at about two o'clock in the morning, having spent until that time working on her final speech – though we could not call it that. The following morning, it was announced. The speech itself was a vintage performance. It was an absolute defence of everything that she had achieved as Prime Minister of her government. She relished the interventions and was served, famously, by Alan Beith, who asked, 'Will the Prime Minister tell us whether she intends to continue her personal fight against the single currency and an independent central bank when she leaves office?' At that point, the hon. Member for Bolsover (Dennis Skinner) interjected, I suspect from a sedentary position, 'No, she is going to be the governor,' to which she quipped, 'What a good idea. I had not thought of that.'[34]

It was the most extraordinary performance. I have to admit I sat with tears running down my cheeks when I watched it. It was the most magnificent exit and, in some ways, it was exactly the right way for her to leave office. She always said that she had never been defeated by the people; she was defeated by her colleagues in the House of Commons, which she felt very strongly was an act of great disloyalty and betrayal. She even briefly contemplated continuing as Prime Minister without being leader of the Conservative Party, which was not an entirely practical idea. She felt very strongly that it was improper that she had been forced to leave office on that basis. To some extent, that dictated her behaviour afterwards.

There has been a lot of criticism that she was disloyal to her successor, John Major – that she undermined him – but I have always said to people that it was a mistake to believe that just because she, against her will, was removed from office, she would stop fighting for what she believed in. She cared passionately, particularly about Europe. She was very strongly opposed to the Maastricht Treaty and the idea that she was going to keep quiet about something that she regarded as so damaging to the country was always wholly impractical. It was not that she was trying to undermine John Major, although I think he felt that she was; it was just that she was continuing to do what she always had, which was standing up and arguing for what she believed.

Conclusion

Finally, I want to say a word about what it was like to work for her on a personal basis. She was immensely demanding – she still is. When I first went to work for her I had to prepare the Christmas message. I had been warned that it was a complete ordeal every year and that almost whatever I wrote would be instantly dismissed and, sure enough, it was. Scathingly, she tore my efforts to shreds and I was made to feel that I was incapable of stringing a sentence together, let alone crafting the Christmas message for the Prime Minister. I said to my secretary, whom I had inherited from my predecessor, 'I think I am going to have to go. She plainly has no confidence in me whatsoever.' My secretary replied, 'No, no; she always does that. Don't worry about it.'

I then went up to see the Prime Minister about an entirely separate matter and sat in on a meeting with about four or five officials. I cannot remember what the subject was. About halfway through, she said, 'John, what do you think about this?' I advanced a fairly anodyne and ill-informed view, but she treated it as a nugget of wisdom, saying 'That's so right'. She knew she had gone a bit too far before and, although she was not going to say 'I'm sorry, I shouldn't have torn you to shreds over the Christmas message', it was her way of making up. She is an immensely kind person.

The people who worked for her on her personal staff are, without exception, completely devoted to her. She showed enormous kindness and was always terribly worried about people at Christmas. To anybody she thought was going to be on their own, she would tell them to come to Chequers – Ronnie Millar used to try to think up reasons why he couldn't go. She worried that one private secretary, who was going through a painful divorce, would be on his own. I remember her receiving a Christmas hamper from the Sultan of Brunei and instructing her private secretary to take it because he was on his own at Christmas, and it would in some way make up for that.

She used to write letters, as I said earlier. I will always remember when she was removed from office. It was an immense trauma. She lost her house, her office, her staff and her job, which she had had for eleven years – all overnight, unexpectedly, and she did not really have anywhere to go. She originally went to live in a flat in Eaton Square, which was lent to her by an American who had never met her, and she then was given an office in Alistair McAlpine's house in Great College Street.[35] I remember something like 20,000 letters arrived from members of the public across the world, and I went in one day to find her writing a very long, handwritten response to one that she had picked out of the pile. Again, it was completely impractical, but she attached great importance to it.

It was an immense privilege to have worked for her. Whatever I do in the House of Commons, I will regard that as something I am most proud to have done. In my view she is, and always will be, one of the greatest Prime Ministers that this country has ever had.

1 Margaret Thatcher, *The Path to Power* (London: HarperCollins, 1995), Chapter 1.
2 The Shops Bill was defeated in 1986 on Second Reading by 296 votes to 282 when 72 Conservative MPs voted with the Opposition. See Francis Bown, 'The Defeat of the Shops Bill, 1986', in Michael Rush (ed.), *Parliament and Pressure Politics* (Oxford: Clarendon Press, 1990), pp.213–33.
3 Thatcher, *The Path to Power*, pp.21–22.
4 The Bill was given a Second Reading by 152 votes to 39. It was enacted as the Public Bodies (Admission to Meetings) Act 1960. On the passage of the Bill, see John Campbell, *Margaret Thatcher, Vol. 1: The Grocer's Daughter* (London: Jonathan Cape, 2000), pp.127–34.
5 Sir Keith Joseph, MP for Leeds North-East (1956–87), served in the Cabinet as Minister of Housing and Local Government (1962–4), Secretary of State for Social Services (1970–74), Industry Secretary (1979–81) and Secretary of State for Education and Science (1981–6). He was credited with being the leading advocate among Conservative frontbenchers of monetarist economics.
6 In his speech on 19 October 1974, Joseph had spoken of the problems of teenage pregnancies and referred to 'the balance of our population, our human stock is threatened'. This apparent suggestion of population control attracted immediate adverse publicity and the realisation among many Conservatives that he would be a potential liability as party leader.
7 Airey Neave was a wartime hero, being one of the few prisoners-of-war to escape from Colditz Castle. He served in military intelligence and was elected as a Conservative MP in 1953. He was alleged to dislike Edward Heath after, it is claimed, Heath as Chief Whip told him that, following a heart attack, his career was finished. Neave was killed in 1979 by a bomb planted under his car, for which the Irish National Liberation Army claimed responsibility.
8 See Philip Goodhart with Ursula Branston, *The 1922* (London: Macmillan, 1973), and Philip Norton, 'The Parliamentary Party and Party Committees', in Anthony Seldon and Stuart Ball (eds), *Conservative Century* (Oxford: Oxford University Press, 1994), pp.97–144.
9 In the first ballot, the results were: Thatcher 130, Heath 119, Hugh

Fraser 16 (abstentions 11). In the second ballot, they were: Thatcher 146, Whitelaw 79, James Prior 19, Sir Geoffrey Howe 19, John Peyton 11 (abstentions 2).

10 See Philip Norton, 'Margaret Thatcher, 1975–79', in Timothy Heppell (ed.), *Leaders of the Opposition* (London: Palgrave Macmillan, 2012), pp.97–108.

11 See, for example, Ian Gilmour, *Dancing with Dogma: Britain Under Thatcherism* (London: Simon & Schuster, 1992). In the foreword, Gilmour made clear that his views had not changed much since 1979.

12 Ian Gow, MP for Eastbourne, was Thatcher's PPS from 1979 until 1983, when he became a junior minister. He was killed in 1990 by a bomb planted under his car.

13 Sir Anthony Meyer, Tory MP for Clwyd North-West, was a Baronet and former diplomat and a strong supporter of European integration. See Anthony Meyer, *Stand Up and Be Counted* (London: Heinemann, 1990).

14 Thomas had been a Labour MP and Secretary of State for Wales. He was Speaker from 1976 until 1983, when he was created a hereditary peer (Viscount Tonypandy).

15 Weatherill had served as the Conservative Deputy Chief Whip. He was Speaker from 1983 to 1992.

16 They came into being following an overwhelming vote by the House of Commons in June 1979 after St John-Stevas persuaded 'a highly unsympathetic Cabinet' to agree to the proposals going forward. Philip Norton, *The Commons in Perspective* (Oxford: Martin Robertson, 1981), p.232. See also Priscilla Baines, 'History and Rationale of the 1979 Reforms', in Gavin Drewry (ed.), *The New Select Committees*, 2nd edn (Oxford: Clarendon Press, 1989), pp.13–36.

17 Kinnock was Labour MP for Bedwellty and served as Labour leader from 1983 until 1992. He was a European Commissioner from 1995 to 2004. He was created a life peer in 2005.

18 Walden was a former diplomat and was MP for Buckingham, before retiring in 1997. He was Minister for Higher Education 1985–87.

19 Gummer was MP for Eye, then Suffolk Coastal, until 2010. He was party chairman 1983–85; he became Minister of Agriculture in 1989 and Environment Secretary under John Major. He was created Lord Deben in 2010.

20 Chris Patten served as Director of Conservative Research Department 1974–79. He was Conservative MP for Bath from 1979 to 1992 and was appointed Minister for Overseas Development in 1986 and Environment Secretary in 1989. He became party chairman the following year. He was Governor of Hong Kong 1992–97, European Commission 1999–2004, and was appointed Chair of the BBC Trust in 2011. He was made a life peer in 2005.

21 Redwood had been in banking and served as head of the No. 10 Policy Unit under Thatcher; he was elected Tory MP for Wokingham in 1987.

22 Wyatt had been a somewhat maverick Labour MP (1945–55, 1959–70) and journalist, but became a noted admirer of Margaret Thatcher. He became a life peer in 1987. His rather indiscreet diaries were published posthumously.

23 Thatcher's role in the campaign was portrayed as constructive 'and she wrote a strong letter to Conservative MPs in early May urging their active support for Europe'. David Butler and Uwe Kitzinger, *The 1975 Referendum* (London: Macmillan, 1976), p.77.

24 Margaret Thatcher, *Britain and Europe* (London: Conservative Political Centre, 1988).

25 Sir Crispin Tickell, diplomat (UK Ambassador to the UN 1987–90) and leading environmentalist, with a particular interest in climate change; he published *Climatic Change and World Affairs* in 1977.

26 House of Commons: Official Report (Hansard): 22 November 1990, Vol. 181, cols 445–53.

27 Conservative MP and a member of the Thatcher Cabinet from 1981 to 1987; Tebbit was party chairman from 1985 to 1987. He was renowned for expressing forthright views on issues, including telling those looking for work to follow the example of his father in getting on his bike.

28 He was seriously injured, and his wife paralysed, in the 1984 IRA bombing of the Grand Hotel in Brighton.

29 Nicholas Ridley was Transport Secretary 1983–86, Environment Secretary 1986–89, and Secretary of State for Trade and Industry 1989–90. Like Norman Tebbit he was seen by Thatcher as 'one of us', but he was prone to unguarded comments. He resigned after making critical comments about economic and monetary union, describing it as 'a German racket designed to take over the whole of Europe'. For good measure, he said that giving up sovereignty to Europe was as bad as giving it up to Hitler.

30 Forth was a flamboyant Tory MP – noted for garish ties and waistcoats – but a skilled parliamentary tactician. Thatcher appointed him a junior minister in 1988.

31 See Philip Norton, '"The Lady's Not for Turning": But What About the Rest of the Party? Mrs Thatcher and the Conservative Party 1979–89', *Parliamentary Affairs*, Vol. 43 (1), January 1990, pp.41–58.

32 On Renton's view of his time as Chief Whip, see Tim Renton, *Chief Whip* (London: Politico's, 2004). As he makes clear, the thought of being Chief Whip had never occurred to him; p.14.

33 Under the rules as they then stood, she needed not only a majority but one that constituted 15 per cent of those entitled to vote. That meant winning by a margin of 56 votes.

34 House of Commons: Official Report (Hansard): 22 November 1990, Vol. 181, col. 451.

35 McAlpine was a businessman who served as Conservative Party treasurer and had been ennobled by Margaret Thatcher in 1984.

Tony Benn

Tristram Hunt
Delivered on 6 December 2011

Biographical note

Tony Benn

Anthony Neil Wedgwood Benn, born 3 April 1925, son of William Wedgwood Benn (Labour MP for North Aberdeen and Gorton, later 1st Viscount Stansgate). Educated Westminster School and New College, Oxford. Married 1949 Caroline Middleton. Pilot Officer, RAFVR, 1945. Labour MP for Bristol South-East 1950–61, succeeded his father as Viscount Stansgate 1961 (re-elected as MP for Bristol SE 1961 but disqualified), renounced peerage 1963, re-elected as MP for Bristol South-East 1963–83; Labour MP for Chesterfield 1984–2001. Postmaster-General 1964–66; Minister of Technology 1966–70; Secretary of State for Industry and Minister of Posts and Telecommunications 1974–75; Secretary of State for Energy 1975–79.

Member of Labour Party National Executive Committee 1959–60, 1962–93; Chairman, Labour Party 1971–72. Contested Party Leadership 1976, 1988, Deputy Leadership 1971, 1981. Chair, Campaign Group of Labour MPs 1971–72. Privy Counsellor 1964. Publications include the multi-volume *The Benn Diaries*.

A campaigning politician, seen as moving from the centre or centre-right of Labour politics to being a leading figure on the left. Noted for campaigning successfully to change the law to enable him to renounce his peerage, he became a combative politician of the left in the 1970s and 1980s, challenging for the party's leadership and deputy leadership. He retired from the House of Commons in 2001 'to spend more time in politics'.

T hank you very much, Mr Speaker, and you may rest assured, I have no intention of following the precedent set by my subject for tonight's lecture who, within only a few years of being elected to the House, had already put down a motion of censure against the Speaker. 'It's the most terrifying thing an MP can do,' Tony Benn later recalled of the events of 1957, following Speaker Morrison's decision to refuse his request to discuss British military intervention in Oman. 'You feel the whole House is against you. The Speaker frowns. Your legs turn to lead as if to hold you forcibly to your seat. Everything inside you says, "Sit down – let it go – it's not worth it."'

But that wasn't the Benn way. Instead, he pursued the matter, offering the House of Commons a mini-tutorial in its rights and privileges – 'the right of free thought and free speech unfettered by the party system'.[1] He continued: 'If you, Mr Speaker, give a ruling which means that an individual backbencher cannot raise a point without the support of his party, then you give to the party a power over the members which I believe would be an imposition on the rights of the House.'[2] Of course, the motion collapsed. As Bernard Levin wrote in *The Spectator*, 'The probability of ignominious failure was high' – but, in fact, Mr Benn gave a speech which was 'witty, graceful, modest, learned, pointed and in some ways deeply moving'.[3]

However, as you know, Mr Speaker, the office of the Speaker – like an elephant – has a long memory. I don't say, 'bears grudges', but has a long memory. So, when in 1960, Benn's father Viscount Stansgate died and the title passed down to Tony Benn, Speaker

Hylton-Foster's response had more than an air of institutional revenge: 'I have made an order, my Lord, that you are to be kept out of the chamber.'⁴ By force, if necessary. The very next day, Benn's salary was stopped, copies of Hansard cancelled, and his travel warrant withdrawn – ah, for those pre-IPSA days...

The ensuing years saw Benn's public life given over to an epic constitutional struggle, which seemed to alternate between Monty Python and Franz Kafka. The battle of Tony Benn, the 'reluctant peer' or 'persistent commoner', to renounce his peerage and reclaim his seat as Member of Parliament for Bristol South East exposes many of the fault lines which criss-cross Benn's career as a parliamentarian. And as this lecture series brings to an end a year-long commemoration of the 1911 Act of Parliament, the trajectory of Tony Benn in and outside of Westminster offers perhaps a broader insight into the place of Parliament in twentieth-century Britain. His struggle against becoming Lord Stansgate – and the passing of the 1963 Peerage Act – saw a new political landscape emerge: his was an extra-parliamentary campaign of petitions, mass media, court cases, fundraising drives and international awareness as well as the traditional legislative battle. All of which was typical of Benn's own relationship with Parliament. For the politician who was often regarded as a quintessential 'Parliament-man' – obsessive from an early age in defending its rights and privileges, and in his later years issuing a video-cassette of his Commons speeches entitled 'Standing up in Parliament' – had, in fact, a more troubled interaction with Westminster than we might believe.

For despite Benn's genuine ardour for Parliament, his belief in representative democracy, the ballot box, the transparency and accountability of the Westminster system, for him politics was always a campaign, even a crusade. As such, Benn came to regard Parliament as a means to an end, a weapon in the broader political struggle. And it increasingly proved as convenient to bypass Parliament as it was to have this place as the fulcrum of politics and engine of social change.

It was a legacy which he, in many ways, would come to rue.

'The chief interest of my family for four generations has been Parliament,' so spoke Tony Benn's father, William Benn, in 1958.[5] And, indeed, it had. William Benn's grandfather, the Reverend Julius Benn, had nominated James Bryce as the Liberal candidate for Tower Hamlets; his father John Benn had been elected as the Liberal MP for the same constituency in 1892; and William Benn took it over in 1906 (before later assuming other seats in Leith and Gorton).

The Benns' enthusiasm for Parliament was shared with their relation (we think) and MP for Newcastle-under-Lyme, Colonel Josiah Wedgwood. It was Wedgwood who began the History of Parliament Trust in the 1930s, the ambition of which was to record the lives of each parliamentarian back to the 1300s. And Wedgwood shared the clan's conviction of the institution's wonder.

> To me, personally, Parliament is everything; the members are the staunchest friends man ever had; the life combines the mental gymnastics of college with the fresh wind of the outer world …
> The man who steps into the English Parliament takes his place in a pageant that has ever been filing by since the birth of English history.[6]

There was, however, another influence in Benn's upbringing which competed with this parliamentary inheritance. 'One of the most significant aspects of my childhood was my mother's deep Christian convictions, which she hoped her children would share.' Benn's mother, Margaret, had been a practising Anglican until the 1940s when a dispute over female representation in the Church saw her move towards Nonconformity. In doing so, she embraced the dissenting Benn tradition, which stretched back to the Reverend Benn's time as a Congregationalist minister. Night after night, Tony's mother read him the Bible stories, in which she was always keen to distinguish 'between the Kings of Israel who exercised power and the prophets of Israel who preached righteousness, and I was brought up to believe in the prophets rather than the Kings'.[7]

Above all, the Protestant belief in individual autonomy and a 'priesthood of all believers' was drummed into the young Benn. Among his favourite bedtime stories was the tale of Daniel's faith, tested by Darius, in a lion's den – which allowed his father, William, to belt out the Salvation Army anthem, 'Dare to be a Daniel, Dare to stand alone, Dare to have a purpose firm, Dare to make it known.'

In short, Tony Benn was nurtured a Dissenter. For a young prince of the Labour movement of the early twentieth century, this was not unusual. The Labour Party was founded at Memorial Hall, Farringdon Road, that great monument to the Dissenting tradition (the expulsion of Nonconformists in 1662), and in 1912 the future Labour Prime Minister, Ramsay MacDonald, felt able to publish a paper entitled *A Plea for Puritanism*. Indeed, this was an inheritance which Benn shared with his sparring partner and later nemesis within the Labour movement, Michael Foot. Just like Benn, Foot was brought up in the Good Old Cause, the Puritan tradition. His father, the West Country Liberal Isaac Foot, endowed him with an equally powerful sense of the Dissenting mission, as it played itself out through English history. 'Poetry and politics, literature and living, the heritage from the past and the onward march of Christian soldiers; for my father the interweaving never ended,' Foot wrote.[8]

> Historical figures and their modern counterparts melted into one; brewers, protectionists, papists, apologists for Lord North and the Chamberlain family; Spanish tyrants and Stuart kings; men of Munich and Suez; sons of Belial and Beelzebub, normally disguised as West Country Tories, an especially reprehensible branch of the species.

But whereas Michael Foot was bequeathed one part of the Puritan inheritance – a love of books, literature and the word –

the Benn bequest was different. 'During my childhood and growing up, no attempt was made to develop the artistic, musical and
literary side of life,' he recounts in a book chapter entitled 'How
I became a Philistine'.[9] Wonderfully, his house at 40 Grosvenor
Road, along Millbank, was right next to the Tate Gallery, but
the family never visited. Instead, what is clearly apparent in the
Benn household is that Puritan mindset of workfulness, asceti-
cism and accounting to God. The house was teetotal and – given
that all time was God's time – full of clocks. 'Father kept a daily
time chart on which he set down the number of hours he worked
every day and the number of hours he slept; in theory it should
equal twenty-four.'[10] Or, as Liam Byrne put it to me, 'Excellent
– an early time and motion study.' Tellingly, Benn's calculations
excluded any time for meals, conversation or social life. Partly
because, no doubt, of the amount of time spent on accruing,
filing and indexing: *The Times* was daily cut up by William Benn
and then filed according to his own Dewey-decimal system.

Here was the modern Puritan spirit at work. Only this can
explain the tea-drinking, vegetarian, ascetic, industrious Benn
personality. As well as what he is arguably most famous for: *The
Benn Diaries*.[11] The modern diary form begins in the post-Refor-
mation era among the Protestant godly sort as a daily accounting
to God: a profit-and-loss score card of sin and salvation, of fail-
ings and achievements along the Pilgrim's path. It is an opening
up to God of one's soul in literary form. And that, for all its diver-
sions into Cabinet splits, NEC meetings, and party politics, is
ultimately what the Benn diaries are about. According to a recent
interview, Tony Benn put his compulsive diary-keeping down to
a moral responsibility to give an account of his life. 'I will present
the Almighty with 18 million words and say, what do you make of
it?'[12] It could be Bunyan or Winthrop, but is in fact Benn.

But such a sense both of worthlessness and egoism, of being
nothing in the face of God but also thinking oneself at the
heart of God's mercy, is what begins to provide – in a secular-
ised format – the sense of mission and crusade behind Benn's

politics: 'Dare to be a Daniel, Dare to stand alone, Dare to have a purpose firm, Dare to make it known.'

These two competing inheritances – parliament and Puritanism; the constitutionalism and the crusading – were apparent from the start, when Tony Benn (after Oxford, the RAF and a brief stint as a BBC radio producer) became the third generation to enter the House of Commons, elected in 1950 as MP for Bristol South East at the age of twenty-five. His maiden speech paid little regard to the niceties of that strange exercise in rhetorical false modesty, with no paean of praise to his predecessors (among them Stafford Cripps) or the constituency – but rather a full-blooded defence of the government's plans to nationalise the iron and steel industry.[13]

In some ways, such ideological fervour was unexpected from Benn. Despite the later caricatures of 'Wedgie Benn' as an unreconstructed Marxist-Leninist, he entered the House as a practical, moderate, reform-minded socialist, a disciple of the municipal socialism his grandfather had once practised on the London County Council. 'It was no good trying to thrust ideology down constituents' throats when they needed a pension or house or job,' he wrote of his political education as an MP, 'you had to tackle the problem as *they* saw it, and then think out what policy change was necessary to prevent similar problems from recurring in the future.'[14]

This is how Tony Benn became a socialist: not through his austere, intellectual upbringing, but by seeking to represent the social realities of post-war Britain. One of his favourite observations was the uniqueness of being an MP – 'the only job where there is one employee and 60,000 employers'.[15] But again, what is so interesting is the religiosity of his analysis – how his Christian mindset interprets the rhythms of democracy. 'Having been to hundreds of polling stations in my life,' Benn wrote, 'I have come to regard them as almost sacred in character.'[16] What was more, his constituency surgeries clearly had the feel of a confessional. 'What I miss most is the constituency,' he admitted on retirement.

'I miss the surgeries. They were very emotional events because people would often burst into tears and unload their problems.'

And Parliament's job was to feed that back into policy-making. As he put it in 2007, 'Parliament is the buckle that links the street to the statute book.' Which was why Benn was so obsessive in the protection of the rights and privileges of Parliament and the role of MPs, not least those of us who reside on the back benches – with its 'invigorating air that stimulates controversy and independence'. By contrast, 'down on the front benches the atmosphere is muggier and the sluggish waters of the "usual channels" give off a faint odour of coalition that is far less exhilarating'.

At the heart of Benn's thinking as a young backbencher was, firstly, a great distrust of patronage and power structures. As a young man brought up in the heart of the British Establishment, in and out of Downing Street and Parliament as a young boy, a gilded public school education and Oxford career – Benn would already start talking of 'them' and 'the Establishment' as something foreign to him. But, secondly, a deep and abiding (passed down from his ancestors) conviction that what happened in Parliament mattered. During the long nights of the Suez Crisis, he wrote in his diary that the battles in the House of Commons 'reminded me once more that politics is not a tea party, even in a parliamentary democracy. It is an orderly and disciplined struggle for power.'[17]

This distaste for archaic systems of patronage and a belief in the centrality of the House of Commons came together in Benn's struggle against the peerage. Famously, he was furious when – in 1941 – he heard that his father William Benn had taken up the offer of a hereditary peerage: not, as Churchill made plain, as a political honour or award, 'but to strengthen the Labour Party in the Upper House'. There were no life peerages at the time and had the natural order of succession taken place, then Benn's much beloved elder brother, Michael, would have inherited the title of Viscount Stansgate. Sadly, Michael died during the war and the title passed down to Benn.

Except, of course, he didn't want it. Jad Adams's biography has a very brilliant account of Benn's struggle against becoming Lord Stansgate – a long and winding tale beginning in 1955 with his signing of an instrument of renunciation, his expulsion from the Commons and barred re-entry and finally concluding, heroically, with the 1963 Peerage Act which allowed the title to be 'disclaimed' (so helping Quintin Hogg and Alec Douglas-Home as well) and Benn returned as MP for Bristol South East.[18]

With that characteristic touch for the dramatic, Benn went to hospital before the final renunciation of the peerage to have a doctor extract a pint of his blue blood, before it went common again. Inevitably, he kept the sample.

In all of this one can see Benn, and he consciously cast himself, as the dogged, lonely outsider battling the Establishment, taking on the systems of patronage and daring to be a Daniel. This was, indeed, a Pilgrim's Progress. And, in many ways, such an interpretation is not wrong as pretty much no one was on Benn's side – not the Speaker, not the PLP, not the courts, not the Prime Minister Harold Macmillan and certainly not Labour leader Hugh Gaitskell or, indeed, the Garter Principal King at Arms.

But, crucially, *the people* were on his side – in the form of the electors of Bristol who returned him to Parliament with a 70 per cent vote share in the 1961 by-election and provided an invaluable moral and political boost to his campaign.[19]

However, in the battle over disclaiming the peerage we also see a stark realisation on Benn's part of the limitations of Parliament – that this august institution, so revered by his ancestors, could be so spectacularly, systematically wrong. What is more, he was never afraid to work outside its parameters: court cases, petitions, popular campaigns, even fundraising drives in America, where Benn tickled US opinion by framing the peerage battle as part of a deeper British malaise: 'Our failure to adapt ourselves to modern life, our fear of the future and our nostalgic preference for living in the cosy afterglow of past glories.'

What Benn used to greatest effect, though, was the mass

media. Newspapers were briefed, columnists squared, journalists kept on side and family interviews offered. One of the
later, self-serving myths – on both sides – of 'Wedgie Benn'
was the notion of an adversarial relationship with the media,
with both sides accusing the other of self-aggrandisement and
manipulation. Famously, Benn would come (like his father) to
add to his clips cupboard by recording all his own interviews and
denounce the unelected power of TV producers. 'We are no longer
even the primary source of debate,' he lamented to the Commons
in 1992, 'as television has taken it over. Mr Speaker Sissons and Mr
Speaker Paxman presumed to tell us what the nation thinks.'

But Benn himself was an adept and masterly media hand. He
began his Labour career as a spin doctor when, in 1950, he wrote
to Herbert Morrison (Peter Mandelson's grandfather no less) offering his skills as a radio producer to assist on the party's election
broadcasts. His offer was soon taken up and Benn was on hand
to help both Hugh Gaitskell and Nye Bevan with their first TV
broadcasts. Then Benn found that he himself was rather good at
media appearances, becoming a regular panellist on *Any Questions?*
before garnering his own Sunday afternoon TV shows. Indeed, if
anyone bolstered – in the post-war years – the democratisation of
politics out from the Commons chamber and into the mass media
it was Benn. Suddenly, Parliament was not the be-all and end-all
of the political process. And as the technology has changed, so has
Benn's mastery of it – from tape to video to the Internet today.

For all *his* later reservations, such a shift in the capacity for
public debate – from Parliament to the people – was, to *my* mind,
no bad thing.

Tony Benn's crusade against the peerage had, time and again,
put him at odds with the stance of the Labour Party leadership.
Gaitskell and much of the PLP wanted this messy constitutional
question of disclaiming hereditary rights – and, quite often, Benn
himself – simply to go away. But he didn't. And that Puritan sensi-
bility, that sense of deep-seated personal righteousness, would be

equally hard to shift when it came to the tricky business of running a disciplined political party in the media age. Daniel never had much to say about collective Cabinet responsibility in the Lion's Den.

Despite all his admiration for the clean air of the back benches, after his hectoring of the government during the Suez Crisis, Hugh Gaitskell rewarded Tony Benn with a frontbench appointment as second spokesman on the RAF. It didn't last long. In March 1958, finding himself unable to support the Labour Party's pro-nuclear defence policy, he quietly resigned as a shadow spokesman. He then resigned altogether more noisily from the National Executive Committee in 1960 on the same question. Although few noticed these comings and goings, it put down a marker for Benn's innate frustrations with systems of party discipline. Time and again, he sided with Richard Crossman's opposition to any notion of collective responsibility extending from the shadow Cabinet to the broader front bench.

Benn's spate of resignations came to a halt in the 1960s and in 1964 he joined Harold Wilson's government as Postmaster General. For all Benn's ardour for the legislature, we should not forget that his time in the executive proved remarkably fruitful. He worked hard to modernise the Post Office, turning a multi-million-pound deficit into a profit, introducing the second-class stamp and all-figure telephone dialling, and even bringing in management consultants McKinsey's to outmanoeuvre the civil service (very much the public-private partnership). Famously, his ambition to remove the Queen's head from the stamps didn't achieve the same success.

In 1966, Benn was promoted to the Cabinet as Minister for Technology, where all his white-heat enthusiasms were given full-rein. Benn's Industrial Expansion Bill, Shipbuilding Industry Act and fiscal support for the Upper Clyde Shipbuilders spoke to an age of industrial activism. But, in reality, the tide of post-war British industry was fast withdrawing and, for all Benn's feverish 'MinTech' activism, Her Majesty's Government would soon be left with a series of beached corporate whales on its hands.

None of which stopped Benn, on his return to office in 1974, from pursuing as Secretary of State for Industry exactly the same strategy of 'picking winners', with Concorde as its most iconic edifice. But, by then, Harold Wilson and Denis Healey had had enough, gutting his Industry Bill and then moving him to the Department for Energy.[20] And, in post there, I think he made one of his more substantive policy suggestions – which was to urge the nationalisation of North Sea oil receipts with all profits to the Exchequer. Maybe, just maybe, if we had followed Benn's advice we could be sitting on a sovereign wealth fund the size of Norway's, with similar capacity for social investment.

What was certainly noticeable about the radical rhetoric of Benn's time in office – support for nationalisation, workers' syndicates, statist intervention – was just how distinct it was from the practical, constituency socialism of his youth. For there had been something of an ideological journey towards the left over the ensuing years and, as a Cabinet minister, he was now finding it ever more difficult to stick either to the party line or his own ministerial brief. At Llandudno in 1968 he set out six conditions for the radical redistribution of political power in Britain – including Freedom of Information, local (electronic) referenda, media regulation, state-funded trade unions and regional devolution. He followed it up with further calls for industrial democracy and populist decision-making, as well as nationalising the top twenty-five UK companies. Defeat in the general election of 1970 only extended Benn's appetite for these clarion calls for socialism.

And, here, the historiography divides: those more inclined to the Bennite view of the world suggest an honest and deep conversion from technocrat to socialist, from the Crossman centre-ground to the Campaign Group left. More cynical chroniclers point to Benn's growing personal, political ambitions and a need to flatter the broader, Labour movement outside the confines of Westminster – an interpretation arguably ratified by Benn's decision to stand (against Michael Foot and Roy Jenkins) for the Labour Party deputy leadership in 1971.

Those suspecting ambition rather than ideology can also point to Benn's decision to campaign so passionately against British entry into the Common Market in the 1975 referendum. In a letter to his constituents, he attacked the Common Market for decisions which would 'make the United Kingdom into one province of a Western European state' – despite being a passionate and committed supporter of Europe only a few years beforehand.

But that, I think, would be unfair because Benn did genuinely start to think about the nature of democracy and liberty in the industrial age during the 1970s. And for inspiration he retreated into the past. During the Labour Party's period in opposition in the 1950s, our other great Dissenting hero, Michael Foot, had sought solace in the literature of the eighteenth century – writing of the great political tussle between the Duke of Marlborough and Robert Harley, with Jonathan Swift centre-stage. Benn, in the 1970s, returned to the seventeenth century and there he found the true meaning of his Puritan inheritance. In the works of John Lilburne and the Levellers, of Winstanley and the Diggers, and the English radical reformation of the late 1640s, Benn found a profoundly prescient political voice. 'I had no idea,' he wrote in his diary, 'that the Levellers had called for universal manhood suffrage, equality between the sexes, biennial parliaments, the sovereignty of the people, recall of representatives and even an attack on property.'[21] In the gloomy environs of the House of Commons tea room, Benn received a crash course in the political thought of the English Civil War from fellow Labour MP and former London University lecturer John 'Jack' Mendelson.[22]

As the lights flickered during the three-day week, Benn immersed himself in the Putney Debates, the New Model Army and the agitators, the struggle over the franchise between the Grandees and the Levellers, and the inspiration of Colonel Rainsborough – 'The poorest he in England hath a life to live as the greatest he.' Rather than Labour Party policy documents, Benn started to quote from the Levellers' 1649 manifesto, 'An Agreement of the Free People of England':

> We, the free People of England, to whom God hath given hearts ... agree to ascertain our Government to abolish all arbitrary Power, and to set bounds and limits both to our Supreme, and all Subordinate Authority, and remove all known Grievances.

And what Benn particularly liked about the Levellers was the role of what Marxists call 'praxis': political radicalisation through lived reality. As he would put it in his Bennite manifesto, *Arguments for Socialism,*

> the Levellers distilled their political philosophy by discussion out of their own experience, mixing theory and practice, thought and action, and by doing so they passed on to succeeding genera- tions a formula for social progress from which we can learn how to tackle the problems of our time.[23]

What Benn admired was the democracy, the equality, the repub- licanism, the attack on patronage and favour, and the earnest discussion. All of this spoke to Benn and he saw himself within the same historical lineage – lamenting how 'the Levellers lost and Cromwell won, and Harold Wilson or Denis Healey is the Cromwell of our day, not me'.

However, once again, the competing inheritances – of Puritanism and Parliament – came into conflict. For part of the Leveller critique was that Parliament was as dangerous a power as King Charles I: that an 'elective dictatorship' (as Lord Hailsham's quintessentially 1970s description had it) was no better than the divine right of kings. And Benn, too, as his ideol- ogy turned leftward and his ambitions for leading the Labour Party grew stronger, started to turn away from Parliament and look to other power bases.

Despite having supported Barbara Castle's White Paper, *In Place of Strife*, and its attempts to limit trade union power, he now (under the tutelage of Eric Heffer) swung behind the trade union movement. He supported the Upper Clyde Shipbuilders work-in of 1971, telling a mass meeting on Glasgow Green, 'We are seeing the birth-pangs of industrial democracy.' He supported 'The Pentonville Five' shop stewards jailed in July 1972 by the National Industrial Relations Court for refusing to obey a court order to stop picketing a container depot in East London. And he actively and proudly supported, by then as MP for Chesterfield, the National Union of Mineworkers' strike of 1984–5.

Increasingly, Benn also used the extra-parliamentary avenues of the Labour Party to forward his political agenda. Realising that his support base within the Parliamentary Labour Party was always fairly limited, he turned to the party structures – the National Executive Committee, the constituency associations, party conference – to pursue his ambitions. It was a strategy designed to carve out his fellow Members of Parliament and give power to the agitators, the rank and file, the russet-coated soldiers of the Labour Party's New Model Army. And it almost worked. In the 1981 battle for deputy leader of the Labour Party, Denis Healey beat Tony Benn by 0.85 per cent – for some, a terrifyingly close shave.

In the process, the Bennites in the Tribune group, the Campaign for Labour Party Democracy, and in the now gently avuncular form of Chris Mullin, unleashed forces within the party which would undermine its capacity for electoral success for over a decade. As in the 1650s, the World was Turned Upside Down as Militant Tendency and Socialist Workers Party activists began to infiltrate the movement – in London, Liverpool and elsewhere – on the back of reselection ballots and extra-parliamentary activism. Denis Healey condemned Tony Benn for doing nothing 'to discourage or condemn' the sometimes violent agitation, while in this lecture series Neil Kinnock has described how Michael Foot – whose love of Parliament never waned – 'declared that the responsibility for transmitting every controversy of the time into an internal Labour Party dispute rested entirely with Tony Benn'.

Whether that was fair or not, it was increasingly clear that the Puritan in Benn was winning out over the Parliament-man; the crusader was trumping the constitutionalist. In 1979, at his audience with Her Majesty the Queen on surrendering the seal of office, he was already complaining to Elizabeth II about the limitations of the Commons. 'Whereas twenty-five years ago we were an empire, now we are colony with the IMF running our financial affairs and the Common Market Commission running our legislation and NATO running our armed forces.'[24] Apparently, the Queen changed the subject.

Benn's disillusion with the House of his fathers only accelerated during the 1990s. Following his retirement as MP for Chesterfield in 2001, he wrote plaintively of how,

> My dad has always been described as a 'good parliamentarian', a man who loved the place and was respected there, and that description has sometimes been applied to me too. I always regarded it as an honour to be so described. But when I look back on my life, I am beginning to see the work of a modern Parliament in a rather different light.

For the two attributes which his father had ascribed to Parliament – controlling the purse and sword; and not binding its successors – were no longer evident. The purse was now controlled not by Parliament, but by global institutions – the WTO, IMF, GATT. The sword was controlled by America, which had the codes for our nuclear weapons programme. And, finally, 'through NATO and our membership of the EU and in many other ways, one Parliament can and does commit its successors'. The power of Prime Ministers now exceeded the divine right of kings and all the patronage structure of the medieval court was held by the Whips Office. The Parliament of Speaker Lenthall was no more.

So, famously, in 2001, Tony Benn quit Parliament 'to devote more time to politics'. He became a stalwart of the Stop the War Coalition; he toured regional theatres with his one-man show, *An Evening with Tony Benn* (telling one interviewer that 'my theatre performances ... are the equivalent of a constituency meeting'); he played Glastonbury; he promoted his *Diaries* and he passed the family baton to Hilary Benn – 'a Benn, but not a Bennite', as Hilary was quick to establish.

In essence, Tony Benn returned to his earliest, childhood inspirations. Having been a king, he now toured the country – from theatres to trade union chapels to *Newsnight* studios to Burford Church (scene of the great Leveller massacre by Cromwell's men) – as one of the Prophets of his mother's Bible stories. Harold Wilson had once unkindly called Benn an 'Old Testament prophet' who 'immatures with age' – but for a new generation, hostile and uninterested in parliamentary politics, that was and is precisely his attraction.

There is, finally, one other way of approaching the political and parliamentary life of Tony Benn. On the riverside site of Benn's childhood home, next door to the Tate Gallery where he watched the tug boats chug up and down the Thames, there was built in 1960 Millbank Tower. Here, in 1996, was where New Labour transplanted the Labour Party from its old, Walworth Road HQ. And another T. B. took charge of the party – Tony Blair.

He too was a moderniser, someone familiar with manipulating the media, an individualist politician happy to work outside traditional party structures, a committed and often messianic crusader for his own political beliefs, a gifted orator, someone unafraid of a fight and, above all, someone who came to be ever more impatient with Parliament and its place within political discourse.

In their skins, both Tonies are Christian Socialists. But the vital difference between Tony Blair and Tony Benn is that the former is Catholic, and the latter a Puritan. Both in Parliament and out.

1   House of Commons: Official Report (Hansard): 29 July 1957, Vol. 574, cols 886.

2   House of Commons: Official Report (Hansard): 29 July 1957, Vol. 574, cols 886.

3   'A very complimentary account', as Benn recorded in his diary. Tony Benn, *Years of Hope: Diaries 1940–1962* (London: Hutchinson, 1994), p.248.

4   Benn, *Years of Hope: Diaries 1940–1962*, p.359.

5   Tony Benn, *Dare to be a Daniel* (London: Hutchinson, 2004), p.32.

6   Quoted in David Cannadine, 'Josiah Wedgwood and the History of Parliament', in David Cannadine, *In Churchill's Shadow* (London: Allen Lane, 2002).

7   Benn, *Dare to be a Daniel*, p.5.

8   Michael Foot, *Debts of Honour* (London: HarperCollins, 1980).

9   Benn, *Dare to be a Daniel*.

10 Benn, *Dare to be a Daniel*.

11 Tony Benn, *Years of Hope: Diaries 1940–1962, Out of the Wilderness: Diaries 1963–67* (London: Hutchinson, 1987), *Office Without Power: Diaries 1968–72* (London: Hutchinson, 1988), *Against the Tide: Diaries 1973–76* (London: Hutchinson, 1989); *Conflicts of Interest: Diaries: 1977–80* (London: Hutchinson: 1990); *The End of an Era: Diaries 1980–90* (London: Hutchinson, 1992). The Diaries were also published in paperback by Arrow Books.

12 *Daily Telegraph*, 12 August 2009.

13 House of Commons: Official Report (Hansard): 7 February 1951, Vol. 483, cols 1778–83.

14 Benn, *Dare to be a Daniel*, p.168.

15 Benn, *Dare to be a Daniel*, p.168.

16 Tony Benn, *Letters to my Grandchildren* (London: Hutchinson, 2009), p.49.

17 Benn, *Years of Hope: Diaries 1940–1962*, p.204.

18 Jad Adams, *Tony Benn – A Biography* (London: Biteback, 2011).

19 The results were Tony Benn (Lab), 23,275, Malcolm St Clair (Con), 10,231, Lab. Maj: 13,044. See *The Times Guide to the House of Commons 1964* (London: The Times Office, 1964), p.44.

20 See, e.g., Harold Wilson, *Final Term* (London: Weidenfeld & Nicolson, 1979), pp.143–4, and Bernard Donoughue, *Downing Street Diary*, Vol. 1 (London: Jonathan Cape, 2005), *passim* and pp.405–11.

21 Benn, *Against the Tide: Diaries 1973–76*, pp.50–51.

22 Benn, *Against the Tide: Diaries 1973–76*, p.50.

23 Tony Benn, *Arguments for Socialism* (Harmondsworth: Penguin edn 1980), p.31.

24 Benn, *Conflicts of Interest: Diaries 1977–80*, p.498.

The authors

ANDREW ADONIS was a Fellow of Nuffield College, Oxford, 1988–91, and a journalist with the *Financial Times*, 1991–96, and *The Observer*, 1996–98. He served in the Prime Minister's Policy Unit, 1988–2005, and was Head of Policy 2001–03. He was raised to the peerage as Lord Adonis in 2005. He was a Parliamentary Under-Secretary in the Department for Education and Skills, 2005–08, and Minister of State in the Department of Transport, 2008–09, before serving as Secretary of State for Transport, 2009–10. He was Director of the Institute for Government 2010–11. He is author of several books, including *Parliament Today*, *Making Aristocracy Work*, *A Class Act* and *Education, Education, Education*, and co-editor of *Roy Jenkins: A Retrospective*.

TRISTRAM HUNT was a Special Adviser in the Department for Trade and Industry, 1998–2001, Research Fellow in the Institute for Public Policy Research 2001, Associate Fellow in the Centre for History and Economics, King's College, Cambridge, 2001–02, a radio and television broadcaster from 2001 and Lecturer in History at Queen Mary College, University of London, since 2003. He was elected as Labour MP for Stoke-on-Trent Central in 2010. His publications include *The English Civil War*, *Building Jerusalem* and *The Frock-Coated Communist*.

DOUGLAS HURD was President of the Cambridge Union and served in HM Foreign Service, 1952–66, and in the Conservative Research Department, 1966–68. He was Political Secretary to Edward Heath as Leader of the Opposition (1968–70) and Prime Minister (1970–74). He was elected Conservative MP for Mid Oxfordshire in 1974. He was Minister of State at the Foreign and Commonwealth Office, 1979–83, and the Home Office, 1983–84. He served as Secretary of State for Northern Ireland, 1984–85, Home Secretary, 1985–89, and Foreign Secretary, 1989–95. He was a candidate in the Conservative leadership election in 1990. He retired from the House of Commons in 1997 and was elevated to the peerage as Lord Hurd of Westwell. His publications include *An End to Promises*, *War without Frontiers*, *Memoirs*, *Robert Peel* and *Choose Your Weapons*.

NEIL KINNOCK was a tutor and organiser for the Workers' Educational Association 1966–70. He was elected Labour MP for Bedwellty in 1970 and was appointed Parliamentary Private Secretary to Michael Foot as Employment Secretary 1974–75. He was shadow Education Secretary 1979–83 and Leader of the Opposition from 1983 to 1992. He left the House of Commons in 1995 upon his appointment as a European Commissioner, serving as a Commission Vice-President 1999–2004. He was elevated to the peerage, as Lord Kinnock, in 2005. He was Chair of the British Council, 2004–09. He is the author of *Making Our Way* and *Thorns and Roses*.

GORDON MARSDEN was an Open University tutor and associate lecturer, 1977–97, and a public relations consultant, 1980–85. He served as Chief Public Affairs Adviser to English Heritage, 1984–85. He was editor of *History Today*, 1985–97, and *New Socialist*, 1989–90. He was elected as the Labour MP for Blackpool South in 1997. He was appointed to the opposition front bench in 2010. His publications include *Victorian Values*.

KENNETH O. MORGAN FBA was Fellow of Queen's College, Oxford, from 1966 to 1989, Professor as well as Principal and then Vice-Chancellor of the University of Wales, Aberystwyth,

1989–95, and Senior Vice-Chancellor, University of Wales, 1993–95. His thirty-two books include six on Lloyd George, and biographies of Keir Hardie, Lord Addison, James Callaghan and Michael Foot. His *Oxford Illustrated History of Britain* has sold over 750,000 copies. His *Ages of Reform* was published by I. B. Tauris in December 2010. He became a Labour peer as Lord Morgan of Aberdyfi in 2000.

PHILIP NORTON is Professor of Government and Director of the Centre for Legislative Studies, at the University of Hull. He was appointed to the chair at Hull in 1986, making him, at thirty-five, the youngest professor of politics in the country. He is editor or author of twenty-nine books, including *The Constitution in Flux, Parliament in British Politics* and *The British Polity* (now in its fifth edition). He was elevated to the peerage in 1998 as Lord Norton of Louth and was the first chairman of the House of Lords Select Committee on the Constitution.

NICHOLAS SOAMES was equerry to the Prince of Wales 1970–72. He was elected as Conservative MP for Crawley in 1983 (Mid-Sussex since 1987). He was Joint Parliamentary Secretary, Ministry of Agriculture, Fisheries and Food, 1992–94, and Minister of State for the Armed Forces, Ministry of Defence, 1994–97. He was shadow Secretary of State for Defence, 2003–05. He is a member of the executive of the Conservative 1922 Committee.

PETER TAPSELL was personal assistant to Sir Anthony Eden as Prime Minister in 1955. He served as Conservative MP for Nottingham West from 1959 to 1964 and in 1966 was elected as Member for Horncastle (subsequently East Lindsey and Louth and Horncastle). He became the longest-serving Conservative MP in 2001 and Father of the House of Commons in 2010. He was the *Spectator* 'Backbencher of the Year' in 1993 and 'Parliamentarian of the Year' in 2004. He was knighted in 1985 and sworn of the Privy Council in 2011.

JOHN WHITTINGDALE was Head of the Political Section of Conservative Research Department 1982–84 and Special Adviser to Secretaries of State for Trade and Industry, 1984–87. He was Political Secretary to Margaret Thatcher as Prime Minister 1988–90 and to Margaret Thatcher 1990–92. He was elected MP for South Maldon in 1992. He was Parliamentary Private Secretary to William Hague as Leader of the Opposition, 1999–2001, and served in the shadow Cabinet from 2001 to 2005. He has been Chair of the Select Committee on Culture, Media and Sport since 2005 and Vice-Chair of the Conservative 1922 Committee since 2006. He was appointed OBE in 1990.

SHIRLEY WILLIAMS was a journalist before being elected Labour MP for Hitchin in 1964, serving in the House of Commons until defeated in 1979. She served as Parliamentary Secretary at the Ministry of Labour 1966–67, Minister of State for Education and Science, 1967–69, and at the Home Office, 1969–70. She was Secretary of State for Prices and Consumer Protection, 1974–76, Secretary of State for Education and Science 1976–79 and Paymaster General 1976–79. She was a founder member of the Social Democratic Party and was returned to the House of Commons as SDP MP for Crosby in a by-election in 1981, serving until losing the seat in the 1983 general election. She was President of the SDP 1982–88. She was elevated to the peerage as Baroness Williams of Crosby in 1993 and was leader of the Liberal Democrat peers in the House of Lords, 2001–04. She was Professor of Elective Politics in the John F. Kennedy School of Government, Harvard University, 1988–2000, and Professor Emeritus since 2000.

Further reading

DAVID LLOYD GEORGE

John Campbell, *Lloyd George: The Goat in the Wilderness* (London: Jonathan Cape, 1977)

Roy Hattersley, *David Lloyd George: The Great Outsider* (London: Little, Brown, 2010)

Kenneth O. Morgan, *Consensus and Disunity: The Lloyd-George Coalition Government, 1918–1922* (Oxford: Clarendon Press, 1979)

Kenneth O. Morgan, *David Lloyd George: Welsh Radical as World Statesman* (Cardiff: University of Wales Press, 1963)

Peter Rowland, *Lloyd George* (London: Barrie and Jenkins, 1975)

Richard Toye, *Lloyd George & Churchill: Rivals for Greatness* (London: Macmillan, 2007)

NANCY ASTOR

Adrian Fort, *Nancy: The Story of Lady Astor* (London: Jonathan Cape, forthcoming)

John Grigg, *Nancy Astor* (London: Little, Brown, 1982)

Christopher Sykes, *Nancy: The Life of Lady Astor* (London: Collins, 1972)

F. E. SMITH

2nd Earl of Birkenhead, *Frederick Edwin, Earl of Birkenhead*, 2 vols (London: Thornton Butterworth, 1935)

2nd Earl of Birkenhead, *F. E.: The Life of F. E. Smith, First Earl of Birkenhead* (London: Eyre & Spottiswoode, 1960)

William Camp, *The Glittering Prizes: A Biographical Study of F. E. Smith, First Earl of Birkenhead* (London: MacGibbon & Kee, 1960)

John Campbell, *F. E. Smith: First Earl of Birkenhead* (London: Cape, 1983)

WINSTON CHURCHILL

Geoffrey Best, *Churchill: A Study in Greatness* (Oxford: Oxford University Press, 2003)

Robert Blake and William Roger Louis (eds), *Churchill* (Oxford: Oxford University Press, 1993)

John Charmley, *Churchill: The End of Glory – A Political Biography* (London: Hodder & Stoughton, 1993)

Martin Gilbert, *Churchill: A Life* (London: Heinemann, 1991)

Roy Jenkins, *Churchill* (London: Macmillan, 2001)

William Manchester, *The Last Lion: Winston Spencer Churchill: Visions of Glory, 1874–1932* (London: Sphere, 1984)

R. A. C. Parker (ed.), *Churchill: Studies in Statesmanship* (London: Brassey's, 1995)

Richard Toye, *Lloyd George & Churchill: Rivals for Greatness* (London: Macmillan, 2007)

ANEURIN BEVAN

Vincent Brome, *Aneurin Bevan: A Biography* (London: Longmans, Green, 1953)

John Campbell, *Nye Bevan: A Biography* (London: Hodder & Stoughton, 1994)

Michael Foot, *Aneurin Bevan*, Vol. 1: *1897–1945* (London: MacGibbon & Kee, 1962; St Albans: Paladin, 1975)

Michael Foot, *Aneurin Bevan*, Vol. 2: *1945–1960* (London: Davis-Poynter, 1973; pub. in 1 vol. London: Faber & Faber, 2009)

Mark M. Krug, *Aneurin Bevan: Cautious Rebel* (London: Yoseloff, 1961)

ENOCH POWELL

Rex Collings (ed.), *Reflections of a Statesman: The Writings and Speeches of Enoch Powell* (London: Bellew Publishing, 1991)

Simon Heffer, *Like the Roman: The Life of Enoch Powell* (London: Weidenfeld & Nicolson, 1998)

Roy Lewis, *Enoch Powell: Principles in Politics* (London: Cassell, 1979)

Andrew Roth, *Enoch Powell: Tory Tribune* (London: Macdonald & Co., 1970)

Robert Shepherd, *Enoch Powell* (London: Hutchinson, 1996)

MICHAEL FOOT

Mervyn Jones, *Michael Foot* (London: Gollancz, 1994)

Kenneth O. Morgan, *Michael Foot: A Life* (London: HarperPress, 2007)

IAIN MACLEOD

Nigel Fisher, *Iain Macleod* (London: Andre Deutsch, 1973)

Robert Shepherd, *Iain Macleod* (London: Hutchinson, 1994)

ROY JENKINS

Andrew Adonis and Keith Thomas (eds), *Roy Jenkins: A Retrospective* (Oxford: Oxford University Press, 2004)

John Campbell, *Roy Jenkins: A Biography* (London: Weidenfeld & Nicolson, 1983)

Giles Radice, *Friends and Rivals: Crosland, Jenkins and Healey* (London: Little, Brown, 2002)

MARGARET THATCHER

John Campbell, *Margaret Thatcher. Vol. One: The Grocer's Daughter* (London: Jonathan Cape, 2000)

John Campbell, *Margaret Thatcher, Vol. Two: The Iron Lady* (London: Jonathan Cape, 2003)

Patrick Cosgrave, *Margaret Thatcher: A Tory and Her Party* (London: Hutchinson, 1978)

Andrew Gamble, *The Free Economy and the Strong State: The Politics of Thatcherism*, 2nd edn (Basingstoke: Macmillan, 1994)

John Hoskyns, *Just in Time: Inside the Thatcher Revolution* (London: Aurum, 2000)

Bernard Ingham, *Kill the Messenger* (London: HarperCollins, 1991)

Russell Lewis, *Margaret Thatcher: A Personal and Political Biography* (London: Routledge & Kegan Paul, 1975)

Nicholas Wapshott and George Brock, *Thatcher* (London: Macdonald & Co., 1983)

Hugo Young, *One of Us: A Biography of Margaret Thatcher*, 2nd revised edn (London: Pan, 1993)

TONY BENN

Jad Adams, *Tony Benn: A Biography* (London: Biteback, 2011)

Russell Lewis, *Tony Benn: A Critical Biography* (London: Associated Business Press, 1978)

David Powell, *Tony Benn: A Political Life* (London: Continuum, 2001)

Index

Also available from Biteback

Enoch at 100
A re-evaluation of the life, politics and philosophy of
Enoch Powell

Edited by Lord Howard of Rising

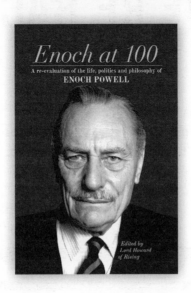

Enoch at 100 is a critical reassessment of the controversial
politician's legacy by some of the leading political figures and writers
of the current age. As well as a history of Powell and his politics it
features contributions, in the form of essays, by figures as diverse as
Iain Duncan Smith, Simon Heffer, Tom Bower, Lord Salisbury, Lord
True, Lord Lexden, Andrew Roberts and Richard Ritchie.

'*This book, friendly to Enoch, but critical too, provides excellent answers.*'
Charles Moore, *Daily Telegraph*

352pp hardback, £25.00
Available now in all good bookshops or order from
www.bitebackpublishing.com